WITHDRAWN

THE SHIPWRECK
THAT SAVED
JAMESTOWN

THE SHIPWRECK THAT SAVED JAMESTOWN

THE *SEA VENTURE*
CASTAWAYS AND THE FATE
OF AMERICA

LORRI GLOVER
DANIEL BLAKE SMITH

A JOHN MACRAE BOOK
HENRY HOLT AND COMPANY
New York

Henry Holt and Company, LLC
Publishers since 1866
175 Fifth Avenue
New York, New York 10010
www.henryholt.com

Henry Holt® and ⬚®are registered trademarks of Henry Holt and Company, LLC.

Distributed in Canada by H. B. Fenn and Company Ltd.

Library of Congress Cataloging-in-Publication Data

Glover, Lorri, 1967–
    The shipwreck that saved Jamestown : the Sea Venture Castaways and the fate
of America / Lorri Glover and Daniel Blake Smith. — 1st ed.
    p. cm
    Includes bibliographical references and index.
    ISBN-13: 978-0-8050-8654-6
    ISBN-10: 0-8050-8654-4
    1. Jamestown (Va.) —History—17th Century.   2. Bermuda Islands—
History—17th century.   3. Sea Venture (Ship)   4. Shipwrecks—Bermuda
Islands—History—17th century.   5. Virginia—History—Colonial period,
ca. 1600–1775.   6. Great Britain—Colonies—America—History—17th
century.   7. Virginia Company of London—History.   8. Seafaring life—
History—17th century.   I. Smith, Daniel Blake.   II. Title.
    F234.J3G58 2008
    973.2'1—dc22   2007042248

Henry Holt books are available for special promotions and premiums.
For details contact: Director, Special Markets.

First Edition 2008

Designed by Meryl Sussman Levavi

Printed in the United States of America

10 9 8 7 6 5 4 3 2 1

CONTENTS

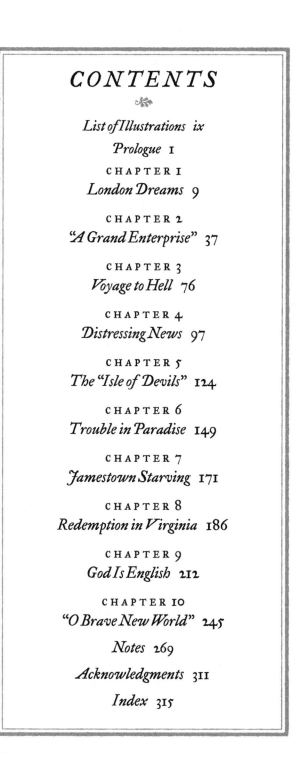

List of Illustrations ix

Prologue 1

CHAPTER 1
London Dreams 9

CHAPTER 2
"A Grand Enterprise" 37

CHAPTER 3
Voyage to Hell 76

CHAPTER 4
Distressing News 97

CHAPTER 5
The "Isle of Devils" 124

CHAPTER 6
Trouble in Paradise 149

CHAPTER 7
Jamestown Starving 171

CHAPTER 8
Redemption in Virginia 186

CHAPTER 9
God Is English 212

CHAPTER 10
"O Brave New World" 245

Notes 269

Acknowledgments 311

Index 315

ILLUSTRATIONS

❧

Sir Thomas Smythe (portrait by Simon de Passe, 1616, courtesy of
National Portrait Gallery, London) 11

Middle Temple Hall set up for a formal dinner (photograph
courtesy of the Masters of the Bench of The Honourable
Society of the Middle Temple) 13

Map of London, 1593 (from John Norden, Speculum Britanniae,
courtesy of Huntington Library) 15

King James I (portrait by Daniel Mytens, courtesy of
National Portrait Gallery, London) 22

Sir Thomas Gates (portrait by C. Jansen,
courtesy of Bermuda Archives) 51

Frontispiece, Robert Johnson, Nova Britannia, 1609
(courtesy of Library of Virginia) 58

Frontispiece, Rev. William Symonds, Virginia. A Sermon
Preached at White-Chappel, 1609
(courtesy of Huntington Library) 64

Sir George Somers (unknown artist, courtesy of
Bermuda Historical Society) 73

Bermuda in the Atlantic World
(map by Rebecca L. Wrenn) 126

Satellite Image of Bermuda Coral Reefs
(courtesy of Paul Illsley] 127

Sir George Somers's Map of Bermuda, ca. 1610
(courtesy of British Library) 157

Replica of the Deliverance (authors' photograph) 169

Bermuda flag 234

Frontispiece, Lewis Hughes, A Plaine and True Relation, 1621
(courtesy of Huntington Library) 235

THE SHIPWRECK
THAT SAVED
JAMESTOWN

PROLOGUE

Late in the evening on June 2, 1609, an impressive convoy of nine ships launched out of Plymouth Sound. Bound for Virginia with six hundred passengers, livestock, and provisions, the fleet was the largest England had ever sent across the Atlantic—an audacious effort born out of the desperate desire to save the dying colony huddled around Jamestown. Three of England's "most worthy, honored gentlemen," Captain Christopher Newport, the nation's most experienced mariner; Admiral George Somers, veteran of campaigns in Ireland, the Netherlands, and the Caribbean; and Sir Thomas Gates, the next governor of Virginia, led the expedition. Peerless in their "ready knowledge in seafaring actions" and fully convinced that their leadership would restore England's fragile claim on America, the commanders on board the flagship, the *Sea Venture,* headed out into the Atlantic looking for a favorable wind; the other eight vessels followed behind, staying close "in friendly consort together."[1]

The *Sea Venture*, a newly built three-hundred-ton vessel, carried some 150 passengers and crew, including an assortment of soldiers, grocers, fishmongers, clothworkers, and tailors. The ship also carried farmers and families; a dozen gentlemen; all the newly appointed leaders of the colony; and an Anglican minister, Richard Buck. Although Rev. Buck was the lone clergyman sailing with the fleet, religion loomed large in the enterprise. In the days and weeks before launching from Plymouth, the rescue effort had been given powerful support from various pulpits throughout England. Still fresh in the settlers' minds were the fervent words of Rev. Daniel Price, whose sermon at St. Paul's Cross just five days before the launch made clear that this expedition was not simply about commerce and national power. "Go on as you have begun, and the Lord shall be with you," Price exclaimed, "go, and possess the Land . . . a land of milk and honey, God shall bless you."[2]

We can well imagine Rev. Buck holding forth in the tiny hold of the *Sea Venture,* imploring the passengers and crew to remember Price's inspiring words and to place confidence in their experienced Captain Newport. A successful privateer and renowned navigator who knew more about the east coast of America than any other Englishman, Newport piloted the *Sea Venture* with a steady hand, making good progress in the first six weeks. By July 24 the fleet was within seven days of reaching Virginia. Then clouds thickened and winds picked up dramatically. Sensing danger, Newport jettisoned the small pinnace he had been towing behind the *Sea Venture.* Despite years of chasing Spanish and Portuguese ships in these Atlantic waters, neither Christopher Newport nor George Somers— nor any of the men under their command, for that matter—was prepared for what came next.[3]

From out of the northeast "a dreadful storm and hideous began to blow . . . swelling and roaring," until it so darkened the sky as to "beat all light from Heaven." This was a "tempest" that in its "restless tumult" would not relent. Even experienced seamen on board struggled with sails whipped around and rendered useless by the merciless winds—sometimes the strength of eight men was insufficient "to hold the whipstaff" and steer the ship. William Strachey, a down-on-his-luck poet seeking a new start in Virginia, had certainly seen fierce storms before—he had traveled near the coast of Barbary and Algiers—yet nothing compared to the suffering he now witnessed: "there was not a moment in which the sudden splitting or instant oversetting of the ship was not expected." And it never abated: "fury added to fury, and one storm urging a second more outrageous than the former."[4]

The *Sea Venture* was facing down a "hurricano." And all the "shrieks" and "hurly and discomforts" that left everyone on board "with troubled hearts and panting bosoms" were about to worsen. Newport and his men lost sight of the rest of the ships in the convoy. Then, passengers discovered that the storm had forced "a mighty leak" in the ship. Within no time, with every joint "having spewed out her oakum [caulking] before we were aware," the water rose to five feet deep above the ballast "and we almost drowned within whilst we sat looking when to perish from above." The rising water ran like terror through the whole ship: "much fright and amazement, startled and turned the blood . . . of the most hardy mariner."[5]

As the water level in the ship rose before their eyes, passengers and crew frantically searched for the source of the leak. With candles in hand, men crept along the sides and corners of the ship looking and listening for water seeping in. At one point, they suspected the leak had begun in the bread room. "Whereupon," Strachey reported, "the carpenter went down and ripped up all the room but could not find it so." Water kept pouring in, so that the leakage "appeared as a wound given to men that were before dead."[6]

Governor Gates, throwing matters of class and rank aside, divided the entire company, except the women, into three groups that worked around the clock bailing water from the sinking ship. He ordered cargo, armaments—whatever weighed down the ship—thrown overboard. Men jettisoned hogsheads of oil, cider, wine, and vinegar, along with ordnance and passengers' luggage, and even considered cutting down the main mast—anything to lighten the load as water flooded the hold. For three full days, not only the "common sort, stripped naked as men in galleys" but every man on board took his turn with the bucket or the pump. And still, "the water seemed rather to increase than to diminish."[7]

Admiral Somers, meanwhile, took charge of the vessel and fought the seas "to keep her as upright as he could." With no food and little sleep, he remained on the poop deck for "three days and three nights together."[8]

Despite these valiant efforts, by the fourth morning ocean water covered the ship "from stern to stem like a garment or a vast cloud." And dread of the inevitable washed over everyone. The wind and rain even drowned out the passengers' prayers, so that there was "nothing heard that could give comfort, nothing seen that might encourage hope." It seemed that the men and women on the *Sea Venture* would never reach the land that ministers at St. Paul's Cross promised God was saving for them. With hearts beating and breaths heaving, the passengers and crew realized they were sinking. "For my part," Strachey confessed, "I thought her already in the bottom of the sea." By Friday, July 28, after futilely bailing water for days, the passengers and crew were ready to give up. A few sailors, resigning themselves to death, broke into the remaining liquor supply for a final toast. Others shut up the hatches and, "commending our sinful souls to God, committed the ship to the mercy of the gale."[9]

As frenzy and fear coursed through the sinking *Sea Venture*, it must have felt like yet another blow to England's effort to stake a claim in the Americas. Despite the hope and confidence that galvanized so much of this rescue mission in 1609, the hard truth was that, for Englishmen, the way west to an overseas empire was littered with false starts and dismal failures.

The English had been latecomers to adventuring in the West; long before them, the Spanish, Portuguese, French, and Dutch had already stretched their own empires beyond the seas. The Spanish virtually dominated the Americas. By the time the *Sea Venture* was sinking in the Atlantic, the Spanish had been extracting enormous wealth from their gold and silver mines in Mexico and Peru for nearly a century. Even worse for Protestant England, every advancing claim of Spain's powerful New World empire strengthened the spreading "menace" of Catholicism.

For its part, England could only point to the enterprising but ultimately disappointing efforts of a few remarkable mariners who probed the North American coast in the last quarter of the sixteenth century. Initially, most of these explorations focused on finding the elusive Northwest Passage to Asia. Nothing came of these efforts, except for a few seasonal fisheries the English managed to establish off the banks of Newfoundland. In 1576, one English mariner discovered what he thought was gold near Baffin Island and wanted to plant a colony there. The idea died when the two hundred tons of ore he carted back to England turned out to be fool's gold. Even a brief moment of modest success turned tragic. Sir Humphrey Gilbert landed at St. John's harbor in 1583 and declared Newfoundland English. But on his way home, Gilbert perished when his ship, the *Squirrel*, went down.[10]

The next year witnessed an even more notorious example of English failure: the tragic debacle of Roanoke. Picking up where his half-brother Gilbert left off, Sir Walter Raleigh, the swashbuckling court favorite, received a charter from Queen Elizabeth I granting him exclusive rights to an enormous stretch of land on the east coast of North America. This enterprise spawned the ill-fated "lost colony" of Roanoke, where 116 settlers, after being deposited on the shores of present-day North Carolina, were never seen by their countrymen again.[11]

Without colonies of its own, England was reduced to attacking and plundering Spanish treasure fleets coming out of the Caribbean in the 1580s and 1590s. In this chaotic era of piracy and uncertain Crown support, it often fell to captains and sailors, men like Drake, Newport, and Somers, to maintain England's otherwise feeble presence in the Atlantic world.[12] Privateers made a living in the Caribbean raiding Spanish and Portuguese ships loaded with gold and silver. But sometimes they returned with little more than trinkets, and sometimes they never returned at all. In more than thirty years of Atlantic adventuring, England's explorers and privateers failed to plant a single viable settlement in the Americas.

Then, amid all the aborted efforts and missed opportunities, an opening for a new venture emerged. An ambitious group of London merchants and gentlemen managed in 1606 to secure from the new king a charter for a colony in North America. They targeted the Chesapeake region very near the area that had been scouted some twenty years earlier during the tragic Roanoke misadventure. In the spring of 1607, a small convoy of English ships reached the mainland of Virginia and claimed the site for King James I.

Like so many of England's earlier overseas enterprises, the dream for a prosperous and thriving colony in Virginia quickly turned into a nightmare. Despite abundant timber and fish and the need to plant crops, it was the allure of finding gold that most excited settlers and investors back in London. While some colonists fished and traded with the Indians, too many others searched futilely for the precious ore. And they quarreled and conspired incessantly—anything to avoid work. Within a year, Virginia was at the point of collapse.[13]

Virginia's near failure is a well-known foundational story in our nation's history. But looming over nearly every telling of it lies the iconic roles of Captain John Smith and Pocahontas and the centrality of race in shaping England's first colony in America.[14] In fact, a great measure of what scholars and the general public know about England's early colonizing efforts in Virginia comes to us from Smith, even though much of what he wrote, especially involving his relationship with Pocahontas, was clearly posturing for history. Yet it has been Smith's history of England's colonial experiences—most notably the drama of his personal bravado set against combative Indians and lazy colonists—that we have largely come to accept as America's beginnings.

While this story offers important insights into the conflicted and increasingly complex racial world that English settlement prompted, a critical part of the broader picture of English survival in early Virginia has been neglected. In fact, by listening to other voices—especially those involved in the *Sea Venture* convoy—a far different picture emerges about England's first efforts at colonizing America. William Strachey, in particular, struggled to make his voice heard but lost out to Smith's larger name and greater ambition. Strachey's personal observations, beginning on board the *Sea Venture*, offer an entirely fresh perspective on the story of Jamestown. He does so by showing how the colony's ultimate success depended on a fascinating array of adventurers—entrepreneurs, seamen, servants, settlers, and politicians—whose daring and moving experiences in seeking out a new life in Virginia emboldened them to undertake a dramatic rescue effort that saved America's first colony. Strachey and the others involved in the odyssey of the *Sea Venture* reveal this poorly understood world of risk-taking adventurers—from investors and clergymen in London to servants and gentlemen on board the ill-fated ship—who never wavered in their commitment to English America. They did so in spite of daunting, often overwhelming, obstacles and lived one of the most surprising adventures in all of American history.

Like most rescue stories, the ordeal of the *Sea Venture* begins with hope mingled with fear. If only the colony in Virginia could be fortified with new colonists, more provisions, and better leaders, then Jamestown—and this fragile beginning for an English America—could survive, and England could meet the grand destiny that many believed God had planned for it. All of which, no doubt, heartened the promoters, passengers, and crew of the *Sea Venture* in the summer of 1609. But as that horrendous storm battered their ship, an unnerving fear doubtless crowded the hopes of the anguished passengers. With all the failures that had brought them to this moment, a devastating question must have crossed their minds as the water kept rising: was their cause—to plant the first American colony for England and Protestant Christianity—truly God's will?

CHAPTER I

LONDON DREAMS

In the spring of 1606, Sir Thomas Smythe's Philpot Lane house fairly buzzed with activity. His family's principal residence served as a gathering spot for London's ambitious merchants and gentlemen who dreamed of spreading their wealth and power and Christian faith beyond the boundaries of their small island nation. Smythe played such a central role in the city's leading overseas trading operations that he used the ground floor of his home for offices for the Levant, East India, and Muscovy Companies, and, most recently, the newly chartered Virginia Company. Upstairs he maintained a museum of sorts, displaying the exotic—and, he no doubt hoped, enticing—discoveries that mariners in his employ brought from the faraway voyages he helped finance. Captains who needed temporary housing between expeditions slept at the Symthe home. Sailors gathered there seeking jobs, and mariners' wives sometimes boarded there while their husbands were at sea.[1]

It was fitting that the architects of England's first empire congregated at Smythe's home. That rare combination of a bold dreamer and a tireless doer, Smythe was at the turn of the seventeenth century the most accomplished businessman in all of London. He served at one time or another as the principal leader of every important commercial enterprise in the city: the Levant, East India, and Muscovy Companies, the Merchant Adventurers, and the French and Spanish Companies. He helped fund expeditions to Ireland, explorations seeking a Northwest Passage, and even a voyage to Senegal. Renowned as a shrewd and supremely competent entrepreneur, Smythe was also respected as a decent and charitable man and a devout Christian. No one was better qualified to oversee the new company that King James chartered that April, the company that would bring about England's American empire.[2]

By the time he involved himself in the Virginia Company, the forty-eight-year-old Smythe knew, from dearly bought experience, how to negotiate the diplomatic and fiscal complexities of launching an overseas enterprise. Monarchs, no less than investors and mariners, had to be won over to the risky idea; exhaustive planning and shrewd promotion were required; lives and fortunes would almost surely be sacrificed before profits came. Overseas adventuring, then, was not for the faint of heart.

Thomas Smythe was the perfect man for the job, because challenges and setbacks—inevitable in foreign trades—did not deter him. Involved in creating the profitable Levant Company at the age of twenty-three, Smythe shortly became a very rich and important man in London. In the 1590s, he worked as a trade commissioner with the Dutch and helped fund the conquest of Ireland, and by 1600 he was an alderman and sheriff of London. But his friendship with the Earl of Essex and Queen Elizabeth's suspicions of Smythe's participation with Essex in a failed coup led to his downfall. He was arrested in 1601, along with Essex and their mutual friend and William Shakespeare's principal patron, the Earl of Southampton, and locked in the Tower of London. Elizabeth's

A leading merchant and one of the most experienced organizers of England's overseas enterprises, Thomas Smythe ran many of those entrepreneurial efforts out of his London home. (PORTRAIT BY SIMON DE PASSE, 1616, COURTESY OF NATIONAL PORTRAIT GALLERY, LONDON)

death in 1603 brought redemption. Elizabeth's successor, King James, pardoned Smythe, knighted him, and the following year appointed him ambassador to Russia.[3]

In a matter of months, Smythe went from tower prisoner to the toast of Moscow. He was commissioned as ambassador in June 1604 and met the emperor in Moscow that October. Thousands of Russians lined the road as he headed into the city. He and his men rode in on horses adorned with "Gold, Pearle, and Precious Stone; and particularly, a great Chaine of plated Gold about his necke." Three emissaries of the emperor attended to Smythe's every need, assuring him "that if his Lordship wanted any thing, they all, or any one of them, were as commanded, so readie to obey therein." Smythe's delegation first saw the emperor "seated in a Chaire of Gold, richly embroidered with Persian Stuffe: in his right hand hee held a golden Scepter, a Crowne of pure Gold upon his head, a Coller of rich stones and Pearles about his necke, his outward Garments of Crimson Velvet, embroidered very faire, with Pearles, Precious Stones and Gold." While at court, they feasted on lavish meals served on silver and gold platters "piled up on one another by halfe dozens." Despite all this impressive pageantry, Smythe did not waste much time at his post. As soon as he secured additional special trading rights for the Muscovy Company, Smythe resigned and returned to London in September 1605. That fall he turned his attention across the Atlantic.[4]

The London that Sir Thomas Smythe returned to in the fall of 1605 was a city for dreamers, with palaces and cathedrals every bit as awe inspiring as what he saw in Moscow. London was unequivocally the cultural and commercial center of the nation. As one visitor aptly put it, "London is not in England, but England in London."[5] For the lucky few born to privilege, London offered a life of elegance and sophistication. The new king's wife, Queen Anne, loved the arts and patronized musicians and poets and painters. She commissioned royal favorites such as Ben Jonson to stage elaborate court masques, and regularly entertained scores of velvet-clad gentlemen and their jewel-draped wives at pageants and lavish feasts at Whitehall Palace. The recently designed Gray's Inn Gardens, laid out by Sir Francis Bacon and using cuttings brought by Sir Walter Raleigh from America, provided the city's elites a setting at once majestic and

The Middle Temple showcased an elegant dining hall for privileged young gentlemen studying law amid symbols of power and achievement.
(PHOTOGRAPH COURTESY OF THE MASTERS OF THE BENCH OF THE HONOURABLE SOCIETY OF THE MIDDLE TEMPLE)

bucolic for evening strolls. St. Paul's Cathedral, with the longest nave in all of Europe, stood at the western end of the city boundary, dominating the skyline. Young gentlemen in training studied law at the Middle Temple. Ornately carved wooden beams framed the main dining hall; light pouring in from stunning stained glass windows, then as now, would illuminate the serving table constructed from timbers taken from the *Golden Hinde*, the ship on which Sir Francis Drake circumnavigated the globe from 1577 to 1580. History, power, and ambition all resided in such places. The kind of men who lived in this part of London, not surprisingly, believed that the world could—and even should—be theirs.[6]

But the real heart of London lay not in landmarks like the Middle Temple or Whitehall, but rather in the vigorous, ambitious, and youthful culture of the city. Some two hundred thousand people called London home at the turn of the seventeenth century. Despite exceedingly high mortality rates, the population had exploded during the Elizabethan era. Even as the plague swept the city in waves, immigrants kept coming: desperate and determined young people left the hinterlands of England to start over and find a different destiny in London. As the city grew, it remained decidedly youthful: a great proportion of citizens were under thirty.[7]

London was still walled then, although its burgeoning population was pushing against the stone boundaries and spilling over into the "suburbs" outside the city proper and across the Thames. Within the city walls, what once had been open fields now bustled with carpenters' shops and glass factories; former churchyards and abbeys became marketplaces. Streets were busy and dirty. Mud, garbage, and even human waste made crowded neighborhoods foul smelling and ripe for disease. And it was very loud: church bells clanged incessantly and wagons clattered along the city's crowded streets all day long, making "such a thundering as if the world ran upon wheels," and competing with the voices of peddlers hawking their wares and preachers giving open-air sermons.[8]

Like the gentlemen who strolled through Gray's Inn Gardens and prayed in the front pews of St. Paul's, the working classes and impoverished newcomers—the "rabble" of London—also dreamed. Many wanted new opportunities, better lives, adventure. And

Even a quick glance at this 1593 map of London suggests how densely settled the city had become in the late Elizabethan era. (FROM JOHN NORDEN, *SPECULUM BRITANNIAE,* COURTESY OF HUNTINGTON LIBRARY)

London gave them the chance to remake themselves. Fifteen times larger than any other city in England, London offered its citizens anonymity and the economic opportunity to achieve more than their "place" would have otherwise allowed. Tudor-Stuart England was fairly obsessed with class: men were born to a status and there they would remain, whether tinker or king. Even a person's attire was supposed to conform to this rigid ranking, and sartorial laws made wearing the wrong fabric or color illegal. Elites successfully policed the social order in the countryside, where everyone knew everyone else, as well as among the coat of arms–obsessed aristocracy in London. But the London street was another matter entirely: there, strangers could remake themselves and escape the rank they had been born to fill. All that was required was a spirit of competitiveness, individualism, and daring.[9]

London's culture reflected the ambitious, risk-taking youthfulness of its citizens. It was, as one resident aptly put it, "the Fair that lasts all year."[10] Taverns, drunkenness, gambling, and violence were everywhere. At least a hundred bawdy houses and brothels operated in the suburbs of London, beyond the city walls or along the south bank. Bear-baiting was wildly popular. For this macabre spectacle, restrained bears were whipped, attacked by dogs, and sometimes gradually slaughtered before cheering crowds. Occasionally bears and bulls were baited together, and owners of the rings could heighten an animal's rage (and a crowd's pleasure) by attaching fireworks to its back. Another imaginative proprietor tied a monkey to a pony's back and then unleashed the dogs. One patron reported, "To see the animal kicking amongst the dogs, with the screams of the ape . . . is very laughable." Cockfights, boar fights, even horse-baiting drew paying customers eager to see the latest, bloodiest game in town. Sometimes they became surprise participants themselves, as did one unlucky spectator at a bull-baiting session: the bull gored a dog and tossed the bloody, dying animal onto her lap. City residents also watched football games and tennis and wrestling matches and frequented neighborhood fairs, where they could see puppet shows, street performers, and human "freaks" while drinking and gambling.[11]

Meanwhile, the city's thriving press offered adventures for the mind. London was home to an active reading public with capacious tastes. Over a hundred publishers and an untold number of booksellers worked there, most within the shadow of St. Paul's. Stationers' Hall, which licensed all books published within the city, sat just a few steps from the cathedral. And more than a dozen bookshops operated in St. Paul's churchyard, with sellers peddling sermons delivered there alongside travel stories that romanticized ocean voyages to foreign places, particularly the widely admired collections of Richard Hakluyt, and plays, including the works of the stage's greatest dreamer: William Shakespeare.[12]

London was the kind of place where the son of a down-on-his-luck glover without a university education could, through talent and drive, become the most celebrated figure in all of literature. The city embraced and inspired Shakespeare, and he in turn entertained and moved its citizens. No man of the theater enjoyed more renown in Tudor-Stuart London than Shakespeare. He drew 1,500 to 2,000 paying customers a day to his theater, the Globe. Everyone in town enjoyed his work, from royals to the "rabble." Six days after his coronation, King James commissioned Shakespeare and his players to perform "for the recreation of our loving subjects" and recognized them as "the King's Men." For the next ten years they mounted plays at court on an average of fourteen times a year.[13]

Shakespeare may have delighted much of London, but some found his work, to say nothing of his customers at the Globe, unseemly. Shakespeare's company attracted the so-called lesser sorts, and, in the eyes of some aristocrats and ministers, served up disgusting spectacles of violence and debauchery. It did not help that his playhouse was located in Southwark, a rather colorful neighborhood. Respectable gentlemen complained about the "vagrant and lewd persons" attending the Globe and the nearby bear-baiting rings and brothels. At St. Paul's Cross, an open-air pulpit just outside St. Paul's Cathedral, popular Protestant ministers such as William Crashaw and William Symonds railed against the craven, sinful playwrights and actors just across the Thames, putting them in the same category as the despised Roman Church. "Papists" and "players" were the enemies of "true" Christians—Anglicans—and were linked together in numerous sermons because of their skilled deceptiveness. By 1606, Crashaw and Symonds were promoting the founding of an American colony as the will of God and con-demning the "papists" and "players" who opposed His mission.[14]

This sort of anti-Catholic vitriol, decades in the making, was born out of both religious conviction and political intrigue. For nearly half a century preceding the founding of the Virginia colony, devout English Protestants increasingly viewed Catholics as a sinister element, spiritually bankrupt and dangerous to the nation. When the Protestant Queen Elizabeth acceded to the throne in 1558, she participated in the growing tendency of evangelical Protestants to link English Protestantism with na-tional interest and view Catholics as their prime enemy. In 1568 Elizabeth imprisoned her Catholic cousin, Mary, Queen of Scots, whom many Catholics believed to be the rightful sovereign of England. Mary's imprisonment so roiled her sympathizers that they embarked upon an unsuccessful rebellion against Queen Elizabeth in 1569. This marked the first of several attempts on Elizabeth's life by members of the persecuted Catholic commu-nity. In 1570, in the wake of the failure of this uprising and the continued incarceration of Mary, Pope Pius V excommunicated Elizabeth and freed English Catholics from any allegiance to her. While Pius hoped to destabilize the Elizabethan regime, he in fact rendered English Catholics traitors to their nation—at least that was how the politically powerful Protestants saw things. By the 1580s, anyone attending Catholic mass could be imprisoned for a year; converting someone to Catholicism was high treason. Meanwhile, English Catholics in exile in Europe began secretly sending Jesuit missionaries to England to keep the faith alive and hopefully bring England back into the fold of the Roman Church. Like the plots against Elizabeth, these missionary efforts only confirmed in Protestants' minds how dangerous and disloyal Catholics were.[15]

The death of Elizabeth and accession of James in 1603 gave momentary hope of toleration to England's Catholics because the new king was the son of Mary, Queen of Scots. But shortly after James's coronation he ratified a law extending Elizabeth's policies regarding Catholics. A small group of Catholics, upset with James's failure to usher in changes, planned to kidnap the king, take over the Tower of London, and hold him captive there until he relented. That laughable folly was followed by a far more dangerous and plausible plot two years later. In the early hours of November 5, 1605, Guy Fawkes was arrested, bringing to light the Gunpowder Plot: an elaborate plan to blow up the House of Lords while the royal family was in attendance. Jesuit missionaries and their converts were quickly singled out as the perpetrators, and a raft of new anti-Catholic legislation sped through Parliament that year. Robert Cecil, the Earl of Salisbury and principal minister to King James (and soon to be an influential leader in the Virginia Company), was vehemently anti-Catholic and shepherded the new laws. After 1605, Catholics were not to come within ten miles of London; they were forbidden from receiving commissions in the navy or army and from working as doctors, lawyers, and clerks; Protestants entertaining or employing known Catholics were fined; Catholic homes could be searched at will, and Catholics were forbidden from owning armor or guns.[16]

The treatment of Henry Garnet, a Jesuit and one of the chief conspirators in the Gunpowder Plot, reveals the depths of Londoners' contempt for traitors and their rage over the Catholic-led effort to attack the English government. It took a jury only fifteen minutes to convict him of treason, and that was how long the executioner let him hang before Garnet's heart was cut out and shown to the crowd that filled St. Paul's churchyard—a poetic location for his execution if ever there was one. Garnet's limbs were severed and displayed to the spectators as well, and his head cut off and impaled on a stake on London Bridge to serve as a warning to other would-be traitors.[17] When Rev. Crashaw preached at St. Paul's Cross against Catholic enemies, his audience would have easily remembered they were standing where the blood of men such as Garnet—an English Catholic and traitor to his country and king—was spilled.

It was this city, of William Crashaw and William Shakespeare, of sophisticated gentlemen and indigent laborers, of bear-baiting and Catholic hating, that imagined and made England's first empire. Men like Sir Thomas Smythe saw riches and glory in America, and he convinced fellow businessmen to wager their money there; Rev. Symonds and his followers interpreted it as a call to fulfill God's greatest design for England; and the out-of-work, wishful artisans and laborers, along with more than a few of the criminals, agreed to sail the Atlantic, dreaming, like Smythe and Symonds, of a new life in Virginia.

And what a fanciful dream it was. Virginia would fulfill the noble ambitions that advocates of colonization had promoted for decades: "the advancement of Gods glorie, the renowne of his Majestie, and the good of your Countrie."[18] It would provide a passage to the Far East and easy access to the world's most desirable markets. Englishmen might discover in Virginia another Mexico, filled with gold and silver mines. Certainly, they believed, they would find endless numbers of "merchantable" commodities, including flax, hemp, silkworms, alum, pitch, tar, turpentine, cedar, walnuts, deer, iron, copper, pearls, dyes, and sugar cane.[19] From this new Eden, England could create a self-sufficient economy, or as promoters explained: "our monies and wares that nowe run into the handes of our adversaries or cowld frendes shall passe unto our frendes and naturall kinsmen and from them likewise we shall receive . . . our necessities." Using the rich resources available in Virginia, England would also build fleets of ships and use them to expand their maritime interests and defend themselves against foreign rivals. And as Walter Raleigh had promised, "hee that commaunds the sea, commaunds the trade, and hee that is Lord of the Trade of the world is lord of the wealth of the worlde."[20]

Advocates for colonizing Virginia also promised many rewards beyond the strictly financial. "True" Christians would convert the "heathen" Indians and introduce them to government and civilization.[21] Down-and-out English subjects could escape the poverty and disease rampant in London and start over in a bounteous, healthy land, where barley and oats grew even when "but fallen casually in the woorst sort of ground." Becoming colonists would be good for artisans unable to compete for jobs in London. Criminals could work for a new life rather than simply rotting in jail. And ex-soldiers had another chance for glory without hiring themselves out as mercenaries. Such men could "rather chose to spend themselves in seeking a new world, than servilely to be hired but as slaughterers in the quarrels of strangers." And, of course, success in Virginia would speed the demise of Spain's domination of the Americas. England's cruel, Catholic enemies would at last be defeated.[22] By way of Virginia, England might rule the world.

Efforts to fulfill those incredible promises began with a simple document. King James issued the charter, or "letters patent," that created the Virginia Company and the American colony on April 10, 1606. It actually defined the boundaries and purposes of *two* colonies, overseen by two separate organizations: one based in London and the other in Plymouth. With the stroke of a pen, James gave the two companies' leaders full rights to "Virginia"—which at the time meant most of the territory north of Spanish Florida. Specifically, they were allowed to found settlements anywhere between the 34° and 45° north latitude, which was, in essence, from the Cape Fear River in North Carolina through Maine. To avoid any potential conflict between the two groups, the London branch

King James I chartered the Virginia Company in 1606 and sanctioned the colony's reorganization in 1609. (PORTRAIT BY DANIEL MYTENS, COURTESY OF NATIONAL PORTRAIT GALLERY, LONDON)

was allowed to create its colony only between the 34° and 41° (somewhere between the Cape Fear and New York City), while the Plymouth group was supposed to settle between the 38° and 45° (more or less from the Potomac River to Bangor, Maine). To guard against overlapping claims, the two groups were required to establish settlements at least one hundred miles apart.[23]

According to the charter, eight men, four in London and four in Plymouth, would lead "divers others of our loving subjects" in attempting "to deduce a colony of sundry of our people into that part of America, commonly called Virginia." Thomas Gates, George Somers, Richard Hakluyt, and Edward Maria Wingfield were the named members of the London operation. Thomas Hanham, Raleigh Gilbert (the son of Humphrey Gilbert and nephew of Walter Raleigh), William Parker, and George Popham ran things out of Plymouth, for "all others of the towne of Plymouth in the countie of Devon and elsewhere" in the West Country.[24]

George Popham headed the Plymouth group, and he got them off to a quick start. Referred to in the charter as the "second colony," they, not the Londoners, actually commissioned the first expedition. Henry Challons, sailing the *Richard* from Plymouth with thirty-one men and bound for the northern regions of Virginia, made it as far as the Straits of Florida before being captured by the Spanish in November 1606 (a month before the London group sent out their first ships). The men on board the *Richard* were imprisoned and the ship sank. It was a total loss to the Plymouth investors, who never fully recovered from that setback. They tried again in June 1607. George Popham and Raleigh Gilbert went themselves this time, along with a hundred or so settlers, to make sure the effort succeeded. Their colony, Sagadahoc, was short-lived. Popham died in February 1608, and Gilbert and the remaining colonists, now fewer than fifty in number, abandoned America after less than a year, escaping on a pinnace they built there, called the *Virginia*. The effort for a "second colony" and the idea of a separate Plymouth group of colonial investors collapsed by the summer of 1608.[25]

As the brief and unhappy experience of the Plymouth group demonstrated, there was a lot more involved in making a colonial dream a reality than simply convincing King James to sign some papers. To be certain, the London group had several advantages over the Plymouth group. The men behind the company were an exceptionally talented—and, it turned out, lucky—lot. Together Thomas Gates, George Somers, and Edward Maria Wingfield had served in virtually every significant foreign cause over the past two decades. Wingfield was a fierce soldier and former prisoner of war who had fought in the Netherlands and in Ireland. Somers had spent most of his life at sea, sailing the Atlantic like Francis Drake and Walter Raleigh and commanding raids in the Caribbean before taking a seat in Parliament. Gates had also fought in the Caribbean and the Netherlands; he studied law at Gray's Inn and served as ambassador to Vienna. Hakluyt, London's famous chronicler of foreign travels and tireless advocate for New World colonies, completed the group. Collectively these four men understood intimately what it would take—in terms of public promotions, domestic and international negotiations, seafaring, and sheer force—to make Virginia happen. In a brilliant move they brought on London's greatest businessman, Thomas Smythe, to oversee operations. And to transport the first voyagers they hired their nation's most experienced captain: Christopher Newport.

Still, believing that Virginia could work required a great leap of faith, for despite all their talents and experience, these men and their project confronted a long history of ill-fated ventures.

The men who acquired the 1606 patent from King James and oversaw the company it created knew well the bleak past of English efforts in America. Many others had tried before them, and all had failed. No one understood that history better than Richard Hakluyt the younger. He was the nation's most prolific compiler of travel narratives, and mariners carried his works around the world, finding in them inspiration and guidance. He was also, along with the elder kinsman who shared his name, a vigorous promoter of colonies—as opposed to simply overseas trading ventures. He felt certain that settling English citizens in America would pay his country rich dividends, and he used his skills as a writer and connections at court to push that dream, knowing well that the odds were not in his favor.[26]

Famous explorers, including the half brothers Walter Raleigh and Humphrey Gilbert, tried to carry out the plans of men like Hakluyt in the late Elizabethan era, with generally demoralizing outcomes. In 1578, Elizabeth granted Gilbert the right to explore America, which he did, raising the ire of Spain and achieving nothing of consequence for England. Gilbert tried to claim Newfoundland, but the English, just like the French, Spanish, and Portuguese who also fished there, could not or would not spare the forces truly necessary to control the trade. He paid for his ambitions with his life. On his way home from Newfoundland in September of 1583, Gilbert was lost at sea.[27]

Raleigh took over Gilbert's charter upon his death, and, with the help of his friend Richard Hakluyt, managed to convince Queen Elizabeth to let them attempt a settlement in America. In 1585, one hundred or so English subjects settled the Roanoke colony, on a small island off the coast of present-day North Carolina. But they had bad luck almost from the start: infertile soil kept them from feeding themselves, and the Indians, quickly disgusted with the colonists and hoping to starve them out, withheld corn. The beleaguered colonists left the colony in 1586, hitching a ride with English privateers on their way home from raiding in the Caribbean. A second group of colonists were deposited in Roanoke the following year, with promises of a speedy return with more supplies. But fate intervened. England and Spain were in a full-scale war by that time, which kept ships and men otherwise occupied for several years.

Raleigh finally sent relief only to find the settlement abandoned again, the colonists' fate then as now unknown. Raleigh's destiny *is* known: King James had him arrested in 1603, retained in the Tower of London for thirteen years, and eventually beheaded.[28]

So while in some quarters enthusiasm for an American colony was strong, the experiences of men who pursued those ambitions were hardly encouraging. When King James took the throne in 1603, decades of plans and expeditions had done little more than invite the wrath of Spain and imperil the lives of sailors. Certainly privateers had made money raiding Spanish ships in the Caribbean, and the fishing off Newfoundland was profitable. But after forty years of talking and trying, the English still had established no colonies in the Americas. In fact, they had failed in every Atlantic enterprise they had tried before 1600. In addition to the debacle in Roanoke, they had pursued futile efforts to discover a Northwest Passage, claim a share of Caribbean trades, and traffic in African slaves. Their sole "success" came in the costly, bloody conquest of Ireland.[29]

Such failures had not deterred the likes of Smythe and Hakluyt. In the face of nearly unequivocal failure, they and a small cohort of merchants and gentlemen continued to keep faith that England could not only break into but eventually control the high seas— and with it, America.

In the five years just before the chartering of the Virginia Company, London's merchants had seen a modest reversal of fortune. They started by successfully challenging Dutch and Portuguese domination of the Indian Ocean trade through the East India Company, which was chartered in December 1600. The first profitable cargoes from that enterprise arrived in London in 1603, and the second followed in 1606. Merchants' experiences with the East India Company gave them hope for the Virginia Company. Many of the same men invested in both projects, and profits from the former encouraged them to pursue the latter. The men who funded both ventures also learned from the East India Company to be patient. Between 1600 and 1606, leaders struggled with shortfalls in capital and subscribers reluctant to pay what they had pledged. The years between the first and second fleets were quite lean, and some nervous investors pulled out.[30] But the resolve of men like Smythe did not falter, and their persistence paid off: by 1606 the East India Company was profitable and the principal backers rich and renowned. Those first difficult years provided a lesson in resolve that the Virginia Company's leaders would need in spades.

Of course, Virginia marked a major shift for London's merchants, from running trading enterprises to creating a colony. The motivations for their other companies were fairly simple: to bring lucrative goods to England and sell English wares abroad. But founding a colony was another matter entirely. Colonies required more money and wider public support and needed to balance the ambitions of both the architects of the effort and the people on the ground.

A successful expedition to the coast of North America in 1602 by Bartholomew Gosnold gave English entrepreneurs the confidence that they could make this transition. The happy news that Gosnold's crew brought back fueled enthusiasm for adventuring to North America. The northern coastline was so filled with valuable fish that Gosnold named it "Cape Cod." One of the men traveling with him published a tract praising the wonderful potential of colonizing the region: it overflowed with trees to be harvested and animals to be hunted and afforded "the greatest fishing of the world." While extracting all the natural resources, the English could, the author assured his readers, "plant Christian people and religion."[31]

And yet for every success, there seemed to be a disheartening setback. Just months after Gosnold's much-celebrated voyage, Captain Bartholomew Gilbert sailed to America, but never saw home again. Gilbert and several of his men had just made it onto the shore when "the Indians set upon them." They died within sight of the rest of the crew, which "had much a doe to save themselves and [their ship]." The survivors made it home in late September 1603; the depressing stories they circulated around London stood in sharp contrast to the cheery Gosnold reports.[32]

London's Fishmongers' Company could not even get their ship out into the Atlantic. In March 1606, just a month before James issued the Virginia Company charter, a group of merchants, including members of the Fishmongers' Company, pooled their resources and hired a ship and captain to exploit the rich fishing grounds off the northern coast of America. But the captain turned out to be a crook. He stole supplies from the ship and sold them, pocketing the money. At one port, he "invited many of the towne on borde to drincke and make merry." It was quite a party: the crew and some thirty guests consumed a hogshead of beer in a single night. The captain, meanwhile, "interteyned" three young "maide servantes." While escorting them back to shore he ordered a cannon fired, whereupon the incompetent crew aimed in the wrong direction and "tore downe" the upper deck. He was finally arrested, but not before all the fishmongers' resources had been squandered.[33]

There was, then, much to lose in wagering on America. But the leaders of the Virginia Company were sure there was also much to gain, and by the winter of 1606 they were ready to take their chance.

The playwrights so popular in London had a field day with the wild promises made about America. In 1605, the play *Eastward Hoe!* went through three printings, demonstrating the popularity of the farcical depiction of pompous adventurers and drunken sailors exaggerating their Atlantic exploits. Blowhard caricatures of men like Hakluyt and Smythe bragged that, thanks to bounteous riches from the New World, even "their chamberpotts are pure gould" and "all the prisoners they take are fetered in gold."[34] For years, Virginia backers would struggle against the "jests of prophane players and other sycophants." Ministers in particular disdained the playwrights and actors who lampooned colonization, calling them "the scum & dregs of the earth." Such denunciation did nothing to temper the popularity of the theater; one contemptuous cleric regretted "some profane persons affirm they can learn as much both for edifying and example at a play, as at a sermon." And what Londoners learned from plays like *Eastward Hoe!* was that Virginia was not a paradise, but a joke.[35]

King James was not quite the friend that Gates, Somers, Wingfield, and Hakluyt needed, either. At first, the accession of James had seemed like an unqualified advantage to the businessmen and explorers eager to colonize America. As long as Elizabeth reigned, Sir Walter Raleigh still retained his exclusive claim to the North American mainland. James changed all that by simply revoking Raleigh's patent. James also negotiated peace with Spain, which helped open the door for the English to settle in America.[36]

But then the new king's first publication after taking the throne denounced tobacco, one of the New World's most lucrative commodities.[37] And James, just like Elizabeth, concerned himself foremost with European power politics; overseas commercial pursuits finished a distant second, and he rejected ideas that threatened his diplomatic agenda. The charter he issued, for example, affirmed Spanish sovereignty over the parts of America they settled and forbade his subjects from entering any such territory. And he offered no financial support to the Virginia Company and no assurance that he would defend them in case of Spanish invasion. Chartering the company was as far as he would go, and even that required a good deal of cajoling. Christopher Newport tried courting the king's favor, bringing two crocodiles and a boar back from the Caribbean in 1605 and presenting them to James at court. The gesture delighted the king but did little to reorder his priorities.[38]

As they planned their colony, company leaders made a number of missteps that turned out to be far more damaging to their prospects than the playwrights' jeers or the king's caution. The governmental structure laid out by the charter in 1606 was overly complicated and an invitation to corruption and chaos. They also failed to exploit the religious zeal and strident anti-Catholicism of the ministers at St. Paul's Cross.[39]

Dreams of an Edenic Virginia furthered their undoing in 1606 and 1607. The men who designed the colony in England appeared to have no idea about the reality that would face the settlers they sent over. The charter spent an inordinate amount of time describing the seal of the colony (which, of course, bore King James's likeness), and the design of the government went into elaborate detail about inheritance laws and judicial processes.[40] The orders drafted by the Virginia Council, the thirteen-man governing body of the company, for organizing their colony were equally unrealistic. They called for the orderly division of men into three work groups: some would construct buildings, some plant food, some serve as guards. As for the colonists' housing, they were advised "to set your houses even and by a line, that your streets may have a good breadth, and be carried square about your market place, and every street's end opening into it." So certain were members of the company of the terrific natural resources in Virginia and the ease with which they could be acquired that they directed Captain Christopher Newport, on his return from Virginia, to bring home "ships full laden with good merchandizes."[41]

The men in London completely misunderstood the native Virginians. The charter gave the colonists full rights to "all the lands, woods, soil, grounds, havens, ports, rivers, mines, minerals, marshes, waters, fishings, commodities, and hereditaments, whatsoever." What of the Indian nations living in those regions? They were dismissed as "such people, as yet live in darkness and miserable ignorance of the true knowledge and worship of God." Furthermore, the charter promised, the colonists coming to America "may in time bring the infidels and savages, living in those parts, to human civility, and to a settled and quiet government."[42] This proved to be as disastrous an idea as it was arrogant.

Finally, Virginia enthusiasts failed to secure widespread public support for their colonial plans. A 1605 petition to Parliament seeking assent to an American enterprise called for the proposed colony to be publicly funded. It was more likely, the petitioners reasoned, that "better men of [be]haviour and qualitie will ingage themselves in a publique service, which carrieth more reputacon with it, then a private, which is for the most parte ignominious in the end." The petitioners were so ambitious as to believe that, with the nation behind colonizing Virginia, quick profits would make it "no harde matter . . . to persuade every County according to the proportion of bignes and abilitie to builde barkes and shippes of a compotent size and to maintaine them."[43]

None of this happened in 1606. Parliament passed on funding the venture, and the Crown also withheld financial support— although it retained the right to one-fifth of any gold or silver found in the colony. The company did not even appear to solicit investments from the general public. Instead, the work of launching the American colony fell to a small group of men, undertaking an adventure, as one observer put it, "as rather beseemed a whole State and Commonwealth to take in hand." Small wonder, then, that many Londoners concluded that settling a colony in Virginia "was a thing seeming strange and doubtfull in the eye of the World."[44]

And then there was the small matter of Spain.

The Spanish ambassador in London, Don Pedro de Zúñiga, took a dim view of the Virginia Company's intention to blatantly violate his country's claim over America. The Spanish, as one diplomat put it, looked out for their American interests "with no less watchful eyes than to the government of their own wives." Not surprisingly, then, as soon as Zúñiga heard about the Virginia undertaking in the early spring of 1606, he sought an audience with James to demand that the king compel his subjects to cease their illegal behavior. He also immediately wrote his sovereign, Philip III, about the necessity of stopping the project in its tracks.[45]

How exactly Spain might go about doing so was the problem. Communications between London and Madrid were slow and unreliable, and Philip, no less than James, wanted to avoid another war. Moreover, officials in Madrid, like their counterparts in London, knew how often Englishmen had failed in executing such bold ideas. There was every reason to believe that the Virginia colonists would doom themselves, as others before them had done, without any need for a Spanish assault.

As plans for Virginia moved from mere conversations in Smythe's home to the actual loading of the ships bound for America, Philip and Ambassador Zúñiga remained unable to decide "what steps had best be taken to prevent" the settlement of Virginia without inviting open conflict. Even after the first colonists arrived in America, Spanish officials were still struggling to acquire accurate information from London and get Philip to act so that "with all necessary forces this plan of the English should be prevented." By that time, however, the plan had become a reality.[46]

Diplomacy was, of course, hardly Spain's only weapon. Philip commanded an awesome military, which could easily destroy the tiny outpost that the English set up in the midst of Spain's vast American empire. Yet, despite the pleas of Zúñiga and other advisers, Philip delayed responding. Ambassador Zúñiga found himself totally exasperated with King James for permitting "his subjects to try and disturb the seas, coasts, and lands of the Indies" and with his own King Philip for refusing to simply quash the colony.[47]

Spanish inaction in 1606 and 1607 must have puzzled Virginia Company leaders who, when they sent out the first colonists, felt deeply (and rightly so) fearful of a full-out attack. James's responses to Ambassador Zúñiga, who repeatedly sought an audience to personally protest the plans to violate Spain's rights, while quite savvy, could not have eased their suspicions. Far from defending the enterprise, James told Zúñiga "that those who went, did it at their own risk and . . . there would be no complaint should they be punished."[48] This cleverly distanced James from what Zúñiga insisted was an unlawful, belligerent act. It also bought the Virginia Company precious time, as Zúñiga and officials in Madrid struggled to decide on an appropriate response to this apparently extralegal colony. At the same time, James affirmed that he intended to go no further in militarily defending the Virginia venture than was mandated by his charter—which was to say not at all.

That Spain neither demanded an end to the Virginia Company before the first boat sailed nor raided and destroyed the settlement once it was founded arguably turned out to be the greatest diplomatic failure of Philip's reign and the greatest gift the Virginia Company ever received. And in truth they needed all the help they could get.

When the ships commissioned to sail to America were "victualed, riged, and furnished for the said voyage," Virginia Company leaders asked Christopher Newport to take "the sole charge to appoint such captains, soldiers, and marriners as shall either command, or be shiped to pass in the said ships or pinnace." Newport was clearly the best man for the job. By 1606, he had acquired more experience sailing the Atlantic than any captain in England. He had fought the Portuguese off the coast of Brazil, raided Spanish ships in the Caribbean, and even explored Florida. Despite losing his right arm while fighting in the Caribbean, Newport remained a fearless, adroit captain, who rightly held the respect of his employers and his crews. Thomas Smythe and the other leaders of the Virginia Company trusted him to safely carry the first colonists to America. From the time the ships left port until they reached Virginia, he alone retained "sole charge and command" of the entire enterprise—which, as it turned out, was not very impressive.[49]

For all their dreams and promises, the Virginia Company sent forth quite a modest force. More an expedition than the foundation of a full-scale settlement, the first band of colonists numbered barely a hundred men, with four boys and no women. Three small ships could carry everyone and all their supplies. The three vessels left London on December 20, 1606. The *Susan Constant*, captained by Newport and lead ship in the convoy, was just over 115 feet long. The *Godspeed*, under command of the experienced Bartholomew Gosnold, measured less than seventy feet long and fifteen feet across at its widest. The fifty-foot *Discovery* was a pinnace under the direction of Captain John Ratcliffe. Thirty-nine crewmen crowded onto the ships with the hundred or so colonists.[50]

The three ships were overflowing with passengers and crew—a harbinger for food running out and disease running rampant. For the superstitious, there was another bad omen, this one relating to the *Susan Constant*. The ship was only a year old when Newport's men readied it for the voyage to Virginia. Loaded in London in mid-November, the *Susan Constant* apparently docked too close to another ship, the *Philip and Francis*. A mariner, Henry Ravens, went to Christopher Newport's house to warn him to move his ship, to no avail. When the tide shifted on November 23, 1606, the two ships collided. The *Susan Constant* suffered damages in three locations, and the *Philip and Francis* fared even worse. A lawsuit ensued, in which Newport and his sailors claimed the *Philip and Francis* was improperly tied down, and the men on the *Philip and Francis* insisted the fault lay with the crew of the *Susan Constant*. The finger-pointing and financial setback—before the ship ever even left England—turned out to be an ominous predictor of England's latest American venture.[51]

Even the most sanguine of onlookers must have found the ragtag bunch of voyagers that turned out for the December launch disappointing. Laborers looking for a new start, out-of-work soldiers, and self-important gentlemen boarded the boats. Almost none of the principal investors in the company made the trip. Richard Hakluyt was supposed to go, but, inexplicably, failed to show up at the dock. Edward Maria Wingfield did go, as did many other gentlemen—too many, in fact—one of them George Percy. Percy packed for Virginia thinking about his status rather than his destination. He bought a new chest and filled it with starched collars and cuffs, fancy gloves, and books.[52] The holds of the two larger ships carried Percy's chest and the other passengers' more meager personal effects; tools for building houses, furniture, and the settlement fort; food and water. But the most precious cargo was a secret set of directions from the Virginia Company.

Newport, Gosnold, and Ratcliffe carried sealed "instruments" listing the names of the colony's council members, to be opened within twenty-four hours of reaching Virginia but not beforehand. No one on the voyage knew the colonial council members' names. Once these men were named, they would elect their president and run the affairs of the settlement. Fatefully, the colonial council was given the prerogative of removing the president "upon any just cause."[53]

In an attempt to promote order in the colony, the Virginia Company required that, before boarding, all passengers take an oath to "beare faith & true Allegeance" to King James. The oath disavowed any allegiances to "ye pope" and "any Authoretie of the Church or See of Rome." Protestant Englishmen would build Virginia—or at least that was the plan.[54]

A launch poem, written to honor the voyage, offered inspiration to the travelers. Poet Michael Drayton praised their "brave hero-ique minds" and reminded them that they "need not feare" the crossing, for "Earth's only Paradise" awaited them in Virginia. And the men funding the adventure offered a final bit of guidance for the band carrying their dreams to America: "Lastly and chiefly the way to prosper and achieve good success is to make yourselves all of one mind for the good of your country and your own, and to serve and fear God."[55] It was excellent advice, if only the Virginians would use it.

CHAPTER 2

"A GRAND ENTERPRISE"

Christopher Newport brought the first happy reports from the American colony home to England in the closing days of July 1607. He reached Plymouth Sound on the 29th and immediately dashed off a note to Robert Cecil, the Earl of Salisbury, assuring him and the other leaders of the Virginia enterprise that "wee have performed our duties to the uttermost of our powers." Newport had safely deposited the colonists on the banks of the river they named for their king on April 26, and then scouted the country some two hundred miles inland. Newport explained in his letter that he much preferred to speed on to London and elaborate on these "glad tidings" in person, but felt obligated to safeguard the *Susan Constant*. Virginia, it turned out, was "very rich in gold and Copper," and Newport's ship held some of that "gold." Leaving it in the hands of an underling seemed too risky, so Newport waited until "winde and weather be favourable" and he could sail the *Susan Constant* on to London and personally deliver his precious cargo to the men of the Virginia Company.[1]

When he finally made it to London around the middle of August, Newport carried along the first letters written by the Virginia colonists, all dated June 22, the day Newport left the settlement. The governing council for the colony, which consisted of President Edward Maria Wingfield, Bartholomew Gosnold, George Kendall, John Martin, Christopher Newport, John Ratcliffe, and John Smith, forwarded an official report to the Virginia Council in London. And a few colonists sent personal letters. Gabriel Archer wrote the most. Archer studied at Cambridge and Gray's Inn before sailing to America with Bartholomew Gosnold on the 1602 exploratory voyage. He apparently served as secretary of the Virginia colony in 1607, for he chronicled Newport's exploration of the James River and offered rosy predictions on "the likelihood of ensuing riches by England's aid and industry."[2]

Collectively, the letters Newport brought home described Virginia as the land of "milk and honey" that London entrepreneurs dreamed about. William Brewster bragged "such a bay, a river, and a land did never the eye of man behold" and predicted that Virginia would soon make England "more rich and renowned than any kingdom in all Europa." According to the council in Virginia, the land "is most fruitfull, laden with good Oake, Ashe, Walnut tree, Poplar, Pine, sweet woods, Cedar, and others," and the waterways "so stored with sturgion and other sweet fish as no man's fortune hath ever possessed the like." Gabriel Archer seconded the promise that "The main river abounds with sturgeon very large and excellent good," and went even further: "at the mouth of every brook and in every creek both store and exceeding good fish of divers kinds; and in the large sounds near the sea are multitudes of fish, banks of oysters, and many great crabs." The soil, he raved, produced better wheat, peas, and beans than that back home, and furthermore "it yields two crops a year." Strawberries, gooseberries, nuts, carrots, potatoes, pumpkins, and melons thrived in Virginia, even if the colonists only "threw in the seeds at random carelessly, and scarce rak'd it." Profits would easily accrue from farming, fishing, naval stores, pearls, and copper.[3]

While never the Garden of Eden depicted by optimistic colonists and opportunistic promoters, coastal Virginia was, in fact, a verdant, fertile land, with thick woodlands full of wildlife and waterways teeming with fish. The leaders of the 1607 voyage located their settlement on an island, some fifty miles up the James River from the mouth of the Chesapeake Bay and connected to the mainland only by a narrow strip of land at the western end. The site of the fort at Jamestown offered strategic advantages against a Spanish invasion from the sea or an Indian assault by land, but it lay surrounded by marshlands and, the colonists shortly discovered, lacked a ready supply of fresh water.[4]

In their letters back home, the settlers assured their London sponsors that they had been good stewards to the mission. The council bragged that in just seven weeks' time they had "fortified well against the Indians" and planted "good store of wheat." The construction of houses continued apace, and they even sent home samples of the clapboard they used.[5]

According to the colonists, much of the credit for the success in Virginia that first summer went to Christopher Newport. It was Newport who refused to bend to the physical hardships: when his exploration met with a waterfall too hazardous to navigate by boat, he led his men on foot. As the colonists struggled to construct their fort, Newport made his sailors help out. Newport negotiated with the werowances, or leaders among the Indian villages, and he sat first among all the white men when they met, signifying his authority. He also settled quarrels between the settlers and members of the colonial council. Because of him, Gabriel Archer said, "We confirmed a faithful love one to another and in our hearts subscribed an obedience to our superiors." The council trusted him to clarify their actions to company leaders: "Captaine Newport hath seen all and knoweth all, and can satisfy your further expectations." And men like William Brewster felt exactly the same, explaining that "our ever-renowned captain, Captain Newport . . . will so justly and truly declare better than I can."[6]

Newport, then, was a man of exceptional ability and resolve, who won the respect of most everyone in Virginia. Unfortunately, his job called him back to England, to transport more people and supplies to Virginia. When he left the settlement, Edward Maria Wingfield took charge. By the time Newport made it back across the Atlantic—and it was a short trip, barely seven weeks—most everything he knew about Virginia and most everything written in the letters he brought home proved to be wrong.

William Brewster, the cheerful colonist so certain that his new home "promiseth infinite treasure," was dead before Newport arrived in Plymouth. The "gold" Newport carried back turned out to be worthless rocks and dirt. And the men he left in charge spent their summer arresting one council member, burying another, and deposing their president.[7]

The letters Newport gave Thomas Smythe and the other leaders of the Virginia Company conceded some difficulties in the colony. Some of the sailors and settlers refused to work. Instead, they dug around in the woods for "Sasafrix roots," ruining some of the company's precious tools. Gabriel Archer's otherwise laudatory account chronicled a violent confrontation with Indians. While Newport traveled into the interior of Virginia, a group of some two hundred Indians laid siege to the fort inhabited by what they viewed as enemy invaders. The offensive against Jamestown came on May 26, a month to the day after the colonists arrived. Only cannon fire from the ships saved the fort from falling during the "very furious assault." For weeks afterward fighting continued, confining the colonists to their fort. Those who strayed outside risked their lives: one man, "going out to do natural necessity," was shot three times.[8]

The ambitious, brash soldier John Smith had also caused all sorts of trouble. First, he tried to foment a mutiny on board the *Susan Constant*. Christopher Newport arrested him and tried to hang him when they stopped over at Nevis for supplies. Bartholomew Gosnold, second in command on the voyage, and Rev. Robert Hunt interceded and saved Smith's life. Then, to Newport's shock, when he opened the secret directions from the Virginia Company, he saw John Smith's name on the list of councilors! Smith, the son of a yeoman farmer, appeared not to know his place and acted as if he knew better than the proper gentlemen on the colonial council. The other councilors initially refused to seat him—or, for a time, even to release him from his chains in the hold of the *Susan Constant*.[9]

Thomas Smythe and the Virginia Company Council members knew, as they planned the first supply of their American enterprise, that some difficulties lay ahead. Clearly, the men they sent over had not been able "to make yourselves all of one mind for the good of your country." Furthermore, the fallacy of Newport's "gold" was quickly revealed. And within days of Newport arriving in London prominent residents were gossiping about the colonists' inability to forge a peace with the Indians.[10]

But Smythe and the councilors in London did not know the whole story. The colonists who wrote home in June were, at best, overly optimistic. They left London in wet, cold December and endured four grueling months at sea before arriving in the Chesapeake in the spring, the most beautiful and temperate time of year. They can be forgiven for initially seeing Virginia as the "New Eden" they had been promised. Furthermore, no one, certainly not Christopher Newport, who was greeted as a hero on his return, wanted to give the London benefactors bad news. And finally, according to their directives, the colonial council censored all the settlers' letters; nothing that might "discourage others" was to escape the shores of Virginia. So, these initial accounts painted a far rosier picture of Virginia than they should have. Most important, few of the 1607 settlers fully understood the gravity of staking their claim in the middle of territory controlled by a powerful confederation of Indian communities, headed by Wahunsonacock, or Powhatan, who gave his name to the peoples under his authority. The Powhatans, which included around thirty tribes living in several hundred villages in the Chesapeake region, numbered some fifteen to twenty thousand. When one hundred or so Englishmen tried to take their land, it produced the bloody results anyone could predict.[11]

After Newport left, the problems the colonists had downplayed in those first reports home spiraled out of control. Smythe did not know—could not know—that while Newport trumpeted the success of his initial voyage and planned for his return trip, the American colony was falling to pieces.

Newport's departure from Virginia on June 22, 1607—and his decision to commandeer many of the colony's provisions for his sailors—left the settlers, in George Percy's words, "verie bare and scantie of victualls." Except for what they foraged, they lived off a pint of wheat and barley a day. Surrounded by swampland, they unknowingly drank brackish, contaminated water and caught dysentery and typhoid fever. Percy began to chronicle the deaths in early August, some from the vividly and aptly named "bloody flux" and others from skirmishes with Indians. John Smith, after finally securing his seat on the colonial council, concluded that "God (being angrie with us) plagued us with such famin and sicknes that the living were scarce able to bury the dead." Percy, while not ready to see God's hand in their plight, otherwise agreed with

Smith's bleak appraisal: "There were never Englishmen left in a forreigne Countrey in such miserie as wee were in this new discovered Virginia." Half the colonists were dead by October, and fewer than forty survived the first winter.[12]

Virginia's leaders, charged with looking out for the settlers, failed miserably at that task. Poor Bartholomew Gosnold, a faithful promoter of America who had also been the only peacekeeper among the fractious council members, died on August 22. With Gosnold dead and Newport gone, the remaining five members turned on one another. Edward Maria Wingfield made a mess of things, and his rivals seized on his every mistake. Within six weeks of Newport leaving him in charge, Wingfield alienated most everyone in the fort. John Smith accused him of hoarding food while working men went hungry and flatly asserted that "he was generally hated of all." In early September, the colonial council, at the instigation of Smith, deposed Wingfield and chained him in the hold of their pinnace to await a disgraceful transport back to England. The gentleman entrepreneur and the ruffian soldier had, in just a matter of months, traded places.[13]

Around the time Gosnold died, George Kendall was accused of treason and thrown off the colonial council. The specifics of the charges remain unknown, but the challenge to the Virginia Company's authority was transparent. Kendall was mentored by and closely connected to Robert Cecil, the Earl of Salisbury, a major investor in the Virginia Company and powerful friend to the enterprise in Parliament. Kendall's cousin, Edwin Sandys, was also an important member of Parliament and advocate for Virginia. They wanted Kendall on the colonial council to make sure they had a reliable friend helping lead Virginia. But he did not last long in the snake pit that was Jamestown. In November 1607, the remaining members of the council—John Ratcliffe, John Martin, and John Smith—ordered him shot to death.[14]

Gabriel Archer apparently spearheaded the accusations against Kendall, and within a month of Kendall's execution Archer had taken a place on the council. In league with Ratcliffe and Martin, Archer then conspired to eliminate John Smith. In early December 1607, the Pamunkey Indians took Smith captive while he explored the Virginia interior. They killed two men traveling with him and turned Smith over to Powhatan. Years later—after all the other people involved died—Smith told that now-famous tale of being rescued from execution by Powhatan's daughter, Pocahontas, during his captivity. Whether that happened or not remains the source of great debate, but Smith did survive his ordeal, and he made his way back to Jamestown around dawn on January 2, 1608. As Smith entered the fort, "each man with the truest signes of joy they could expresse welcommed mee," except for Gabriel Archer "and some 2 or 3 of his." Archer's cohort, dismayed to see their arrogant and accomplished rival safely returned, blamed Smith for the deaths of his two companions and made plans to rid themselves of him. By a fluke of fate, Christopher Newport sailed up the James River on the *John and Francis* that very night and stopped the plot against Smith. If Pocahontas did not save Smith's life that winter, Christopher Newport surely did.[15]

Newport returned to Jamestown with a boat full of supplies and around a hundred new colonists, fully expecting to see a thriving settlement. Instead, he found the colony in a state of mayhem and the fort in utter disarray. While some of the colonists had planted and others had traded with the Powhatans, their efforts had been inadequate to properly supply the entire camp. Newport fed the hungry colonists with provisions he had brought and put his men to work reinforcing the fort and storehouse. He also sorted things out among the leaders. After freeing Smith, Newport released Wingfield—still captive on the pinnace after nearly four months. Wingfield singled out Archer as the "ringleader" of all the troublemaking; he was allegedly "always hatching of some mutiny" and "spewing out his venomous libels and infamous chronicles" against someone. Whether or not Newport agreed with this assessment, he decided to take Gabriel Archer back to England.[16]

As if things were not bad enough, on January 7 a fire swept through the fort. It destroyed all but three buildings and most of the settlers' provisions and clothes. Francis Perkins, one of the new colonists Newport brought over, lost everything he owned except for one mattress he had not yet unloaded from the ship. Some 140 people faced January's "bitter colds and such severe frosts" with little more than the clothes on their backs. John Smith recalled "many of our old men diseased, and of our new for want of lodging perished."[17]

John Smith liked imagining himself as the savior of the Virginia colony, and he appeared increasingly jealous of Christopher Newport's popularity among the settlers. Conveniently ignoring the fact that Newport had saved his life, Smith claimed that the captain's continued presence in Virginia only worsened the colonists' troubles. Newport and his men gave lavish gifts to Powhatan and sold everything they could to the Indians, which, Smith complained, "cut the throat of our trade." The crew of the *John and Francis* stayed for fourteen weeks, when Smith believed they "might as well have been gone in 14. daies." And during that time, Newport's sailors "spent the beefe, porke, oile, aquavite, fish, butter, and cheese, beere and such like; as was provided to be landed us." Finally, Newport, like the investors in London, continued to hunger for gold, which Smith suspected did not exist in Virginia. Newport brought over two gold refiners and two goldsmiths, and with "golden promises" set the colonists on a fool's errand: "there was no talke, no hope, no worke, but dig gold, wash gold, refine gold, load gold."[18] When Newport weighed anchor on

April 10, 1608, carrying another load of "gold" to England, Smith was glad to see him go and no doubt doubly glad that Gabriel Archer was sailing with him. Maybe now things would get better in Jamestown—surely they could not get worse.

The news Christopher Newport brought back from his second trip to Virginia—of famine, infighting, warfare with the Indians, and the deaths of better than half the colonists—would have been devastating to the investors and company leaders. Nothing seemed to be going right in America for the London wing of the Virginia Company. And things were even worse for the Plymouth group. When Newport arrived in England in late May 1608, news of failures in the "second colony" had already reached London. Half the colonists had fled Sagadahoc in December 1607, and the winter killed many of those who remained, including George Popham, one of the principal leaders of the Plymouth group. About the time Newport reported on the dire situation in Jamestown, the last of the Sagadahoc settlers were abandoning Virginia's sister colony.[19]

Aware that his continued prominence now depended in no small measure on Virginia's success, Newport appeared desperate to produce some good news. He first bragged about bringing gold from America. Newport had assured company leaders that he had simply loaded the wrong material in 1607, a mistake he corrected on his second trip. But John Smith was right. The colonists had once again filled Newport's ship with rocks and soil. Newport also brought home Namontack, a young servant to Powhatan who knew English and acted as a mediator between the colonists and the Indians. Powhatan sent Namontack to England to learn all he could about the newcomers' land, but Newport passed him off as a prince—the son of the great "emperor" Powhatan—hoping that Namontack's presence would drum up excitement over the faltering colony.

Spanish Ambassador Zúñiga, who had been gleefully reporting on the hardships in Virginia, saw through this immediately. Namontack appeared to be merely "a little boy" and a "very ordinary person." Zúñiga scoffed at Newport's transparently bogus claim about his royalty: "it has amused me to see how they esteem him."[20]

Equally embarrassing and far more devastating to the Virginia Company was the ignominious return of Edward Maria Wingfield. One of the eight charter members of the company and the only one in Jamestown, Wingfield was supposed to ensure the order and profitability of the enterprise. Instead, he returned to England in disgrace. How humiliating it must have been for Wingfield to try to explain his absolute failure to his friends on the Council of the Virginia Company. Attempting to absolve himself of responsibility for the chaos in Virginia, he wrote a blistering review of the settlement. Wingfield's "Discourse of Virginia" detailed the dreadful illnesses and deprivations of food that beset the colonists, the conspiracies plotted among the colonial councilors, and the general laziness and venality of the men sent to America. Only Newport escaped his rebuke. Unfortunately, in the process of condemning all his enemies, Wingfield also revealed their grievances (many of which appear legitimate) and his own incompetence. The only saving grace was that London's publishers did not get their hands on Wingfield's "Discourse," so the shame was fairly contained.[21]

The Virginia Company's luck at keeping the appalling news about Virginia off the streets of London ran out in August 1608. A personal letter written by John Smith became, without his consent or knowledge, the first report from the Virginia colony ever published. *A True Relation* made public all the troubles in Jamestown: the "want of sufficient and good victualls," the "famin and sicknes," the deposing of Wingfield because he "was generally hated of all." Smith also described how, after Newport first left them in America, the colonists lived in rotten tents and that most "would rather starve and rot with idelnes, then be perswaded to do any-thing for their owne reliefe."[22] Predictably, Smith made himself the hero of the story. He negotiated with the Powhatans for corn and explored the region, describing it as filled with great bounty but ineptly exploited by the ill-equipped, quarrelsome colonists.

The Virginia Company quickly sent a second supply under Newport's command in the fall of 1608. That operation, which transported the first women to the colony, did nothing to change the growing suspicion among company insiders that their enter-prise was going badly astray. Newport arrived in the colony in October and returned to England in January 1609 with more of the same disappointing information: John Smith, if more effective than other leaders, remained an arrogant bully; the councilors quarreled incessantly; the Powhatans resented the colonists and struck at will; many of the colonists refused to take orders or even work to feed themselves, and they suffered from famine and devastating ill-nesses; neither precious ores nor a passage east had materialized.

When he reported all this to the Virginia Company Council in London, Christopher Newport also delivered a scathing rebuke of the company penned by their colony's newest president, Captain John Smith. Smith rose to power by capitalizing on the factional-ism rife in Virginia and the deaths or departures of several of his chief rivals. He wasted little time in exercising his power. The company's directives for the second supply—for Newport to hunt gold and a passage to the East and to crown Powhatan a tributary prince of King James—Smith declared ludicrous. His letter also condemned Christopher Newport's "unnecessary wages"; he com-plained that Newport earned "an hundred pounds a yeare for carry-ing newes," and argued that that money should be used to feed the hungry settlers. In the second supply, Newport brought barely twenty pounds' worth of food, with which Smith was somehow supposed to feed two hundred people. Smith also explained why he was expelling John Ratcliffe, and warned "if he and Archer returne againe, they are sufficient to keepe us alwayes in factions." Smith sarcastically suggested that next time the company try sending "Carpenters, husbandmen, gardiners, fisher men, blacksmiths, masons"—in other words, useful men rather than their conniving gentry friends.[23]

Unfortunately for John Smith, Thomas Smythe talked to Smith's critics before he read his words. Christopher Newport's relationship with John Smith had grown increasingly strained in the months after he saved Smith from execution; by 1609 their rivalry had devolved into undisguised mutual disdain. And Newport reported to Smythe upon his return to England. Gabriel Archer and John Ratcliffe, each removed from Virginia because of Smith, also met with Smythe. Both men felt bitterly contemptuous of Smith, a point they would not have hidden when they talked to Smythe. So, what Smythe knew about Virginia came predominately from John Smith's enemies, who depicted him as arrogant and domineering and as the cause of Jamestown's failures.

With his reproachful letter, John Smith confirmed Newport, Archer, and Ratcliffe's stories; his language was self-aggrandizing and insolent. Clearly he had never learned his "place." Smith's letter helped convince the leaders of the Virginia Company that extraordinary changes were required to save their American venture.

By January 1609, Thomas Smythe knew beyond a doubt that his Virginia enterprise was failing in every conceivable way and that Englishmen in America were paying for those failures with their lives. But reading John Smith's condemnation that month only solidified his and the other leaders' resolve to see their investment through. At the same time, Smith's letter affirmed that almost nothing the company and its colonists had attempted over the past two years had worked. Turning things around in America would require the Virginia Company essentially to start over.

Which is precisely what they did. Everything changed in 1609: Smythe and his colleagues undertook a complete reorganization of the Virginia Company and its Council, planned a different route to America, designed a new government for the colony, expanded the colony's boundaries and relocated the principal settlement, recruited a different and far larger collection of colonists, and demoted John Smith and appointed a proper gentleman to lead Virginia.

Along with a new plan came remarkable serendipity. Sir Thomas Gates, one of the four charter members of the London wing of the Virginia Company, had been fighting in the Netherlands until 1608. In April, he secured a leave of absence from his military post so that he could take an active part in the Virginia Company. Gates had just settled back in London when Newport arrived with Wingfield and the initial reports of chaos in the colony, and he happened to be there when Newport brought further bad news from his second supply in the winter of 1608–9. Gates knew the way west from his privateering days, he learned how to fight the Spanish during his long military service, and his ambassadorship to Vienna taught him the art of diplomacy. And Gates—unlike the upstart Smith—was a gentleman: educated at Gray's Inn, knighted by Queen Elizabeth in 1596, and allied to London's most influential merchants and politicians. Sir Thomas was everything John Smith was not, and everything that the Virginia colony needed in 1609.[24]

Gates, Smythe, and the other leading men of the Virginia Company had been considering how best to reconceive the design of their American colony since the summer of 1608, but after Newport brought still more bad news and John Smith's letter in January

An experienced military commander and well-connected political leader, Thomas Gates determined to make his mark establishing an orderly settlement in Virginia. (BERMUDA ARCHIVES, CABINET OFFICE COLLECTION, NEG. 3876)

1609 they moved with haste. By mid-February 1609, the Virginia Company secured from King James a second charter, radically restructuring the company and colony.[25]

The new charter created an expanded fifty-man council for the Virginia Company, seated in London. Thomas Smythe was named treasurer, and he continued to run the company's operations. But the new charter brought on board great numbers of powerful men: the Earl of Pembroke and the Earl of Southampton (William Shakespeare's patron), Lord De La Warr, Oliver Cromwell, Francis Bacon, Edwin Sandys, and several dozen other prominent leaders. All of them were named when the charter was published, so that each had a vested interest in the colony's success. The council held "full and absolute power and authority, to correct, punish, pardon, govern and rule" everyone in the American settlement. Their authority extended over all of Virginia and "upon the seas in going, and coming." The charter forbade the councilors from violating any English law in their colony, but otherwise they could do whatever "they, in their good discretion, shall think to be fittest for the good of the adventurers and inhabitants there."[26]

What they saw "fittest to do" was replace the colonial government. Company insiders blamed the trouble in Virginia primarily on the "outrages, and follies" committed by various leaders in the colony. Incompetent, self-interested men had failed to supervise the settlers and exploit the boundless natural riches of Virginia. Such "misgovernment of the commanders, by dissention and ambition among themselves" led directly to "idleness and bestial slouth, of the common sort, who were active in nothing but adhering to factions and parts, even to their own ruin." The Council of the Virginia Company determined to restructure the colonial government so as "to reform and correct those [problems] already discovered, and to prevent such as in the future might threaten us." Their solution: investing power in "one able and absolute governor." That governor would be the "able and worthy gentleman" Sir Thomas Gates, and he would lead a rescue mission to America as quickly as possible.[27]

As soon as Governor Gates and the new representatives of the company arrived in Virginia, according to the 1609 charter, "the government, power, and authority of the President and Council . . . and all laws and constitutions, by them formerly made, shall utterly cease." Moreover, the president in Virginia—that would be John Smith—was required to "forthwith be obedient" to Gates. As governor, Gates enjoyed wide latitude in defining and defending the law in Virginia. He was told to act "as shall in your discrecion seeme aptest for you" and could "proceede by martiall lawe" if he felt it necessary.[28]

Once in America, Gates would preside over an unprecedented number of colonists. Sending a few settlers at a time had not worked, so the company audaciously determined to work on a much larger scale. As one insider explained it, "We always thought at first we would send people there little by little, and now we see that the proper thing is to fortify ourselves all at once."[29] Six hundred would sail with Gates—more than had gone to Virginia in the three prior years combined. Thomas West, the Lord De La Warr, was to follow in August, bringing another thousand colonists and succeeding Gates as governor. Gates and then De La Warr would also control a vast amount of territory. The new charter expanded the boundaries of the Virginia colony from ten thousand square miles to over one million square miles—two hundred miles north and south of Point Comfort, from "sea to sea," and one hundred miles offshore.[30]

To assist Governor Gates in reordering this greatly expanded colony, the Council of the Virginia Company created a new colonial council. But they made clear that this group, unlike their predecessors, could never override Gates: "they shall not have, single nor together, anie bindinge or negative voice or power uppon your conclusions." In an odd move, sure to perpetuate the very factionalism they wanted to curtail, the councilors in London named both John Ratcliffe and John Smith to serve on the first colonial council.[31]

The objectives set for Gates's new government were as far-reaching as the new boundaries. Gates's responsibilities included removing the principal settlement from Jamestown, which the men in London knew to be "unwholsome," and constructing three settlements, including one at Point Comfort, far from the seat of power, that a demoted John Smith could command. The council in London gave long, detailed suggestions about how to deal more effectively with Powhatan. But since they continued to believe the Virginia Indians "are so wrapped up in the fogge and miserie of their iniquity and . . . chained under the bond of deathe unto the divell," their plans had little prospect of securing peace.[32]

Gates was also going to regiment life in the colony. Settlers would be required to work a prescribed number of hours each day, and even eat together, called to those activities by a bell. Finally, but hardly surprisingly, the 1609 charter forbade immigration of anyone "suspected to effect the superstitions of the church of Rome." The governor had to make sure the colonists worshipped "accordinge to the constitucions of the Church of England." Atheism and "popery" should "be exemplarily punished to the horror of God."[33]

According to the grand design of 1609, Thomas Gates would shortly lead a Virginia that was, unlike the chaotic outpost it had been, profitable, peaceful, and Protestant. It was a vision promoted by London's leading men that the whole of the nation could get behind.

The 1609 plan to save Virginia—and with it all hope for a Protestant, English America—was unprecedented in scope in England's history. Six hundred passengers, with nearly two hundred crewmen, would travel on the largest fleet ever to leave Plymouth. The nation's most renowned captain would sail the lead ship, carrying an entirely new government and more colonists than had ever been to Virginia. London's preeminent businessman used all his talents to plan the voyage in less than one hundred days. And the city's nobility, entrepreneurs, and ministers came together to promote the adventure, which they depicted as God's will and England's destiny.[34]

What had begun in 1606 as a modest business effort became in 1609 the whole nation's mission: "henceforth this will be done, now that it is no longer the business of any one person, nor of a few private individuals but of the whole state . . . all of them sharing the same privileges and determined to venture, some their person, and some their fortune in it."[35]

So sweeping an endeavor would be extremely expensive, more costly than the original investors could afford, so the redesigned company operated as a joint-stock corporation. Individuals and guilds paid twelve pounds, ten shillings per share—or "bill of adventure"—in the stock that would be reinvested for seven years. In 1616, dividends, in the form of land and profits, were promised for each investor. Men and women lacking the resources to sub-scribe could also "adventure" their persons: colonists could go to Virginia for shares in the company, the precise number determined by their skill and potential value to the settlement. While King James and company leaders agreed upon the new charter in Febru-ary, they did not publicize it until May 23, so that all the investors could be named and they, just like the new council members, would be forever publicly bound to the mission.[36]

Selling subscriptions to an overseas enterprise was no simple matter, particularly since many Londoners already knew about the troubles in Virginia. So Smythe and his friends orchestrated a brilliant public relations campaign, tying their company to na-tional pride and Protestant faith.

In 1606, the Virginia Company's leaders had failed to solicit

widespread public support for their business, and, even more important, they missed the potential of tapping into the powerful convictions of the Protestant ministers at St. Paul's Cross and their zealous
followers. Smythe and the other council members had initially
viewed their Virginia adventure in exclusively commercial terms. But
profit alone did not move a nation to action. So in 1609 company
leaders coupled their bold new plan for Virginia with an unprecedented fundraising campaign that corrected all the missteps of 1606.
Virginia would, of course, turn a profit for investors. But company literature also promised that preserving the colony would fulfill God's
will and bring glory to England and immortality to those daring
enough to adventure there. The campaigning began as soon as King
James agreed to the charter. It reached out to every class of citizen in
London and to Englishmen throughout the nation and abroad.[37]

Members of the Virginia Company Council started raising
funds in February, within days of James's acceptance of the new
charter. Along with several other nobles, Henry Wriothesley, the
third Earl of Southampton, agreed to serve on the expanded council and invest in the new Virginia Company. Southampton was
dashing and handsome, if unfortunately excessively hot-tempered,
with a mane of auburn hair and an adventuresome spirit. By the
time Jamestown was founded he had been freed from the Tower of
London by King James and was so much favored by the king that
he kept a suite of rooms at Whitehall. Southampton was connected
to the players at the Globe as well as to the ministers at St. Paul's
Cross; both William Shakespeare and William Crashaw dedicated
works to him. In addition to his enthusiasm for the theater—he
became Shakespeare's patron in 1593—Southampton had long
been interested in North America. In 1609 he became a dedicated
promoter of the company he had joined, using his extensive political connections to draw in other investors. Just days after James
agreed to the new charter, Southampton and a group of noblemen

wrote the English ambassador to The Hague and the English military commander in the Low Countries trying to drum up subscriptions and entice soldiers to sail to America. That same week, representatives of the Virginia Company wrote the mayor and aldermen of Plymouth ("our very loving Friends"), asking them to support this latest effort. The letter assured the leading men of Plymouth that they could recover their losses from Sagadahoc if they would "joyne your indeavors with ours."[38]

The day after that letter was sent, the first promotional tract of the fundraising campaign, *Nova Britannia*, was entered at Stationers' Hall. The dedication to Thomas Smythe and the Council of the Virginia Company apparently attempted to disguise the company's involvement in the publication. But the campaigning could not have been more transparent: "I wish and intreat all well affected subjects, some in their persons, others in their purses, cheerefully to adventure, and joyntly take in hand this high and acceptable worke." Author Robert Johnson promised his readers that funding the redemption of Virginia would "advance and spread the kingdome of God, and the knowledge of the truth, among so many millions of men and women, Sauage and blind . . . as also for the honor of our King, and enlarging of his kingdome." Johnson painted a rapturous picture of Virginia, with "sweete Springs" flowing across a countryside full of "hidden treasure, never yet searched" and soil that yielded every crop "in great aboundance." As he explained in elaborate detail the religious and economic benefits of colonizing Virginia—the tract runs nearly twelve thousand words—Johnson never failed to remind his audience of their duty (and his real purpose in writing). The company needed "people to make the plantation, and money to furnish our present provisions and shippings now in hand." And he pushed potential investors to act fast: "the sooner and more deeply men engage themselves, their charge will be the shorter, and their gaine the greater."

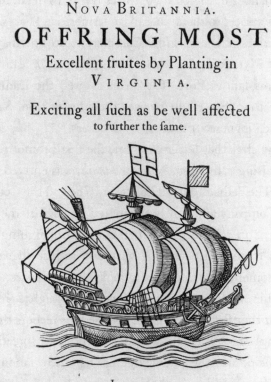

NOVA BRITANNIA.

OFFRING MOST

Excellent fruites by Planting in
VIRGINIA.

Exciting all such as be well affected
to further the same.

LONDON
Printed for SAMVEL MACHAM, and are to be sold at
his Shop in Pauls Church-yard , at the
Signe of the Bul-head.
1 6 0 9.

*Typical of the promotional tracts issued by Virginia
Company boosters,* Nova Britannia *promised wealth and
glory for those who contributed to the 1609 fundraising
campaign.* (COURTESY OF LIBRARY OF VIRGINIA)

All investors would be named in the final published patent, so for a
very modest price a man could forever link himself to this glorious
cause. Johnson hit all the right notes: religiosity, philanthropy,
national pride, and self-interest.[39]

As *Nova Britannia* went to press, broadsides flooded London. While tracts such as Robert Johnson's targeted the literate investor class, the short broadsides aimed to recruit colonists. *Concerning the Plantation of Virginia New Britain* assured readers that "many noble persons, Counts, Barons, Knights, Merchants and others" had already committed to sail to Virginia under the new mission. But the enterprise needed settlers: "Therefore, for the same purpose this paper has been made public, so that it may be generally known to all workmen of whatever craft they may be . . . men as well as women, who have any occupation, who wish to go out in this voyage" could do so. They simply needed to go to Thomas Smythe's home on Philpot Lane, "and there will be pointed out to such persons what they will receive for this voyage." The advertisement named blacksmiths, carpenters, coopers, shipwrights, fishermen, bakers, weavers, and shoemakers among the desired trades, and promised all adventurers would receive "houses to live in, vegetable-gardens and orchards, and also food and clothing at the expense of the Company." In addition to getting all their basic needs met, every settler "will have a share of all the products and the profits that may result from their labor."[40]

In mid-March, Smythe turned to London's guilds, or companies as they were called, as potential investors. While most butchers and tailors lacked the resources to individually invest, skilled craftsmen collectively held great potential. So the Virginia Company Council asked Humphrey Weld, the Lord Mayor of London, to intercede on their behalf and try to sell bills of adventure to "the best disposed and most able of the companies." Their letter closed by reminding Weld that rescuing Virginia was "an action concerning God, and the advancement of religion, the present ease, future honor and safety of the Kingdome, the strength of our Navy, the visible hope of a great and rich trade, and many secrett blessings not yett discovered."[41]

Weld, a former grocer and new member of the Council of the

Virginia Company, happily obliged. He immediately forwarded the letter to every company in the city with a directive "that you call before you your said Companie and acquainting them with the contents of the said letter to deale very earnestly and effectually with every of them to make some adventure in soe good and honourable action." Weld even bought three shares himself.[42]

The fishmongers met on March 20 and were "persuaded to adventure." The grocers, Humphrey Weld's company, soon followed, then the clothworkers, the stationers, and the merchant tailors. Not everyone was immediately convinced. When the clothworkers first met on April 4, only one man—who already owned a share himself—seemed especially interested. They tabled the matter so that members could "have some tyme to deliberate uppon this matter." When they reconvened eight days later, the company agreed to invest £100, most likely swayed by the growing momentum behind the Virginia adventure. The more companies that met, the more enthusiasm built. The stationers gave £125, and over 120 members of the merchant tailors company invested over £500. In all, fifty-six city companies bought shares, along with many individual ironworkers, drapers, and haberdashers.[43]

It is impossible to calculate how many artisans and small businessmen contributed to the 1609 fundraising effort, because some of the records have been destroyed, and in the surviving sources some of the companies listed all the members pledging money, but many others did not. Clearly though, Smythe and Weld's effort paid off in a big way, for it committed hundreds and hundreds of ordinary Londoners—musicians and masons, vintners and coopers, butchers, bakers, and even candlestick makers—to saving English America.

Even King James, while less than zealous about the matter, did his part. In May, just before signing the final version of the charter, he directed the customs office to show the Virginia enterprise special status: the company could "shipp and carrie awaye such goods and Merchandizes" as the colony needed without the government levying "anie Custome Impost or other duties."[44]

Throughout the spring of 1609, James effectively stalled Ambassador Zúñiga, who understandably felt incensed at learning of Smythe's newest plan. Through spies in the English government, Zúñiga knew almost immediately about the second charter, and he acquired copies of all the Virginia Company's propaganda, which he faithfully passed along to King Philip of Spain. James avoided meeting Zúñiga when he could and, when he could not, continued to disavow any involvement in Virginia. Zúñiga knew from all the publicity the company generated that spring that King James was misleading him. From tracts such as *Nova Britannia*, the ambassador could easily see James's complicity in the effort, and the charter disclosed that he stood to earn 20 percent of profits from any mining operations. In Zúñiga's mind, the 1609 effort was nothing more than "a swindle and a robbery" and the colony "should be destroyed with the utmost possible promptness," and he begged Philip to *"give orders to have these insolent people quickly annihilated."*[45] But from Madrid, King Philip could not appreciate the energy spreading through London and the threat to his monopoly over America.

Ambassador Zúñiga, like everyone else in London that spring, could feel the excitement in the air. "The people," he observed, "are mad about this affair." And for good cause. The Virginia Company's propaganda promised that investing would serve God's will and bring glory to England. Those who adventured their money and their lives were promised that future generations of English men and women would "Uphold your names and memories so long as the Sunne and Moone endureth."[46]

It worked. In a matter of weeks, Zúñiga saw the Virginia Company raise "a sum of money for this voyage which amazes one." By

May, no fewer than 659 individuals had bought shares in the recon-
ceived Virginia Company, along with 56 companies and guilds,
representing hundreds of other investors. Some were rich, like the
Earl of Southampton. Some, including the mayor of London, had
impressive political connections. And a few, most notably Smythe,
were savvy businessmen. But the majority were unexceptional, like
Stephen Powle, who walked to Smythe's home around ten o'clock
on the morning of March 9 to deliver his money into the hands of
the company clerk and to watch the clerk record his name among
those to be remembered for "so long as the Sunne and Moone endureth." Powle trusted Smythe with his investment, but declared,
"The success of whitch undertakinge I referre to god allmighty."[47]
And it was faith in "god allmighty" more than anything else that
distinguished the campaign of 1609 from all the earlier efforts and
made Englishmen believe they should make America their own.

The genius of the 1609 campaign lay in Virginia Company promoters' masterful marriage of their colony to national pride and
Protestant faith. Four hundred years later, with a full understanding
of the manipulative nature of the writing, the language remains
compelling: "A right sure foundation therefore have you (My Lords
and the rest of the most worthie Adventurers for Virginia) laid for
the immortalitie of your names and memorie, which, for the advancement of Gods glorie, the renowne of his Maiestie, and the
good of your Countrie, have undertaken so honourable a project, as
all posterities shall blesse."[48]

London's presses had never worked so much on behalf of America as they did in early 1609, and they continued to turn out broadsides and essays extolling the material benefits of the Virginia
colony. Unlike in 1606, however, company leaders now saw clearly
the power of faith to motivate investors. Promoters depicted En-

gland's presence in America as the will of God; their propaganda highlighted the providential design of colonizing Virginia and the obligation to spread Christian faith among the native peoples. As Robert Johnson wrote in *Nova Britannia*, "wee seeke nothing lesse than the cause of God."[49]

The Virginia Company found superb allies in tethering their colony to Christian duty and national honor among the fervent Protestant ministers sharing their faith at St. Paul's Cross. Ambassador Zúñiga was appalled to see that company leaders "have actually made the ministers in their sermons dwell upon the importance of filling the world with their religion and demand that all make an effort to give what they have for such a grand enterprise." Sure enough, in sermon after sermon during the spring of 1609, prominent ministers such as William Crashaw and William Symonds gladly proclaimed the virtues of the Virginia adventure. Just as Robert Johnson depicted the Virginia Company seeking the "cause of God," preachers declared that God was calling English Christians to pursue the business of Virginia. As Rev. Daniel Price proclaimed, the new Virginia Company was planning "a voyage wherein every Christian ought to set his helping hand."[50]

There was no line between duty to God, glory for England, and the salvation of Virginia in these promotional sermons. In a typical appeal, Rev. Robert Gray beseeched his followers to "seeke after such adventers whereby the Glory of God may be advanced, the teritories of our Kingdome inlarged, our people both preferred and employed abroad, our wants supplied at home, his Maiesties customes wonderfully augmented, and the honour and renown of our Nation spread and propagated to the ends of the World." Daniel Price likewise spoke rhapsodically about "a great part of the glory of God, the honour of our Land, Joy of our Nation and expectation of many wise, and noble Senators of this Kingdom, I mean in *the Plantation of Virginia*."[51]

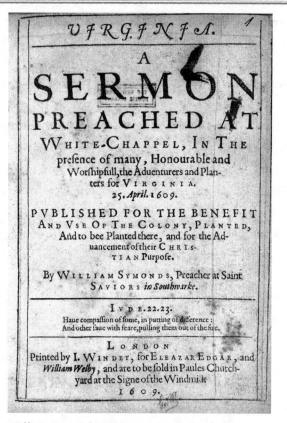

William Symonds's stirring sermon, preached in
support of the Sea Venture *fleet, argued that it was*
God's will for English Christians to colonize
Virginia. (COURTESY OF HUNTINGTON LIBRARY)

These sermons described the English as God's chosen people, called to sacrifice and eventual greatness in the New World. William Symonds gave one of the first sermons in support of the Virginia Company on April 25, 1609. It was quickly published and dedicated to the company. Symonds relied on Genesis, chapter 12, in which God told Abram, "get thee out of thy Countrey, and from thy kindred, and from thy fathers house, unto the land that I will shew thee. And I will make of thee a great nation, and will blesse thee, and make thy name great, and thou shalt be a blessing."[52] God, who stood firmly on the side of Protestant England, wanted to make it a great nation. Ministers such as Symonds used all their skill to convince Christians to go to Virginia to answer that call.

Symonds and others promised that those faithful enough to do God's work in America could expect His favor in heaven. Daniel Price insisted "whosoever hath a hand in this business, shall receive an unspeakable blessing . . . [and] *shall shine as the stars for ever and ever.*" Robert Gray offered the same sort of assurance, telling the "Adventurers for the plantation of Virginea" that when they died, to honor their dutifulness to God's will, He would "make you members of his Church triumphant in Heaven."[53]

Revs. Price and Gray just as confidently condemned anyone opposing the Virginia venture as an enemy of the nation and of God. They did not mince words. Price charged that "If there be any that have opposed any action intended to the glory of God, and saving of souls . . . let him know that he is a persecutor and an adversary of Christ." Gray agreed, warning anyone who would listen that "every opposition against it [Virginia] is an opposition against God, the King, the Church, and the Commonwealth." Gray offered a dire prediction for those too stingy to invest and too cowardly to sail: "they which preferre their money before vertue, their pleasure before honour, and their sensuall securitie before heroicall adventures, shall perish with their money, die with their pleasures, and be buried in everlasting forgetfulnes."[54]

The heart of this Christian mission in America lay in converting Indians, whom promotional writers and preachers depicted as savages, living without religion and civilization. Despite their countrymen's nearly three years' experience with the Powhatans, enthusiasts in London remained profoundly, willfully ignorant of Indian ways. Rev. Symonds told his congregation that Virginia was nothing but "a waste country, where the people doe liue like Deere in heards . . .

[and] where they know no God but the diuell." And in *Nova Britannia*, Robert Johnson promised investors their money would help "advance the kingdome of God, by reducing savage people from their blind superstition to the light of Religion." Company promoters expected the Powhatans to welcome this "help," and largely ignored what the settlers' experiences in America should have taught them: that Virginia Indians held firmly entrenched religious values and social traditions and that they wanted to interact with the colonists and make use of English ways only to the extent that doing so advanced their agenda. These writers, conversely, depicted the Indians as uncivilized heathens. Ultimately, by claiming Virginia and converting the Indians to Protestant Christianity, the English would save themselves. As Rev. Price explained it, once the 1609 colonists helped "a savage country to become a sanctified country," they would "obtain the saving of their souls," and angels in heaven would rejoice.[55]

As an added bonus, making Virginia a "sanctified country" kept it from falling into the hands of the English Protestants' most reviled foe: the Roman Church. Alongside the unchecked contempt they showed toward Indians, the preachers who sold Virginia as God's business used their sermons to excoriate Catholics. To be certain, the secular writings on Virginia in 1609 joined in with this strident anti-Catholicism. The new charter forbade the immigration of Catholics, because they would undermine "the conversion and reduction of the people in those parts unto the true worship of God and Christian religion." *Nova Britannia* reiterated that the colony forbade all "papists" and suggested that "if once perceived, such a one, weede him out, and ship him home for England, for they will ever be plotting and conspiring."[56]

None of the company literature, however, compared with the vitriol in Protestant sermons. William Symonds considered Catholics traitors, and assured his audience that the men leading the 1609 mission "are carefull to carry thither no Traitors, nor Papists that

depend on the Great Whore." Further into his sermon he attributed much of the evil in the world to "ATHEISTS and PAPISTS" who
"haue gotten out of their serpents holes."[57] From pulpits throughout London devout Protestant clergymen promised city residents
that national glory and God's favor awaited those who helped build
a Protestant English America.

In the end, words were all these clergymen had to offer.
William Crashaw invested thirty-seven pounds, ten shillings in
the Virginia Company, but Price, Gray, and Symonds did not give
any money to the campaign they so aggressively promoted. And
for all their zealous appeals on behalf of the colony, none of the
four signed up to sail to Virginia. Oddly enough, God apparently
did not need any of them to leave the comforts of their homes in
London and security of their ministerial appointments to carry His
word to America.[58]

As the preachers of London who backed the Virginia enterprise
from the safety and security of their pulpits demonstrated, it required a special kind of courage to adventure one's person in America. Investors in Virginia risked twelve pounds, ten shillings a
share. Some bought one or two shares, while others spent as much
as a hundred pounds. But most wagered no more than they could
afford to lose. Boarding the boat was another matter entirely. Sailing to Virginia required staking your life.

In recruiting settlers, promotional writers willfully ignored the
parade of bad reports out of Virginia. Typical of the campaigning,
Rev. Symonds assured his audience that the colony offered a bounteous and safe environment; in his sermon Virginia was again a
New Eden. At the same time, he understood that English men and
women feared leaving home—and for good reason. "I am not ignorant," he explained, "that many are not willing to goe abroade and

spread the gospell, in this most honorable and christian voyage of the Plantation of *Virginia*."[59]

Symonds was convincing; he tapped into his countrymen's ambitions to alleviate their doubts about moving to Virginia. First and foremost, he insisted that God called Christian Englishmen to settle America: "Neither can there be any doubt, but that the Lord that called *Abraham* into another Countrey, doeth also by the same holy hand, call you to goe and carry the Gospell to a Nation that neuer [never] heard of Christ." Those willing to fulfill that mission could expect God's favor. For the more secularly minded, he claimed that Virginia promised glory in this life: those who moved to America "shalt bee more eminent and famous in a yeare, then at home halfe of thy ranke shall bee all their daies."[60]

To entice the many laborers the colony required, Symonds made the most practical pledge: Virginia offered impoverished workers a fresh start. It was, Symonds argued "a necessity to seek abroad," for England had grown so crowded "that there is very hardly roome for one man to liue by another." Opportunities for a better life were so rare that even soldiers who had valiantly fought for their country "can hardly scape [escape] the statute of rogues and vagrants," and "The rich shop-keeper hath the good honest poore labourer at such aduantage, that he can grind his face when he pleaseth." But in Virginia, exploited, crowded English workers would find "a Land more like the garden of Eden: which the Lord planted, then any part else of all the earth."[61]

Several authors of the 1609 promotional campaign made no bones about their contempt for London's poor. In *Nova Britannia* Robert Johnson pointed out "our land [is] abounding with swarmes of idle persons, which having no meanes of labour to releeve their misery, doe likewise swarme in lewd and naughtie practices." He saw in Virginia England's best chance "to rid our multitudes of such as lie at home, pestering the land with pestilence and penury, and infecting one another wich vice and villanie, worse then the plague it selfe." Robert Gray also blamed London's poor people for the city's problems. He warned that the city's growing population threatened its future by producing "oppression, and diverse kindes of wrongs, mutinies, sedition, commotion and rebellion, scarcitie, dearth, povertie, and sundrie sorts of calamities." Gray shrewdly failed to mention that this was exactly what awaited them in Virginia. Instead he, like Johnson, promised that shipping "idle persons" to Virginia would be good for the poor, because they got a fresh start, and good for the nation they left behind. Johnson went so far as to predict that, beyond simply redeeming the poorest Englishmen, relocating in Virginia "will make them rich."[62]

The company, while ultimately forced to accept whatever settlers they could attract, preferred skilled workers. Thomas Smythe and his colleagues needed to recruit men and women to build their colony basically from the ground up. Following John Smith's advice, they advertised for carpenters, shipwrights, masons, farmers, fishermen, blacksmiths—men "of every trade and profession." Given the undisciplined settlers already making a failure of Jamestown, it was little wonder that the feverish campaign of 1609 focused on gathering a skilled workforce. And since company leaders knew from the last two years' experience that "by discord great things soone come to nothing" they tried their best to attract dutiful, upright settlers.[63]

The drive to recruit colonists worked nearly as well as the fundraising. By May 1609, some six hundred people had pledged their lives to rescuing Virginia. Some went for wages and some for shares in the company, apportioned according to their skills. A few were gentlemen seeking glory, but more were small investors and artisans. The ship logs unfortunately included more desperate and shady characters—"irregular persons"—than the colony needed.[64]

Remarkably, in three short months Virginia Company leaders raised enough money and recruited enough colonists to save their

American enterprise. In May, seven ships and two pinnaces were outfitted to carry the settlers and their supplies to America. Now only one thing stood in their way: the Atlantic crossing.

Despite warnings from John Smith, the Virginia Company hired John Ratcliffe and Gabriel Archer to sail two ships in the fleet. Their friend John Martin captained a third. While clearly difficult men, they possessed invaluable experience. All three knew the passage west and knew Virginia. Their experience appeared to trump John Smith and Edward Maria Wingfield's reports about their propensity for "hatching of some mutiny."[65] In any event, better men than them commanded the mission. Governor Gates's authority would not be easily challenged once the voyagers made land: the new charter and his forceful personality made sure of that. During the crossing, Martin, Archer, and Ratcliffe answered to Admiral George Somers, commander of the fleet, and followed the lead of Christopher Newport, who commanded the flagship: a three-hundred-ton vessel, better than twice the size of the *Susan Constant*, christened the *Sea Venture*.

Captain Newport knew all about Martin, Archer, and Ratcliffe's conniving ways, and he had already shown he could best them. Besides, overseas adventures attracted ambitious men. Power struggles inevitably arose among the kind of individuals daring enough to sail thousands of miles from the known world. Still, there could be no doubt that Newport kept a close watch over these three as he readied for the crossing to America.

The passengers were likewise a bold lot, drawn to the enterprise by a host of factors, including the pursuit of their own interests. Whether religion or patriotism or desperation drove them to board the *Sea Venture* and other ships in the fleet, the voyagers would have thought of themselves as full partners in the redemption of Vir-

between the three commanders regarding authority during the crossing, a disagreement that would have powerful consequences for the voyage and the future of Virginia. If they had followed maritime tradition, the three leaders would have traveled on separate ships in the fleet. That way, if one or even two of them happened to be lost at sea, the third commander would survive to lead the company for the rest of the mission. But when it came time to depart, suspicions and jealousies between the sea and land commanders surfaced, with Somers enjoying the loyalty of the sailors, Gates controlling the soldiers, and Newport overseeing the crew of his ship. And "because those three Captaines could not agree for place, it was concluded they should goe all in one ship," the *Sea Venture*.[3]

It was also concluded that they should go quickly. Company leaders did not want to wait for more temperate weather. The commanders knew the sun would be directly above the ships as they sailed, and that storms were more intense in the summer months. But Thomas Smythe had decided that rescuing English America could not be delayed. If Newport, the most experienced of the commanders, thought differently, he kept his concerns to himself or got outvoted; they would take the risk of leaving in June.

In the weeks before they sailed, Gates and "men of the best experience" debated taking a new route. The standard course to Virginia took ships south to the Canaries, from there to the West Indies, then north from Hispaniola, by the Bahamas, to catch the Gulf Stream on up to the coast of North America. This was a slower route that brought English ships through Spanish-dominated waters, and a fleet as large as the *Sea Venture* was all but certain to attract attention. Captains—including Newport in his three prior crossings—followed this perilous and longer course based on the assumption that the Gulf Stream above Florida was simply too strong to cut across. But some mariners doubted this, and company leaders believed that the delay involved in taking the lengthy route would only exacerbate troubles in Virginia. So in the spring of 1609 the Virginia Company hired Samuel Argall, a young but accomplished captain, "to attempt a direct and cleare passage, by leaving the Canaries to the East, and from thence, to run in a streight westerne course." Argall left on May 5, sailing south to about the thirtieth degree, and then headed directly west across the Atlantic, "in the longitude of the Barmudos." He made Virginia on July 13, and "found no currant, nor any thing else which should deter us from this way."[4]

But no one was willing to wait on Argall's report before launching the fleet. Gates's direction from the Virginia Company Council called on him only to seek the advice of knowledgeable mariners to determine "what way is safest and fittest for you to take." He did not know when he departed on June 2 about Argall's successful voyage. He knew only about the real peril one route posed and the feared danger of the other.[5]

Fatefully, he, too, chose the path near Bermuda.

As the fleet prepared to sail from Plymouth Sound on the evening of June 2, there was good reason for hope. The voyage, company officials had promised them, "is neither long nor dangerous." Within six weeks they could expect to arrive in Virginia, "over the great ocean, without encountering rocks, shallows, narrow straits, or the lands of other princes, who might interfere with us." Ministers also exhorted settlers to view the crossing from England to Virginia as natural and easy: "This passage into *Virginea* is in true temper so faire, so safe, so secure, so easie, as though God himselfe had built a bridge for men to passe from *England* to *Virginea*."[6]

Those on board the flagship, the *Sea Venture*, were sailing on a sturdy, well-built, nearly new vessel. A large ship, nearly one hundred feet stem to stern, gleaming with new paint, the *Sea Venture* had been built just five years before. It was well armed, with some twenty pieces of ordnance and harquebuses on the upper deck. Facing the breeze as it sailed out of Plymouth was its figurehead, the "Hound of the Vikings." The admiral's large pennant flew at the mizzen, the flag of St. George's Cross at the fore, and the Union flag on the mainmast.[7]

The *Diamond*, under the command of Vice Admiral John Ratcliffe, went out just behind the *Sea Venture*. Gabriel Archer, captaining the *Blessing*, followed along with the *Unity*, the *Lion*, and the *Swallow*. George Somers owned part of the *Swallow*, and his nephew, Matthew Somers, sailed on it as master. Two smaller boats, including the pinnace *Virginia*, built in the failed Sagadahoc colony, joined the larger vessels. The *Falcon*, commanded by John Martin, brought up the rear.[8]

The fleet soon encountered a reminder that nature, rather than all their elaborate preparations and seafaring skills, controlled the outcome. After setting sail from Plymouth they found themselves "crost by South-west windes," and had to put in at Falmouth. They waited six long days, with the summer heat growing ever stronger. On June 8, they finally found friendly winds for getting out to sea.[9]

As the voyagers left behind family and friends, they did so knowing that any ocean crossing, no matter how new and sturdy the ship, carried dangerous and disquieting prospects—seasickness, food shortage, disease, storms, and shipwrecks loomed on the horizon of any Atlantic journey. They all knew perfectly well that an ocean separation could become permanent. As a result, some voyagers made wills before embarking, fearful they might die thousands of miles from the friends or family who otherwise could oversee the dispersal of their estates. Tom Verney, for example, sailed for Virginia several years later with his casks, barrels, servants, and muskets, and gave authority to William Webster, who "in case of mortality of the asaid Mr. Thomas Verney" was instructed "to sell and dispose of his goods, provisions, and servants."[10]

Given the obvious dangers of a long Atlantic voyage, why would some six hundred people risk "removing" to Virginia? The flood of religious-based promotional literature certainly would have influenced some settlers. Few ordinary passengers left behind evidence revealing their precise motives, but, given the huge push for emigration from leading ministers, we can reasonably speculate that boarding the *Sea Venture* fleet was in part an act of faith. In addition to the devout, there were the desperate. For many passengers practical necessity animated the move to Virginia. Poor servants, for example, voyaged in hopes of starting a new life in a new land, even if it required years of indenture. Some skilled laborers traveled for paid wages, others owned shares in the company, gambling on the trip as a way to improve their situation, especially if they came with a valuable trade. Stephen Hopkins, for example, who, in addition to his Puritan sensibilities, belonged to a London woolen guild, hoped to tap into the growing demand for hats and broadcloth in Jamestown. Others, from the three commanders to men like William Strachey and Rev. Buck, saw in the voyage a unique opportunity for honor for themselves as well as for God and England, all of which fostered a common spirit of hope in the enterprise, and a sense of investment in it among many on board. Many of the soldiers working for the Virginia Company and under the control of Gates expected to be profitable settlers in Virginia, and so would have shared in that vision. But the sailors under Newport and Somers's command made the voyage for wages with no long-term interest in the colony.[11]

With only a handful of women on board the *Sea Venture*, and perhaps twenty-five or thirty in the entire convoy, single men dominated this voyage, as they had for the past three years. Those few colonists who traveled with family and friends carried with them a social network to cushion them against the shocks and perils of voyaging. But the young and single voyagers who predominated likely confronted an even harsher reality—shipboard relationships would have to be formed quickly to provide any help in the face of dangerous circumstances.[12]

Traveling to this unknown world without family and kin, most passengers clung all the more tenaciously to what was known and familiar: the belongings they brought on board. Those who brought wealth and high standing to the voyage made sure to carry possessions that suggested the stature they expected to assume in Virginia. George Percy packed his clothes in a new chest, bought especially for his 1606 voyage to Virginia and filled with two dozen "silke points" and two pairs of "sweete gloves."[13]

Ordinary travelers relied on the Virginia Company to subsidize their new start in America. Company broadsides advertised that they would supply the adventurers, no matter how poor, with all the basic necessities of life. This required the Virginia Company to send with the 1609 voyagers plants and seeds, cloth and leather, bedding, farming and gardening tools, and breeding animals.[14] Ship logs for the *Sea Venture* fleet have not survived, but other ships that traveled to America in this era normally carried all sorts of tools, household supplies, and foodstuffs. Ships also carried iron and lead; hogsheads of meal; barrels of peas, oatmeal, and butter; an assortment of tools—scythes, shovels, spades, axes—and blankets, rugs, and cloth. With 150 people crammed into the *Sea Venture*, there was precious little room for large items like furniture and livestock. The fleet as a whole transported only a few animals—such as Somers's horses—mainly for breeding. The *Sea Venture* carried some pigs, perhaps a few sheep, and a dog.[15]

As they settled into the ship's cramped quarters early in the voyage, passengers instantly surrendered any hope of privacy. Comfort on board such an overcrowded vessel was nearly impossible to find, particularly for the poorest travelers and the crew. Sailors and lesser hands stayed in the bottom deck, just above the hold, where the ceiling was perhaps four feet high in the middle—a congested mix of men and belongings. The upper and poop decks, controlled by the commanders, provided the only spaces with any sort of solitude. Cabins represented the one privileged piece of privacy for the master and one or two other officers—everyone else had to lie where they could, sleeping in any space they could find for a mat or in a small hammock hung on a nail. The "great cabin" on the upper deck offered the largest room on the ship and the best lighting and breezes from its windows. Here Newport, Somers, and Gates, along with their senior officers, ate and plotted their course. They most likely kept the sealed box containing the list of Virginia's new leaders in the great cabin as well.[16]

For the three commanders to maintain control of the ship and authority over its passengers and crew required a clear hierarchy of positions on board. The most important officer under the captain was the master, who served as the navigating officer of the ship, expert in using the astrolabe, the backstaff, cross-staff, quadrant, and other navigational instruments. He was in charge of sailing the ship and thus controlled the whipstaff, the lever by which the ship was steered. Beneath the master were the master gunner, carpenter, and boatswain. The high boatswain stood watch at sea, maintaining all ropes, rigging, cables, and flags. He also meted out punishments to seamen. Below him ranked various petty officers or quartermasters who oversaw the steward in delivering food to Thomas Powell, the cook, and in pumping and drawing beer. The cockswain looked after the pinnace. The master gunner and his mates ate and slept in the gunroom. Besides seamen, most ships carried one or two boys, or "younkers," who learned the ropes and served as lookouts, and a swabber who kept the ship clean.[17]

The world of sailors in this era offered a hard life and was strictly for young men with little to lose. Ship logs from the period reveal that most companies consisted overwhelmingly of the young and unmarried. When Drake sailed for the West Indies in 1572, the oldest of seventy-three voyagers was age fifty-two; none of the rest was over thirty years old. Despite a world of adventure, the young mariner faced harsh conditions on a regular basis: "a hard cabin, cold and salt meat, broken sleeps, mouldy bread, dead beer, wet clothes, want of fire, all these are within board."[18]

For passengers, simply being at sea meant enduring sometimes severe bouts of seasickness and frequently unhealthy living conditions. Tacking and sailing through rough seas could easily lead to a ship full of violently ill people. Just a few miles off the English coast, for example, Rev. Robert Hunt became miserably seasick in the initial voyage to Virginia in 1606.[19]

Within a week or so at sea, most passengers and crew became hard-pressed to practice basic cleanliness. Fresh water for washing was unavailable, and with gun ports and hatches battened down in bad weather, fresh air rarely filtered into the lower decks. The atmosphere stank of filthy travelers, livestock, and garlic, which voyagers chewed to mask the fetid stench of waste and decaying supplies.[20]

In seventeenth-century voyages, travelers frequently rejoiced at the end of a trip simply if no one died. The weather was especially worrisome—and utterly beyond anyone's control. One ship traveling through the West Indies in the 1630s was struck by lightning, killing five men. Even those who survived ferocious storms could lose basic equipment and livestock necessary for survival in America.[21]

As the passengers settled in for the long voyage, maintaining a sufficient food supply began to loom larger among the many challenges of an Atlantic crossing. Daily rations for most passengers and crew depended mainly on preservable items: salted beef, pork, and fish; oatmeal; biscuits; peas; and beer. Travelers might supplement this diet with bread, vegetables, fruits, and cheese they brought from home or bought in foreign ports. But food often ran short, especially if ships had to wait for fair winds—as the *Sea Venture* fleet did—or got delayed by poor weather.[22]

Like much else, class and rank determined how and what one ate aboard ship. Only the captain and his officers dined in any sort of comfort. Officers in the great cabin sat down at a relatively well-stocked table complete with napkins and tablecloths, pewter plates and tin spoons, with ship boys bringing food and serving wine. At the captain's table, food was not rationed; meat or fish was likely served most every day, and officers enjoyed a private supply of wine and spirits. Meanwhile, passengers and crew ate where they slept or sat on their sea chests, eating from wooden dishes with wooden spoons. Their food was closely rationed; usually for the week they received biscuit or bread, two pounds of salted beef or pork, and beans, washed down with weak beer.[23]

Within a few weeks at sea, the victuals all too often went bad and the beer soured. Without refrigeration, the food, kept in the hold, could quickly turn rancid, and spoiled food supplies could produce epidemics of dysentery. Amid the hold's stifling heat and unventilated air, casks could rip open, spewing their contents. When rain and water seeped into the hold, food decayed or became moldy. "Our greatest store of food was peas," one earlier voyager to Virginia complained, "and those were so corrupted, moldy, rotten, worm-eaten that there was no substance left in them but being stirred would crumble into dust." All of which helped breed an army of rats down below. In the hold, rats could thrive, scampering about, gnawing into supplies and casks of meat. Even more worrisome, rats could chew through the hull's planking, causing dangerous leaks.[24]

Lack of food could provoke mutiny among passengers and

crewmen on long voyages. The food-starved company aboard one ship trying to make it back to England in 1608 grew so desperate due to "wante of victualles" that they were forced to stop in the Azores and pawn their masts for food even as a rebellion was breaking out. In extreme cases, mutinying sailors murdered their masters for food. Rancid water was also a constant worry. One traveler among the original 1606 company vividly recalled how bad the water became: it "was so stencheous that only washing my hands therewith I could not endure the scent thereof." He was not alone in his disgust: the water stank so bad that "none of our men was able to endure it."[25]

The crowded, often fetid, lower decks became spawning ground for all manner of contagious disease, including dysentery, yellow fever, smallpox, and, most deadly of all, the plague. Bubonic plague spread easily and could have a mortality rate of upward of 90 percent. It is unknown what shipboard illnesses may have struck the *Sea Venture*, but on the *Diamond* and the *Unity* passengers brought aboard plague. By July, "the infection was somewhat hote" on both vessels.[26]

The plague, which raged in London in 1603, continued to afflict ships making Atlantic crossings, especially those on longer voyages into tropical regions. Typhus also overtook English ships, especially when large numbers of ill-fed men crowded together for long periods. One ship leaving Barbados a few years after the *Sea Venture* with 350 passengers on board became so infected with contagious disease that 200 fell ill at one time, and the crew "have thrown overboard two and three in a day for many dayes togeather that in all we lost fourescoare of our people." Well-to-do passengers on the ship fared no better than the common folk: six of ten in the great cabin died within three weeks at sea.[27]

In every sense, then, a transatlantic voyage such as the 1609 expedition offered up a harsh world of daily discomfort and dangerous risk. But it was also an opportunity, especially for the desperate and the driven.

After the *Sea Venture* fleet set sail from Falmouth "with prosperous winds," they managed to stay together for better than six weeks. Trumpets sounded to keep the convoy together, and for most of the trip the ships were able to stay "in friendly consort together." Nothing slowed the crossing through June and most of July.[28]

In the middle of the summer, after running "a Southerly course from the Tropicke of Cancer," the fleet "bore away West." Directly under the "fervent heat" of the July sun, many of the passengers in the convoy contracted yellow fever, or "the Calenture." Gabriel Archer, piloting the *Blessing*, which thankfully "had not any sicke," reported that so many travelers fell ill that crewmen from two of the other ships had to throw thirty-two bodies overboard. And the *Diamond* "was said to have the plague in her." The *Sea Venture*, like the *Blessing*, appeared to stay free of all serious illness and death.[29]

But all ships had to struggle with a key navigational problem: determining exactly where they were at sea at any given time. Latitude, the ship's distance from the equator, could be reasonably assessed by measuring the angle the sun made with the horizon at its highest point. So in terms of north versus south, Somers, Newport, and Gates knew their location with some accuracy. But longitude—their position east and west—was a far more difficult matter. By using an hourglass they tried to assess the passage of time, but that method was far too imprecise a way of measuring time from a known spot (such as Plymouth) to a location in the Atlantic. This left them with "dead reckoning": trying to plot their progress westward by estimating distance since last landfall. Mariners were reduced to calculating their position by changes in the color of the water, the appearance of seaweed, and birds circling overhead. They also tried estimating their progress by tossing a piece of wood into the sea and timing its movement between two notches on the gunwale. This gave them a way to calculate their speed, and thus estimate their position.[30]

The trumpets that kept the fleet together served both symbolic and practical purposes: the trumpet's sound announced the admiral's authority and conveyed signals and orders. The trumpeter stationed himself on the poop deck to announce the admiral's going ashore and coming aboard, to hail other ships, and, along with other musicians brought on most expeditions, to serve as entertainment. Musicians not only encouraged and sustained morale on board, they also were to be used to attract Indians, once the English made land. As one of the men on an early Virginia crossing noted, "Besides, for solace of our people and allurement of the savages, we were provided of musike in good variety: not omitting the least toyes, as Morris dancers, Hobby horses, and Maylike conceits to delight the savage people, whom we intended to winne by all faire meanes possible." On their final voyage in 1598, Francis Drake and Richard Hawkins took "sundry instruments of music for eight musicians and nine trumpeters." When Drake dined, trumpets sounded.[31]

But trumpets could not drown out the boredom: for most passengers aboard the *Sea Venture*, the biggest and most unavoidable problem lay in the ceaseless monotony of the long days and nights at sea. As the fleet sailed slowly west at the typical pace of two and a half miles per hour amid the heat of an Atlantic crossing in June and July, the tedium would have been severe. Frustration and boredom would have intensified on days when the ship was becalmed; days, occasionally weeks, wasted waiting for winds that never came could drive some passengers crazy. Gossip and games provided the most common diversion from the long voyage. In calm weather some might go swimming; others told stories, sang, played with the ship's dog, or indulged in gambling.[32]

At least two people on the *Sea Venture* found the trip anything but tedious: the cook, Thomas Powell, found time to court Elizabeth Persons during the voyage, and they soon decided to marry. A few officers and religious men such as Rev. Buck and Stephen Hopkins would have spent time reading the Bible and other religious works. In his earlier voyages, Sir Francis Drake reportedly passed time coloring the pictures in his copy of John Foxe's *Book of Martyrs*.[33]

Such stretches of languor, particularly amid the heat and over-crowded conditions, could also flare up into angry confrontations. Shipboard tension might erupt over arguments on subjects as small as where to lay sleeping mats or as large as religion. The devout Stephen Hopkins, who helped Rev. Buck lead daily prayers on board the ship, may well have used the many slack moments at sea to discuss some of his intense religious views at length with members of the company. Hopkins likely found on board a receptive audience for his strident Protestant faith, especially among passengers such as John Want and Nicholas Bennett. We can only wonder if the call so forcefully sounded in Rev. Symonds's stirring sermon back in London to those venturing on this expedition found expression in the shipboard prayers and conversations of Buck and Hopkins. Did they see themselves as latter-day Abrahams, sent from home to spread God's word?[34]

In the great cabin, a rather different set of concerns animated Gates, Somers, and Newport. They doubtless worried about violent storms, attacks by Spanish ships, disease, shortages of food and water, and difficult relations with angry, even mutinous, passengers and crews. And we can well imagine that all three men privately pondered what names they would find inside the sealed box from the Virginia Company.

Perhaps because he had lost an arm in a violent uprising, Newport was keenly aware of the need for strong shipboard discipline. Above all, he wanted to make sure the often dissolute habits of the many sailors and soldiers on board did not undermine morale. After all, drunkenness, brawls, and violence were commonplace among English mariners. Traditionally, the sailors working a ship expected a measure of respect in how to conduct the voyage. But the presence of unskilled landsmen and colonists living in crowded shipboard conditions undermined a mariner's sense of independence and deepened the stress of dangerous Atlantic crossings. Seamen were accustomed to rule by consensus—hence the classic cry of the mutineer "One and All." So when their voices went unheard, they would often become unruly.[35]

Mutiny, the ultimate clash of authority on the high seas, nearly always grew out of severe discontent between the chief officers and some or all of their sailors. Although each depended on the other, a wide gap of authority and different priorities complicated the relationship between commanders and crew. For one thing, masters such as Newport and Somers were usually part owners in the ships they sailed, typically holding a one-eighth share. They were responsible to the other owners for making a profit on the voyage as well as for the ship's safety. Control over their crewmen—workers for hire—depended mainly on force of personality, age, and skill.[36]

Full-fledged mutinies, though, tended to be rare, because they required careful planning and access to weapons, which commanders wisely kept under lock and key in the ship's armory. Mutineers also needed the cooperation of an officer who could sail the ship. And the stakes were high: in a successful mutiny, the rebels usually felt compelled to murder most of the officers and many of the men. Their actions, the rebels understood, could never be forgiven.[37]

Desperate circumstances, however, sometimes led to deadly measures. Henry Hudson's crew, on a tragically misguided exploration for a passage east over the top of the world in 1611, ran out of food and water and sailed so far north they no longer even saw seals. They were reduced to eating moss to survive and determined finally they would take no more. The mutineers set Hudson, a handful of his faithful crewmen, and Hudson's young son adrift in a small boat in the ice-packed far North Atlantic to suffer a frigid, tortured death.[38]

When their men rebelled, captains meted out the punishment, usually imprisoning the unruly. Two years before taking command of the *Sea Venture*, Newport had had to shackle the fractious John Smith in the hold of the *Susan Constant*. Other offenses demanded more physical remedies, such as flogging or ducking from the yardarm. The death penalty, however, was rarely invoked.

Fortunately, whatever shipboard tension over personal or class differences may have surfaced on the *Sea Venture*, there was no evidence that Somers and Newport had to punish unruly passengers or disgruntled sailors—not yet, anyway. The hot sun bearing down for so long in this midsummer crossing produced more than the usual amount of sunburn and discomfort, but this ship was led by men determined to keep order and fulfill their duty to England.

The fleet, after reaching a position between 26° and 27° latitude, had turned due west to find a "friendly" wind to carry them straight toward Virginia. Both Somers and Newport approved of this more northerly, direct course that avoided the usual, more dangerous passage through the Spanish-controlled West Indies. By Newport's reckoning, on Monday, July 24, the fleet was within seven days of reaching landfall at Cape Henry on the coast of Virginia. The new route had, as hoped, made for a quicker and safer passage.

But later that day, everything began to change. The clouds thickened and the wind picked up dramatically, "singing and whistling most unusually." Concerned, Newport cast off the small pinnace that he had been towing behind the *Sea Venture*. Gathering out of the northeast blew "a dreadful storm and hideous" that soon began "swelling and roaring as it were by fits" until the sky grew so dark it "beat all light from Heaven." The sky suddenly "turned black upon us," filling everyone aboard with "horror and fear." This storm soon became a "tempest" whose "restless tumult" never abated, as "fury added to fury, and one storm urging a second more outrageous than the former."[39]

The violence of the storm was such that "men could scarce stand upon the Deckes, neither could any man heare another speake." Unable to communicate between the ships amid the torrential storm, "every man steered his owne course," and the captains quickly lost sight of one another. The *Sea Venture*, much to the horror of passengers and crew, had sailed into the middle of a disastrous hurricane in the western Atlantic, separating the ship from the rest of the fleet. Indeed, all the other vessels managed to fight their way around the hurricane, while the passengers and crew of the *Sea Venture* were pulled toward the heart of the storm.[40]

The *Sea Venture* quickly found itself thrown into a frightening odyssey at sea. Few passengers knew anything about hurricanes, let alone had encountered one; only those who had sailed the Caribbean would have had any experience with such a powerful storm. This catastrophic force of nature unleashed deathly fears in the hearts of those aboard the *Sea Venture*. As the ship tossed wildly in the ocean, cries and shrieks issued from the passengers who "look[ed] one upon the other with troubled hearts and panting bosoms," their screams and prayers "drowned in the winds and the winds in thunder."[41]

William Strachey numbered among the rare few, along with Somers and Newport, who had encountered terrible weather, having sailed near "tempests" around the coast of Barbary and Algiers and once in the Adriatic. Yet nothing he had ever seen prepared him for the storm raging around him now: "there was not a moment in which the sudden splitting or instant oversetting of the ship was not expected."[42]

With their sails ripped down and wound around the mast, there was little the sailors could do to guide the ship through the storm. The crew struggled mightily to maneuver the ship. The storm's rage, Strachey recalled, produced something far worse than rain: "the waters like whole rivers did flood in the air. . . . Winds and seas were as mad as fury and rage could make them." The *Sea Venture* was facing a storm so ferocious that "the sea swelled above the clouds and gave battle unto Heaven."[43]

And then the news turned even worse. "It pleased God to bring a greater affliction yet upon us": the fearsome storm, the passengers soon discovered to their horror, had created "a mighty leak" in the ship. With every joint in the ship, according to Strachey, "having spewed out her oakum before we were aware," the *Sea Venture* soon filled with water, "and we almost drowned within whilst we sat looking when to perish from above." The rising water ran like terror through the whole ship "with much fright and amazement [that] startled and turned the blood and took down the [bravado] of the most hardy mariner of them all."[44]

With the water rising rapidly in the ship, passengers and crew scrambled to find the source of the leak. Men of all ranks—from master and boatswain down to coopers and blacksmiths—frantically searched the ship, looking and listening for leaks. Small holes were detected here and there and quickly sealed with whatever could be found. One desperate man tried shoving pieces of beef into a leak. But nothing the passengers and crew tried slowed the flooding. Admiral Somers calculated that the ship took on better than nine feet of water, flooding the lower holds and threatening at any minute to sink the ship.[45]

Governor Gates decided that, since the leak could not be found, the only thing left to do was organize a massive effort to bail the flooding water out of the sinking ship. Ignoring issues of rank, Gates divided the entire company of nearly 150 people, excluding the handful of women on board, into three groups who worked around the clock bailing water. He stationed groups under the forecastle, in the waist (or main deck), and next to the compass box in the stern with each man given a one-hour watch for working the buckets or pumping water. With their lives literally at stake, everyone took part, from "the better sort, even our governor and admiral themselves, not refusing their turn . . . [and] to give example to other." Amid the frantic effort, then, a rare moment of egalitarian cooperation sprang into view: "The common sort, stripped naked as men in galleys" to fight the salt water that "continually leapt in among them." For the next three days and four nights, "destitute of outward comfort and desperate of any deliverance," the whole company battled the rising water that poured into the ship. With Gates down below at the capstan "heartening every man unto his labor," the entire company exerted itself against the raging storm. Even accounting for necessary breaks to eat and rest, never fewer than one hundred men at a time furiously bailed the seawater.[46]

But the enormity of this "most sharp and cruel storm" proved overwhelming. Silvester Jourdain reported that "with the violent working of the seas our ship became so shaken, torn, and leaked that she received so much water as covered two tier of hogsheads above the ballast; that our men stood up to the middles with buckets, barricos, and kettles to bail out the water and continually pumped for three days and three nights together without any intermission." Strachey felt overwhelmed by the immense intensity of the storm, yet he could not resist poetic imagery: "So huge a sea," he recalled, "covered our ship from stern to stem like a garment or a vast cloud." Robert Rich, another passenger on the *Sea Venture*, likewise gave lyrical expression to their plight: "The Seas did rage, the windes did blowe, distressed were they then: Their Ship did leake, her tacklings breake, in daunger were her men."[47]

But more than anything, the violence of the water shocked the voyagers. Such brutal waves of water, Strachey reported, "rushed and carried the helm-man from the helm and wrested the whipstaff out of his hand" and tossed him from side to side "as it was God's mercy it had not split him." Other men rushed in to replace him at the helm, but despite their feverish efforts to steer the ship, the whipstaff was soon "rent in pieces and absolutely lost." When one particularly powerful wave crashed into the ship, Gates himself, laboring below with the other men, was thrown to the floor facing what looked like a violent end. There "our governor" lay, "all us about him on our faces, beating together with our breaths all thoughts from our bosoms else than that we were now sinking."[48]

Still, the passengers and crew bailed and pumped water in a spontaneous burst of cooperation born out of desperation. "There was not a passenger, gentleman or other," Strachey insisted, "after he began to stir and labor, but was able to relieve his fellow and make good his course." Even men who had "never done hour's work before (their minds now helping their bodies)" labored together for four days and nights under the most extreme circumstances.[49]

If rank and class had been obliterated in their storm-tossed world, day and night had also become blurred: the "heavens looked so black" that neither "a star by night nor sunbeam by day was to be seen."[50]

Except for one eerie moment. While on watch on Thursday night, Admiral Somers caught sight of a fiery apparition in the distant night sky. A tiny, round light, "like a faint star, trembling and streaming along with a sparkling blaze," shot across the cloud-filled sky, producing an electrical storm that seemed to emanate from the ship's main mast, "shooting sometimes from shroud to shroud." The strange light show continued for half the night, and

Somers called several men up to take a look at it, "who observed it with much wonder and carefulness." Strachey and no doubt Somers knew that the "sea fire" they were witnessing, known as "St. Elmo's fire" to Spanish mariners, could sometimes appear in violent thunderstorms. Superstitious seamen also viewed it as an "evil sign of [a] great tempest."[51]

Somers and his officers closely watched the "apparition" all night. They did so in hopes that, despite the usually ominous sign such a "sea fire" portended, in this one instance, it might suggest a miraculous, positive way out of the wild waters raging around them. Perhaps, they hoped, it would lead the company "more to our known way," instead of on the random course the storm-tossed ship was following. Morning came, though, and the "sparkling blaze" in the sky disappeared.[52]

The men could not bail the water fast enough; the *Sea Venture* was slowly but surely sinking. Reducing the weight of the ship in any possible way became an urgent necessity, so crewmen began throwing the passengers' luggage overboard—"many a trunk and chest"—along with casks of beer and hogsheads of oil, cider, wine, and vinegar. As the ship listed badly to the starboard, they tossed all their ordnance off that side and were ready to cut down the main mast. By this point, after some four days and nights without sleep or food, exhaustion overwhelmed the passengers and crew: "we were much spent and our men so weary as their strengths together failed them with their hearts." The hold was now filled with water so that neither beer nor fresh water could be retrieved out of it. The men on the *Sea Venture* had made a valiant effort over four days, pumping by Strachey's estimate some one hundred tons of water every four hours out of the ship. But after so many sleepless nights of fighting water that poured in relentlessly from above and below, the sailors and passengers, now "without any hope of their lives," realized that they could not go on.[53]

Despite the situation aboard the *Sea Venture* growing ever bleaker, Sir George Somers refused to give up. He had been "sitting upon the poop of the ship . . . three days and three nights together, without meal's meat and [with] little or no sleep" trying to keep her as upright as he could. But on Friday morning "there had been a general determination to have shut up hatches and, commending our sinful souls to God, committed the ship to the mercy of the gale." Some of the men broke into the remaining liquor supply and offered up a final tragic toast, "taking their last leave one of the other until their more joyful and happy meeting in a more blessed world."[54]

Dispirited and exhausted, the passengers and crew of the *Sea Venture* watched the cold, dark water rising in their sinking ship. As they faced near certain death, many likely looked within their souls and wondered: Was God testing their faith or punishing them for their sins? Would He deliver them to paradise or to hell?

CHAPTER 4

DISTRESSING NEWS

When at last "God shewed his mercy, and his power in rebuking the winde," John Ratcliffe, Gabriel Archer, and the other captains checked their vessels: each had suffered damages, some more severe than others, but, thankfully, all appeared seaworthy. That was the only good news. By delaying their passage to Virginia, the storm had worsened shipboard illnesses, including yellow fever, flux, and plague. Ratcliffe's *Diamond* and the *Unity* suffered more than the others, but none were untouched by disease. Passengers and crew survived the ordeal of the hurricane only to find that when the winds battered their ships and seawater flooded their holds, "much of our provision was spoyled." And the lead ship, which had been the hardest hit by "the violence and extremitye of the weather," was nowhere to be seen.[1] As the waters calmed and the dread of drowning passed, different fears set in: Was everyone on the *Sea Venture* dead? Could the damaged and now poorly provisioned ships survive the rest of the ocean voyage? And, having apparently lost the leaders and company directives, what would happen if they did make Virginia?

Gabriel Archer commanded the *Blessing*, and his friend John Martin sailed the *Falcon*. Before leaving London, they and the rest of the captains had received clear written directions from Thomas Gates about what to do if separated from the *Sea Venture* by a storm. Each captain was to "steer away for the West Indies," anchor at the island of Barbuda, "and there to have their rendezvous, and to stay seven days one for another." A few days after the storm passed, Archer's *Blessing* met up with the *Lion* and then with Martin's *Falcon* and the *Unity*. But rather than heading for the designated meeting point, Archer and Martin—in a clear act of insubordination—"lay away directly for Virginia."[2] Later, some Virginia Company promoters, seeking to stifle rumors about rebellions in the colony, insisted that, once at sea, Gates "countermaunded those directions by word of mouth, and assigned them, (that if they were scattered) that they should make with all speede for Virginia." Therefore, the captains "proceeded originallie from his advise and authoritie." But Archer's account never mentions this change, and other company leaders admitted that the four captains, "wearied and beaten," decided to head on to Virginia "and to decline their commission"—a necessary consequence of defying Gates's orders.[3]

It took another week to get to Virginia; the *Lion, Blessing, Falcon,* and *Unity* sailed into the Chesapeake Bay on August 11. Spying land no doubt answered many prayers aboard the damaged ships; the surviving passengers saw at last relief from the perilous seas.

The view from the shore was another matter entirely. The beleaguered Virginia colonists, waiting months for relief, anticipated welcoming a majestic fleet carrying full holds and hardy workers. Instead, they got one letdown after another. The ships appeared "all much weather beaten" and had suffered, from disease and the storm, "*great loss of men.*" The *Unity* was "sore distressed . . . [and] of seventy land men, she had not ten sound, and all her Seamen were downe" except "the Master and his Boy, with one poore sailer." The other three ships had fared little better in the hurricane: all seemed "much distressed."[4] As newcomer William Box reported, "Some [ships] lost their Masts, some their Sayles blowne from their Yards." Many of the passengers were sick, and they brought few of the supplies—and little of the hope—desperately needed by the long-suffering residents of Jamestown. Even such thankful survivors as Box recognized that they arrived in Virginia in a "miserable estate."[5]

One can scarcely imagine the heartbreak of the waiting colonists who had been promised that this, the third supply from the Virginia Company, would be their deliverance. Things got no better when John Ratcliffe, in the *Diamond*, arrived a few days later with most of the men onboard "very sicke and weake" and "having cut her maine Mast over boord." Three or four days more brought yet another demoralizing blow: a similarly damaged *Swallow* staggered into the bay, badly leaking with her main mast gone. Not one of the six vessels had seen the *Sea Venture*.[6]

Henry Spelman, an impoverished, wayward teenager, relieved to have survived his horrendous passage on the *Unity*, remembered that, despite all the difficulties, "we were joyfully welcomed by our countrymen, being at that time about 80 persons under the government of Captain Smith, the president." Spelman had been sent to the American settlement after earning the "displeasure of my friends."[7] Perhaps his troubled past, or maybe his youth, made him sanguine about Virginia. It is equally plausible that the sick, overworked, and isolated colonists genuinely welcomed the newcomers, despite disappointments about their cargo and overall health. The prospect of more hands to work the ground, fight the Indians, and fish and hunt, not to mention new companions bringing information from home, would certainly have heartened many of the forlorn colonists. But not for long.

Immediately the number of newcomers posed a problem: Where would they live? And what would they eat? More than four hundred people—most sick and hungry—crowded into Jamestown, home to eighty settlers already straining to feed and shelter themselves. The first migrants had been, they bitterly complained, "slenderly provided for" from the moment they arrived in 1607, and each subsequent group came "worse every way provided for than the former." Food from the second supply, brought by Christopher Newport in the fall of 1608, had lasted less than two months. By wintertime, the colonists were surviving mostly off oysters they foraged, supplemented by a measly ration of one pint of corn per person, per week. That diet, reported by survivors once they could get their writings past Virginia Company inspectors, "caused all our skins to peel off from head to foot."[8] Colonists bristled years after the fact when they recalled how the inadequate provisions sent by the company were usually "moldy, rotten, full of cobwebs, and maggots, loathsome to man and not fit for beasts." And that was if stores actually made it to the settlement. Company ships had not returned in the spring of 1609 with long-promised and desperately needed supplies. Now nearly five times the number of people struggling against this deprivation had flooded the colony, and these migrants, thanks to the hurricane, arrived with only "a small proportion of victual" needed to feed themselves.[9]

The initial joyful welcome that Henry Spelman and his shipmates experienced thus proved short-lived. In the fort, the empty-bellied newcomers found "houses few or none to entertain them" and so were "quartered in the open field." As for poor Henry, not two weeks after the boy arrived in Jamestown, John Smith traded him to the Powhatan Indians. Spelman lived with them for two years, which, as it turned out, offered a far better fate than staying in Jamestown.[10]

Communicable diseases, rampant on cramped, filthy ships,

worsened the problems in the colony. The typical lack of clean water and safe food near the end of the voyage, coupled with the maladies contracted along the way, left the passengers in a feeble state. Most arrived in Virginia too sick to work, susceptible to other diseases, and highly contagious.[11]

Even had they arrived in better physical condition, the hurricane survivors had missed the planting season. Mid-August would have been sweltering in coastal Virginia, a time to reap, not to sow. Despite the abundance so widely advertised in London, the Virginia colonists found little to harvest that year. Too many settlers had spent the summer hunting for gold or bowling in the fort; too few had planned for the coming winter. Those who had tried planting found themselves vexed by their own limited experience and by continuing drought. And no one anticipated the arrival of some four hundred ill-equipped, unhealthy, leaderless newcomers. John Smith, who tried his best to sustain the settlement, saw firsthand the potential of the Chesapeake Bay region, and he blamed the deprivation in Jamestown on the sick, inept migrants: "Though there be fish in the Sea, foules in the ayre, and Beasts in the woods, their bounds are so large, they so wilde, and we so weake, and ignorant, we cannot much trouble them."[12]

It did not take more than a few days for the first fight to erupt between the deprived recent migrants and the beleaguered earlier settlers. "With great penury and sufferance" the colonists had managed to cultivate during the summer some "small quantity of corn, not being above seven acres." It represented months of labor and hope for sustenance come winter. But they made the mistake of not guarding it from their new neighbors, who "fell upon that [corn] . . . and in three days at the most wholly devoured it."[13]

Trouble just as quickly spilled over into Indian country, disrupting the tenuous peace John Smith had managed to forge with the Powhatans and therefore endangering the colonists' safety and food supply. Smith complained that the newcomers harassed the Indians: "that disorderlie company so tormented those poore naked soules, by stealing their corne, robbing their gardens, beating them, breaking their houses, & keeping some prisioners." Smith, who propped up his controversial authority in Virginia by emphasizing his savvy negotiations with Powhatan leaders, claimed that the Powhatans complained to him that, "he had brought them for protectors worse enimies than the Monocans [a rival nation] themselves."[14]

For their part, the 1609 voyagers felt shaken when they saw their countrymen, the supposed vanguard of their nation and God's presence in America, living "in much distresse." Captain Archer reported his dismay at learning that some settlers "were dispersed in the Savages Townes, living upon their almes," while others who remained faithful to the colony "fed upon nothing but oysters eight weekes space."[15] It would have been a grievous sight: "civilized" Englishmen reduced to trading with and even begging from the Indians they had been sent to save; colonists unable to exploit the bounteous environment, with open sores on their malnourished bodies. The newcomers must have questioned how, if experienced settlers could fare no better than this, they would ever survive this terrible place. And the trouble had only begun.

The man-made storm that hit Virginia that August proved far more destructive than the one that struck the *Sea Venture* fleet in the Atlantic. Even Virginia Company supporters conceded that "The broken remainder of those supplies made a greater shipwrack in the continent of Virginia, by the tempest of dissention." The conflict engulfed everyone in Virginia, from the president of the colony to the poorest servants; it surged among the white-cuffed gentlemen as well as the sailors and soldiers; it ran far into the interior of Virginia, to Powhatan and Monacan towns, and across the Atlantic Ocean, all the way to the Philpot Lane home of Sir Thomas Smythe, the grocers' guild, and the royal courts of James of England and Philip of Spain. John Smith, at the center of the storm, later wished that the hurricane had sunk the whole fleet: "Happy had we bin had they never arrived; and we for ever abandoned . . . for on earth was never more confusion, or miserie, then their factions occasioned."[16]

Political infighting among the colony's leaders commenced as soon as Archer's *Blessing* and the three other damaged ships made land. George Percy, one of the original settlers in Virginia, watched as "the passengers being no sooner well landed but presently a dissension did grow between them and Captain Smithe, then president."[17] Captains Archer and Martin no doubt reveled in settling the score with their old enemy, John Smith, and they said they had the Virginia Company on their side. Archer and his supporters claimed that the new charter—aboard the delayed *Sea Venture* with the new governor—immediately ended Smith's presidency. Smith, disgusted to see these troublemakers back in Jamestown, refused to believe them. He knew his term expired in September but felt obligated to lead during those last few weeks. Smith's opponents insisted he accede to company directives and resign; he refused to do so until Gates and the new charter materialized. The disagreement quickly spiraled out of control.

Smith claimed that Archer, Martin, and then Ratcliffe had no sooner stepped on shore before they began "railing and exclaiming against Captaine Smith, that they mortally hated him, ere ever they see him." Which is entirely plausible. After all, Smith had abetted the ouster of Archer and personally expelled Ratcliffe. Determined to "rule all or ruine all," the three ringleaders, according to Smith, "led this lewd company" on "1000 mischiefes." Throughout August, Smith felt constantly besieged: "It would bee too tedious, too strange, and almost incredible," he insisted, "should I particularly relate the infinite dangers, plots, & practices . . . amongst this factious crue" whose craven desire for power seemed to Smith boundless. They would not cow him.[18]

The self-appointed new leaders, meanwhile, found Smith's demand to see the new charter spurious and his refusal to share power entirely self-serving. They also swore that only their loyalty to the Virginia Company and determination to carry out the planned reorganization of the colony's government lay behind their actions. Hopeful that Gates would shortly arrive, they resented Smith's refusal to step aside, particularly since they realized he knew about the company's plan to replace him.

In fact, John Smith understood, even before Archer and Martin arrived, that his days as president were numbered. The Virginia Company had sent Captain Samuel Argall to the colony earlier in the summer to test the shorter, northern passage and give the Virginians advance notice of the coming fleet. Argall arrived on July 13 only to watch the famished colonists steal his ship's provisions. Smith admitted the fish and wine that Argall carried "was not sent us" but "our necessities was such as inforced us to take it."[19] Smith's relief at being able to feed his people with the purloined supplies would have doubtless been balanced by his disappointment upon hearing news of his political fate. Nearly a month before any ship in the *Sea Venture* fleet made Virginia, Argall told Smith that Thomas Gates was on his way to replace him as the colony's principal leader.

So why did Smith not relent? He later maintained that he would have much preferred to surrender his duties and return to England. But he stayed and resisted his adversaries out of the "smal hope this newe commission would arive" and stabilize the colony, and the conviction that, in the meantime, he might prevent the "factious spirits" imported with the newcomers from tearing apart the colony. While apparently prepared to surrender power to

Gates, Smith refused to recognize Archer, Ratcliffe, and Martin as lawful representatives of the Virginia Company.[20]

Although Smith's opponents were telling the truth about the company's intended ouster of Smith, they hardly had the legal authority to overthrow him in Gates's absence—certainly not until his term expired in September. While Ratcliffe and Martin had been named to serve on the newly created council that would aid Governor Gates, so had John Smith.[21] Until Gates showed up in Virginia—which seemed less likely with each passing day—both factions technically held a valid claim to authority over the colony, but neither side had the practical power to override the other. The fact that Smith and the Archer cohort shared a long history and mutual contempt for each other only exacerbated an underlying crisis of political legitimacy caused by Gates's disappearance in the western Atlantic.

The men running the Virginia Company had anticipated problems of succession, and so they chose a replacement governor should Gates die during the passage or early in his term. Also foreseeing the dangers of publicizing this information (what would keep the successor from killing the governor in order to seize power?) they kept the next governor's identity a secret. Not even Gates knew whose name company officials had written on the paper secured inside the black box "marked with the figure of one and sealed with our sealle." His instructions from the company required him to "keepe secret" the box and never to break the seal until "you shall find your self unlikely to live or determined to returne." Only then could Gates hand over the box—and only to the entire colonial council assembled together. They could open it only after he died or left Virginia.[22]

It was quite a clever plan, with but one flaw in execution: Gates carried the box with him on the *Sea Venture*.

There was reason—and precedent—for keeping faith that

Gates would shortly arrive in Virginia. When Christopher New-port came back to the colony with the first supply in January 1608, another vessel in his convoy, the *Phoenix*, met with bad weather. The captain was forced to spend the winter in the West Indies and arrived in Virginia several months later.[23] But whether Gates was lost at sea or merely delayed mattered less and less as tensions in Jamestown reached the boiling point.

Growing daily more disquieted with Smith, the anti-Smith fac-tion tried to take matters into their own hands. At one point, Archer explained, they drafted Francis West, brother of Thomas West, the Lord De La Warr, to be their leader "in the absence of Sir Thomas Gates, or if he miscarried by sea, then to continue till we heard newes from our Counsell in England." Fearful that the com-pany might side with the Smith party and interpret their actions as mutinous, Archer insisted that "Master West, Master Percie, and all the respected Gentlemen of worth in Virginia, can and will tes-tifie otherwise"; they simply refused to submit to Smith and "onely subjected ourselves to Master West." Another day, Martin emerged as president, but according to John Smith, "knowing his own in-sufficiencie, and the companies scorne, and conceit of his unworthi-nesse" he quit within three hours.[24]

For his part, Smith was not a man easily outdone, and he had a good number of the original colonists and newcomers on his side. His enemies charged him with subverting the social order by con-spiring with the sailors and servants. George Percy, allied with the Archer-Martin-Ratcliffe party, accused Smith of manipulating the sailors with "feastings, expense of much powder, and other unnec-essary triumphs" so that they would not side against him. Archer echoed this charge, writing to Virginia Company leaders that Smith "to strengthen his authority, accorded with the Mariners." Worse yet, he "gave not any due respect to many worthy Gentle-men, that came in our Ships."[25]

Smith countered that Archer, Ratcliffe, and Martin used the "unruly Gallants" they transported from England to try and "dispose and determine of the government." Exploiting the passengers whose minds they poisoned against Smith while at sea, these "lewd Captaines," Smith alleged, "did what they could to murther our President, to surprise the Store, the Fort, and our lodgings, to usurpe the government, and make us all their servants and slaves."[26]

In fact, neither Smith nor his adversaries really controlled the colonists; the more the leading gentlemen fought for power the less there was to claim. The laborers and soldiers did not know one day from the next which commander to follow. Some of the colonists resented Smith's domineering style, while others recognized him as an effective, hard-working president. Then, Archer and his cohort arrived and confirmed Argall's report of a new charter, which seemed to depose Smith. But they produced no proof or lawful successor, as all the official documents were with Gates—wherever he was. Mired in such chaos, the colonists "fell first into factions, and at last into plain distractions."[27]

Even had there been more clarity and consistency in authority, the settlers, particularly the 1609 voyagers, were not as a rule an especially deferential lot. Eager to fill their boats, company leaders had given little scrutiny to the emigrants. For all their advertisements trying to recruit respectable artisans and devout Christians, the company wound up with no small number of con men, criminals, and other "irregular persons." Packed off to Virginia, they thrived in the political bedlam of that fall and indulged "in al kind of looseness." As one man succinctly put it: "A more damned crew hell never vomited."[28]

Many of the migrants who adventured their lives in America in 1609 were a combination of ambitious and desperate. They had been promised the sun and moon by propagandists and celebrated as brave partners in pursuing their nation's glory. But after a near-deadly ocean crossing they arrived in Jamestown to find only deprivation. And what did their leaders, the so-called better sort do? The "chiefe and wisest guides among them (whereof there were not many) did nothing but bitterly contend who shall be first to command the rest."[29]

Not surprisingly, soon no man in Jamestown "would acknowledge a superior nor could, from this headless and unbridled multitude, be anything expected but disorder and riot." And "every man overvaluing his own worth, would be a Commander: every man underprising an others value, denied to be commanded."[30]

John Smith concluded that the men and women sent by the Virginia Company in 1609 were "ten times more fit to spoyle a Common-wealth, then either begin one, or but helpe to maintaine one." He felt sure that "neither the feare of God, nor the law, nor shame, nor displeasure of their friends could rule them here." Few followed orders and fewer still worked. One group of men, sent to trade for corn with the Indians, instead stole the *Swallow* and headed out to sea. Some joined bands of pirates, while others sneaked back to England, carrying some of the first news of the pandemonium in Jamestown.[31]

While the *Sea Venture* foundered in the western Atlantic, the fractious colonists in Virginia, "not being able to subsist and live together," split up.[32] John Martin, with George Percy and around sixty others, headed down the James River toward Nansemond. Francis West took a party of some one hundred men northwest, toward the falls on the James River, near present-day Richmond. Smith remained at Jamestown, as much in control as someone presiding over this quarrelsome and estranged lot could be—which was barely at all.

Martin's and West's incursions quickly aggravated the Powhatans—which may have been Smith's intention all along. Smith had long promoted himself as the only man able to negotiate effectively with the Powhatans, and it would not require a giant leap to imagine that he foresaw Martin and West failing and needing him to intercede.[33] Whether Smith calculated for trouble or not, it did not take long before the Indians' resentments of the colonists' encroachments provoked violence. Just after Martin and Percy settled into their fort, they sent a trading party to the nearby village at Nansemond. Martin and Percy never heard from their men again, "but understood from the Indians themselves that they were sacrificed, and that their brains were cut and scraped out of their heads with mussel shells." Martin responded with a greater show of violence: his men attacked the Indians, burned their village, and raided the graves of their leaders for valuables as well as corpses, which they desecrated. Relations, understandably, deteriorated.[34]

Up at the falls, West's men also clashed with the Indians, and some fled back to Jamestown, wounded and bringing reports that many others "were cut off and slain by the savages." Smith went to investigate for himself, and fought again with Francis West. Some colonists claimed that an irate Smith then conspired with the Indians to kill West. As Percy charged, Smith "incensed and animated the savages against Captain West and his company, reporting unto them that our men had no powder left them than would serve for one volley of shot."[35] Accounts more favorable to Smith disavowed any such conspiracy, but all parties agreed that the troubles only worsened after this confrontation.

Unable to resolve his quarrel with West, an exasperated Smith headed back to Jamestown. While he slept on the boat, one of his powder bags suddenly, inexplicably exploded. Smith and his critics always maintained that this was an accident, but given the fervor and venality of his enemies, there is good reason to suspect a more sinister cause. Whether mishap or plot, the explosion nearly killed Captain Smith. He later vividly recollected (referring to himself, as usual, in the third person) that the blast "tore his flesh from his bodie and thighes, 9. or 10. inches square in a most pittifull manner." In utter anguish, Smith threw himself overboard to "quench the tormenting fire." He very nearly drowned, saved only when his men pulled him from the water. Smith arrived back in Jamestown at the point of death and "neare bereft of his senses by reason of his torment." His wounds were so severe and his pain so excruciating that "few expected he could live."[36]

Unbelievably, his situation then got worse. Martin, Ratcliffe, and Archer—at least in Smith's version of events—conspired to take advantage of Smith's incapacitation and "plotted to have murdered him in his bed." Only a last-minute bout with his conscience kept an assassin from shooting Smith. Having survived one attempt on his life if not two, and unable even to stand, much less fend off his rivals, Smith resigned himself to abandoning Virginia. The day after the aborted murder scheme he sailed for England.[37]

While Archer and his allies from the *Sea Venture* fleet never admitted to any plot to kill the bedridden Smith, they readily exploited the situation. Smith's injuries, whether by design or happenstance, gave them the leverage they needed to seize power. Even their supporters admitted that, lacking any empathy whatsoever for the tormented Smith, "captains Rattliefe, Archer, and Martin practiced against him and deposed him off his government." Not content with just unseating Smith in Virginia, the three tried to discredit him in London as well. Archer had already reported Smith's supposedly corrupt and self-serving behavior in a letter he wrote just weeks after arriving in Virginia. In October, he and the others refuted Smith's claim that Smith was returning to England because of his injuries. Ratcliffe—expelled from Virginia less than a year earlier by Smith—now took his revenge. He wrote Robert Cecil, the Earl of Salisbury, that Smith was being *"sent home to answere some misdeamenors, whereof I perswade me he can scarcely clear himselfe."*[38]

As Smith's replacement, the Archer faction turned to the effete George Percy. Educated at Eton and Middle Temple and the brother of the Earl of Northumberland, Percy made sure to pack the sartorial signs of his gentility when he left for Virginia in 1606. His brother furnished him with items necessary for a man of his standing, including books and a feather bed with a tapestry covering. Percy was an honorable and refined gentleman, dedicated to the cause of English colonization, with powerful connections in London and long experience in Jamestown.[39] But he was no leader. His appointment numbered among the most ruinous mistakes made in Virginia that autumn.

Captain Smith somehow managed to survive the passage back to England, arriving in London in November 1609, just as winter began to set in at Jamestown. Despite encouragement from Smith's enemies, the Virginia Company Council did not pursue any charges against him.[40] Instead, the distressing news that he and others brought back from Virginia occupied their time and attention.

In the fall of 1609, shareholders in the Virginia Company expected to hear that Thomas Gates had turned Virginia around, that the colonists were diligently pursuing God's work in converting the Indians to Protestantism, that the settlement now produced varied and lucrative commodities, and that they could shortly expect a tidy return on their investment. Instead, ship after ship arrived in England *"laden with nothing but bad reports and letters of discouragement."*[41]

The most discouraging report of all: a rumor that the *Sea Venture* had gone down in the western Atlantic. Some of the earliest stories of the loss of the flagship and the consequent turmoil in Virginia came from the men who fled Jamestown early in the fall, including the band that stole the *Swallow* and others who had joined up with pirates. Company leaders rebuked them as the "scum of men" and dismissed their stories as self-serving fabrications believed only by the most foolish of Englishmen. These liars, company promoters charged, returned to England only "after their wilde roving upon the Sea, when all their lawlesse hopes failed." Bitter and impoverished, they "bound themselves by mutuall oath . . . to discredit the land." In a bid to conceal their own contemptible behavior, these men falsely claimed that "their comming awaie, proceeded from desperate necessitie." And the "stupidity and backwardnesse" of some men in London led them to actually believe these lies.[42]

But tales of the storms at sea and on land continued to trickle into London, and from sources not so easily dismissed. Captain Argall arrived in England in October, having sailed from Virginia around the first of September, and he reported that Gates had still not appeared when he left. He most likely brought along Gabriel Archer's full accounting of the hurricane as well as the whole sordid mess regarding John Smith.[43]

As the stories multiplied, the finger-pointing began. The character of the American colonists was much disparaged in London that fall. Company insiders continued to blame the exaggerated tales of trouble on the sorry colonists living there. In a typical appraisal, Virginia Company loyalist Robert Johnson complained that far too many "wicked Impes" and "ungratious sons that dailie vexed their fathers hearts at home" had gone to Virginia in the first place. Too lazy to work there, some gutlessly came back home. Then, "to cover their own leudnes," they decided to "fill mens eares with false reports of their miserable and perilous life in Virginea." Such deceitful, indolent men simply could not be trusted, insisted Virginia Company supporters. Any real problems in Jamestown were also the fault of "such an idle crue, as did thrust themselves in the last voiage" to Virginia.[44]

John Smith, back in London if not back in the good graces of company leaders, told a very different tale. Having invested so much in Virginia, he never faltered in his faith in the colony. He blamed the failures there on his rivals. "Had we beene in Paradice it selfe (with those governours)," he argued, "it would not have beene much better with us." Smith, however, had fallen too far out of favor among the leading men of London to command their attention. While Virginia Company Council members dismissed calls to prosecute him, they seemed equally uninterested in any future involvement with him. They ignored Smith's ideas, and he never received another commission from them. After recuperating, Smith worked on his *Map of Virginia*, a history of the colony's earliest years. But his estrangement from the city's principal entrepreneurs seems to have scared off potential publishers. No one in London would print Smith's *Map*; he published it in Oxford instead. Ostracized in London and barred from going back to Virginia, Smith shifted his interests northward in America. A group of West Country investors subsidized his 1614 voyage to survey the region he named New England.[45]

Although company insiders snubbed Smith, many other Londoners shared his low opinion of Virginia's leaders. And they found plenty of men to fault, including the once-celebrated Governor Gates. Questions about Thomas Gates's leadership grew so widespread in London that the council felt compelled to publish a defense of him. Critics condemned Gates for charting a dangerous course in the first place, which caused the passengers to contract the plague and put them in the path of the hurricane. He was disparaged for foolishly carrying "all the principall Commissioners" in one boat, and therefore undermining stable government in Virginia. Even the minister in Virginia shared in the culpability. One man blamed the troubles in Virginia on Rev. William Mease, "who being, as they say, somewhat a puritaine, the most part [of the colonists] refused to go to his service, or to heare his sermons." Dissenting church services were, of course, the least of the colonists' problems. But the letter illustrates how speculative the rumors about Virginia's troubles had grown by November 1609.[46]

While Londoners blamed the colonists—either the craven, lazy workers or the inept leaders—the colonists themselves found another culprit: Sir Thomas Smythe. Some charged him personally with causing the "great miseries and calamities" they endured. First, he neglected "providing and allowing better means to proceed to so great a work." He then compounded this failure by "hindering very many of our friends from sending much relief and means." Smythe, some asserted, lied to their friends in London, falsely assuring those who tried to aid the colonists "that we were in no want at all, but that we exceeded in abundance and plenty of all things." So their allies not only decided not to send supplies, but they also came to distrust reports of deprivations coming from the colony. Smythe tried to counter negative rumor-mongering with a positive public relations campaign on behalf of the Virginia enterprise. The effort sometimes veered into overt censorship. He required all letters from the colony inspected, and anyone caught sending word to England of the dire straits in America was "severely punished." And, to further obscure the harsh reality of life in Virginia, "Neither was it permitted to any to have pass to go home, but by force were kept here."[47]

The more accusations investors heard that fall, the more nervous they got. While it was easy to discount the wild stories of a few embittered former colonists, respected ships' captains and gentlemen were another matter entirely. They had no ax to grind. What, besides truth, would motivate men like Argall and Archer to give such bleak reports on America? And with so many people of so many different ranks telling so many similar stories, how likely was it that all were confused or lying? Suspicious stockholders began to reconsider their commitment to the Virginia Company.

In their haste to raise funds for the *Sea Venture* fleet, the Council of the Virginia Company had agreed to sell shares, or subscriptions, on time, to be paid in installments. This allowed more people to invest more easily. It also, quite unintentionally, gave shareholders a way out of their full financial commitment. As gossip about the most recent failures in America spread through London, some subscribers simply refused to pay.[48] They were then publicly lambasted by Virginia Company leaders, much like the "liars" maligning Virginia, for their lack of integrity and faith.

Throughout the closing months of 1609, a dwindling number of optimists in London—persuaded by Virginia Company propaganda—continued to hope that Gates's ship was only delayed in reaching Virginia, not lost at sea. From time to time, investors heard rumors that the *Sea Venture* had finally reached land. But in late November 1609, the remnants of the fleet reached London with the demoralizing confirmation: Gates, Somers, and Newport had never been seen. The letdown was all the greater because of the promises made for the rescue mission. One Englishman poignantly reflected how "that Virgine voyage . . . which went out smilling on her lovers with pleasant lookes, after her wearie travailes, did thus returne with a rent and disfigured face."[49]

Londoners watched their enemies thrill to "insult and scoffe" in this, their darkest hour. Spanish Ambassador Zúñiga happily sent news to Madrid of the failure of the *Sea Venture* fleet less than two weeks after its return. And in early December he added: "the sailors are not well pleased because they suffer much from hunger

there." News of the loss of the Virginia colony's leaders and the ensuing chaos in the settlement quickly spread across Europe. Word
that "From Virginia wee hear that the 2. best shippes with Sir
Thomas Gates are separated from the other five and are in danger
to be lost" reached Brussels in November. And in early 1610, a
London printer released a translated Dutch tract in which the
author, Emanuel van Meteren, recounted all the troubles in
Jamestown.⁵⁰

By late November 1609, Virginia Company leaders trying to
squelch rumors and hold on to investors saw they were fighting a
losing battle. Pleas to forebear, assurances of future success,
dismissals of negative reports—nothing could stop the spreading
belief that things had gone horribly wrong in America.

It is not clear exactly what Thomas Smythe and the other councilors knew and when they knew it—and so, therefore, where to
draw the line between optimism and deception. Even after Archer's
August letter, the leaders could still reasonably hope that Gates
was simply delayed. We know that John Ratcliffe wrote the Earl of
Salisbury in early October, confessing there had been still no sign
of the *Sea Venture* "and we much feare they are lost." That devastating confession would have reached the council around late November, the same time as some of the ships in the separated fleet
returned with their negative reports. By late November, then, if
there had been earlier duplicity, such ploys were now pointless.⁵¹

Whether acting in good faith based on new and reliable information or cunningly abandoning ineffectual deceptions, one thing
is clear: in December 1609 the Council of the Virginia Company
made a remarkable reversal of course.

The high-pressure sales tactics long employed by the Virginia
Company no longer worked by December 1609. Grandiose prom-

ises made in publications such as *Nova Britannia* now appeared transparently bogus, and not only to the most skittish investors. Even experienced businessmen who had waited several years for profits in earlier ventures such as the East India Company lost faith in ever getting their money out of Virginia. Certainly they were not about to pay even more toward subscriptions when every report from the colony seemed more disturbing and more reliable than the last. Artisan guilds and small individual investors also refused to pay because they, like everyone else in London, heard only disheartening news from America.[52]

Thomas Smythe found himself caught between the absolute necessity of raising money to save the colonists in Virginia and the refusal of increasing numbers of investors to support the failing enterprise. He could no longer deny the troubles in Jamestown, but Londoners' growing knowledge of those troubles undermined all his ability to help. Desperate, the Council of the Virginia Company decided to make a bold move: tell the truth.

On December 14, 1609, the Virginia Company entered a remarkable publication at Stationers' Hall. Entitled *A True and Sincere Declaration of the purposes and ends of the plantation begun in Virginia*, the tract conceded that many of the rumors running through London, while spread by "ignorant" and "impious" enemies of the endeavor, were not inaccurate. For example, regarding the reports of widespread hunger in the colony, the company explained, "though the noise have exceeded the truth, yet we do confess a great part of it." They spread the blame far and wide for deprivation in the colony: the Indians "cunningly" withdrew all trade; the leaders in the colony "by dissension and ambition among themselves" failed to oversee farming; and "the idleness and bestial sloth of the common sort" exacerbated the shortages. Human failure, nothing inherent in the land, caused the trouble. Therefore, if a better group of colonists went over with better leaders and "a supply of victual for one year . . . they will never need nor expect to charge us with more expense for anything."[53]

The document also ratcheted down earlier grand hopes by explaining to city citizens that they should expect setbacks as a natural consequence of so vast and perilous an undertaking as colonizing Virginia. As the tract reminded readers, "every action hath proportional difficulties to the greatness thereof." And the plans for Virginia were great indeed. The colony had a threefold mission. First, the Virginians intended "to preach and baptize into Christian religion and . . . to recover out of the arms of the devil a number of poor and miserable souls." Besting the devil was, understandably, no simple matter. Second, Virginia would "provide and build up for the public honor and safety of our gracious king and his estates." This included shipping the excess population from England, where it was fast becoming "a burthen" for the nation, to America to build a colony that would provide "a bulwark of defense" against other colonizing nations, namely Spain. National glory, particularly when tied to challenging Spain's dominion over America, would not easily be won. Finally, Virginia was expected to produce commodities that would free England from economic dependence on foreign rivals. Again, no mean feat.[54]

Furthermore, the Virginia Company differed from earlier enterprises such as the Muscovy and East India Companies, because it involved not simply commercial exchanges but also the permanent transplantation of large numbers of English men and women. This only added to the difficulties posed by the religious, political, and economic objectives. Clearly, the council was ready to admit by December, the heady optimism of the first year or so of Virginia's existence needed to be reconciled with the monumental difficulties of implementing so sweeping a plan.

They presented this as a challenge, a test of Christian fortitude. God himself, the tract intimated, had written the history of the

English in America. Christians enacting His will in Virginia must continue "the constant and patient prosecution thereof, until by the mercies of God it shall retribute a fruitful harvest to the Kingdom of Heaven and this commonwealth." Faithful men had, after all, persevered through setbacks over the prior three years, learning from their mistakes. *A True and Sincere Declaration* pointed out two particular problems that the Virginia Company had confronted in the summer of 1609: "the form of government and length and danger of the passage." To correct the latter, Argall had charted another course in May and June, and he had "succeeded almost beyond our hopes." To rectify the former problem, the council had redesigned the colony's government, appointed the new Governor Gates, and sent hundreds of settlers in the *Sea Venture* convoy.[55] God, however, had interceded in that part of the company's plans.

The author reminded readers that it was not the place of men to question God's will as related to the *Sea Venture*: "Who can avoid the hand of God, or dispute with Him?" Rather, it was their duty to rise to the challenge that God had set before them, otherwise they would reveal themselves as unworthy of His mission: "Is he fit to undertake any great action whose courage is shaken and dissolved with one storm? Who knows whether He that disposed of our hearts to so good beginnings be now pleased to try our constancy and perseverance." If God was testing the English, and it appeared that He was, then failing to follow through in Virginia was not only a poor business and diplomatic decision, but a sin as well.[56]

Apparently aware that not all subscribers would be moved by this religious call, the author of *A True and Sincere Declaration* then artfully turned to other selling points. National interest might move some skeptical investors, so the tract called on readers to consider the history of their most bitter rival, Spain: "how abundant their stories are of fleets, battles, and armies lost . . . and yet with how indefatigable industry and prosperous fate they have pursued and vanquished all these." If Spain could transcend so many terrible hardships, surely England would not throw away its colonial dreams after only one storm.[57]

The author then laid out the logic and the plan for saving Virginia. First, he reminded readers that Gates's fate "is in suspense, and much reason of his safety against some doubt." After all, in the prior three crossings "no man miscarried in the way." Most likely, Gates was either repairing his ship or already in Virginia. Moreover, regardless of Gates's whereabouts, the physical reality of Virginia remained unchanged: it was a land of unrivaled plenty, and, with the right governance, would produce many lucrative commodities and therefore great profits for investors. Thomas West, the Lord De La Warr and a model of "courage, temper, and experience," had agreed to lead another rescue effort; investors could rest assured he would do all in his power to bring stability to Virginia and glory to England.[58]

The tract explained how Thomas Smythe and other Virginia Company leaders devoted themselves to thoughtfully preparing for De La Warr's voyage. In particular, they were screening potential colonists to avoid sending more of the dissolute, lazy, corrupt people they blamed for the current troubles in Virginia. Blacksmiths, joiners, fishermen, masons, and other craftsmen interested in adventuring to America were urged to consult with Smythe. But they were warned that each man would be required to prove his skill in his trade as well as "bring or render some good testimony of his religion to God, and civil manners and behavior to his neighbor with whom he hath lived."[59] The company could, of course, hardly afford to be so choosy given the dire straits of their enterprise. The list, which conspicuously included no gentlemen, offered savvy salesmanship: more assurances for potential investors that the problems of the past would not be replicated in the 1610 voyage.

Then, in a brilliant, audacious move, the author of *A True and Sincere Declaration* implicated his readers in the fate of the Virginia colonists. If religious faith, patriotism, and logic failed to persuade, perhaps guilt would work. The tract likened English citizens who possessed knowledge of the desperate circumstances confronting their countrymen in Virginia and still failed to send relief to an experienced swimmer ignoring a drowning man. "Let not any man flatter himself that it concerns not him," charged the essay. The trouble in Virginia was put to the "souls and consciences" of all English subjects, who were reminded, "what was at first but of conveniency and for honor is now become a case of necessity and piety." Investors "have promised to adventure and not performed it." And on those promises, "600 of our brethren by our common mother the Church, Christians of one faith and one baptism" had wagered their lives. If England failed to fund De La Warr's relief effort, they were condemning the men and women in Virginia "to a miserable and inevitable death." The language was unequivocal and chastening: "he that forsakes whom he can safely relieve is . . . guilty of his death."[60]

The company followed up *A True and Sincere Declaration* with a shorter broadside targeting a wider audience. It reiterated all the claims about "unruly youths" spreading "vile and scandalous reports." The separation of the *Sea Venture* from the remainder of the fleet was conceded, but pitched as a problem of timing: "they could not in so convenient time" make it to Virginia. And the broadside assured readers that wise businessmen and faithful ministers still stood squarely behind the Virginia enterprise: "many of them both honourable and worshipfull have given their hands and subscribed to contribute againe and againe to new supplies if need require." The promise of steady supplies was particularly important since the broadside targeted potential colonists, not delinquent investors. All that remained for success in Virginia, proclaimed the broadside, was "honest and good" artisans. A similar list of desired workers as appeared in *A True and Sincere Declaration* was included along with directions to Smythe's house for interviews. That December, then, the company made every effort to coax gentlemen, Christians, investors, and workers to adventure either their money or their lives in De La Warr's rescue mission.[61]

The effort, imaginative, impassioned, and inspiring, fell short. Even King James, in whose name the entire enterprise was ostensibly devoted, showed far less concern than Virginia Company leaders would have wished. The same week as *A True and Sincere Declaration* appeared, Henry Wriothesley, the Earl of Southampton and one of the most influential members of the council, paid a visit to the king to report the news from America. Far from being distressed over the situation in his namesake town or the spreading fear that Christopher Newport and Thomas Gates had died, James instead pressed Wriothesley about acquiring for him a flying squirrel from America. Wriothesley reported his exchange with King James to the Earl of Salisbury: "hee presently & very earnestly asked mee if none of them was prouided for him, & . . . sayinge that hee was sure you would gett him one of them. I would not haue trobled you with this but you know so well how hee is affected to these toyes." Southampton asked Salisbury to find some way of getting a squirrel to present to King James when he came to London in late December.[62]

Investors also failed to turn up in the numbers Virginia Company leaders anticipated. Shame, unfortunately, worked less effectively than they had imagined. Despite the moving moral appeals in *A True and Sincere Declaration*, subscribers continued to ignore their obligations that winter. Similarly, the five to six hundred colonists De La Warr hoped to carry to America never materialized.

Short funds forced him to delay his departure until the spring of 1610. When he left, only about 150 passengers sailed with him; they needed only three ships. No doubt as potential migrants contemplated the possibility of meeting the sad fate they assumed had befallen their countrymen on the *Sea Venture,* discretion got the better part of valor. For many prospective colonists and investors alike, fear overwhelmed hope. Even devoted supporters of the Virginia campaign had a hard time convincing themselves that the De La Warr rescue attempt could succeed. Robert Johnson, a faithful investor, admitted that "we had nothing left but hope, and this hope of ours we fixed much (if not too much) upon that honourable Lord Governour." Many earnestly prayed for De La Warr that spring, including a chancery clerk and investor in the Virginia Company, who asked God to "blesse his worthy endeauours."[63] Whatever part God played in that spring departure, He did not send the men and money that De La Warr and Smythe wanted.

As the fund-raising campaign in London dragged along and De La Warr and Smythe worked on scaling back their plans, the situation in Virginia grew ever more miserable. In the weeks after John Smith's departure from Jamestown, the leadership in the colony collapsed, as did relations with the Indians and the resolve of the settlers. Around the time the Virginia Company issued *A True and Sincere Declaration,* the colonists began "to feel that sharp prick of hunger." By the time De La Warr's small convoy left London, they were trapped in an inconceivable "world of miseries."[64]

And still, no one in America or England—no one in the world—yet knew the fate of the *Sea Venture.*

CHAPTER 5

THE "ISLE OF DEVILS"

By Friday, July 28, 1609, even Rev. Richard Buck and the most faithful Christians must have questioned why God had brought them three thousand miles from home only to bury them in a watery grave. When they left England seven weeks earlier, in June, the true believers felt confident—inspired by seductive Virginia Company propaganda spread throughout London's neighborhoods and zealous sermons delivered at St. Paul's Cross—that God stood with Englishmen seeking to save Virginia. But from Monday afternoon, July 24, to Friday's dawn, the powerful hurricane battered the *Sea Venture* so intensely that passengers and crew eventually gave up bailing and commended their "sinful souls to God, [and] committed the ship to the mercy of the gale."[1]

But God, it turned out, did indeed work in mysterious ways. The voyagers' story was not ending at the bottom of the Atlantic Ocean. It was only beginning—at the most feared place in the known world.

Admiral George Somers, the nearly sixty-year-old commander

of the fleet, faced the storm from the poop deck of the sinking flag-ship. For three days he watched the seas from that vantage point and, with 150 crew and passengers below readying themselves for a grisly death, struggled "to direct the Shippe as euenly [evenly] as might be." Then, on Friday morning, Somers spotted something in the distance and cried, "Land!" At first barely audible above the winds, Somers's call soon roused the men to action. Some rushed to the hatches to see for themselves, which unfortunately only wors-ened the immediate problem: "they gaue such aduantage to their greedy enemye, the salt water . . . they had well nigh swallowed their death." Then quickly everyone resumed bailing water, as one man recalled "with will and desire beyond their strength," aware that they might now with valiant effort save their lives.[2]

Had they known where they were, some might have worked less zealously.

Like Somers, Captain Christopher Newport understood precisely where they were headed. By 1609, he had already made three successful trips to the Virginia colony, and, over the course of his storied career, had led more Atlantic crossings than any other Englishman of his era. So when Somers cried land, Newport would have known instantly what land the Admiral meant. They had been hit at around 30° latitude by a northeastern storm. Even given the ferocity of the hurricane and the chaos of the past week, for knowledgeable seamen like Somers and Newport there could be no mistaking: the salvation of the *Sea Venture* depended on Bermuda, "the Ile of Devils, that all men did shun as Hell and perdition."[3]

Somers and Newport understood—but initially kept to themselves—that their only hope rested on "that dreadfull coast of the Bermodes," which was supposedly "inchanted and inhabited with witches, and devils." So fearful was the reputation of the small string of islands that Somers and Newport, alongside Thomas

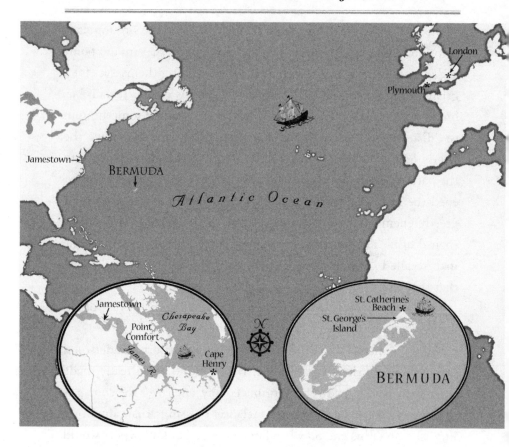

Gates, even with no other option than the certain deaths of 150 souls, actually discussed whether to attempt to make land. In "a kinde of desperat resolution" these three men "agreed of two evills to chuse the least" and Newport steered the *Sea Venture* toward the fishhook-shaped island chain.[4]

Bermuda's infamy as a dangerous, even diabolical, place had spread across Europe for over a century. The more superstitious among mariners saw it as "an inchanted den of Furies and Devils, the most dangerous, unfortunate, and forlorne place in the world." Sailors told of evil spirits that inhabited both the island and its surrounding water, sinking ships and stealing men. Bermuda, they maintained, was "so fearful, hideous, and hateful

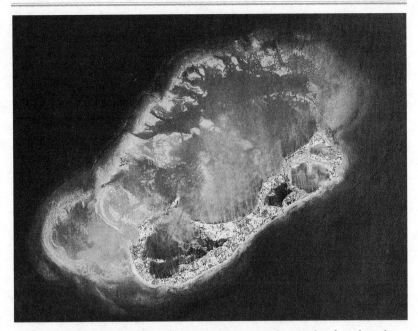

This satellite image of coral reefs surrounding Bermuda reveals why colonial-era ships approached the island chain at great risk. (COURTESY OF PAUL ILLSLEY)

as it seemed a place abandoned of God and man, and given up to the devil's power and possession, and to be of all known places in the world a very hell upon earth." Even men skeptical about such purported demonism avoided Bermuda. Samuel de Champlain, the founder of Quebec, sailed by Bermuda in 1600 and condemned it as "a mountainous Island which is difficult to approach on account of the dangers that surround it. It almost always rains there, and thunders so often that it seems as if heaven and earth were about to come together. The sea is very tempestuous round the said Island and the waves as high as mountains."[5]

The true source of Bermuda's dreadful reputation was neither demonic possession nor a bizarre climate. Coral reefs—the northernmost in the world—surround the chain of some 150 small islands. On the northern side of Bermuda, the coral reefs extend as far as ten miles from shore, while to the south they lie in shallow waters just off the coast. These treacherous, rocky formations—not devils—ripped into the hulls of passing ships. The ocean floor, not fairies, conspired with the reefs. Off Bermuda's shore the depth of the Atlantic can shift in less than one mile's distance from five thousand feet to waist level.[6]

The captain and crew of the *Sea Venture* knew none of this. Somers and Newport, seeing only two terrible options, picked the devil over the deep blue sea. Making the choice was only the first difficult task. Safe passage to the "Isle of Devils" would require all of Captain Newport's skill and, as Englishmen later saw it, divine intervention.

By late morning the sea calmed, and some of the passengers made their way to the main deck. They were close enough to see wind-whipped trees on the distant shore when Newport commanded the helmsman: "bear up." Anchoring the sinking ship, it turned out, was impossible. The only hope for survival lay in running aground—a decidedly dangerous proposition. Too forceful a crash would tear the hull apart and leave no time to evacuate. (A half-century later when an English ship, the *Virginia Merchant*, wrecked just off the southwest shore, only 10 of 179 passengers survived. And by that time, ships' captains knew well the outline and dangers of Bermuda's coast.)[7]

The boatswain, at his first sounding, reported a depth of thirteen fathoms, then seven, and then four. By now, the island chain lay within a mile, and the potential for catastrophe was immediate. Then came the first in a series of what the English interpreted as miracles: by "Gods divine providence," the *Sea Venture* floated to safety. Around a half-mile from the northeastern tip of the chain (today, St. George's Island), the ship, as passenger Silvester Jourdain explained, "fortunately in so great a misfortune fell in be-tweene two rockes, where shee was fast lodged and locked, for fur-ther budging."[8]

Sailors rushed first the handful of women and children on board and then the male passengers into skiffs and headed for the shore. They rowed through deep waters of brilliant cobalt blue into shal-low areas colored a vivid turquoise. Volcanic rocks, scattered where the waves broke, would have made it necessary to walk the last yards to the faintly pink seashore. St. Catherine's Beach, where the first castaways came ashore, is still a breathtaking place today: a narrow strip of pinkish beach strewn with boulders and bordered by high rock shelves. But for the crew of the *Sea Venture*, this was hardly the time to ponder the wonders of their new home. As soon as one boatload of passengers made the beach, the crewmen sped back for another, until, as the survivors acknowledged, "by the mercy of God unto us," every person on board—and their dog—made it safely to shore. Even then, Gates, who asserted primary au-thority once they made land, and Somers, who still commanded the sailors, gave their men little time to rest. They needed to re-trieve everything on board the ship before it sank. So the crew, doubtless weary beyond words, returned again and again, searching for tools, clothing, food, household supplies—anything they could carry.[9]

The *Sea Venture*'s log has not survived, but it is possible to piece together a likely catalog of their recovered supplies. Lists from sim-ilar contemporary ships suggest that the castaways would have had all sorts of tools and household supplies, cloth, paper, staples, and food, including grains and salted meat, and seeds for planting. Very little furniture would have been carried—it occupied too much space, and migrants assumed there would be plenty of wood in the colonies to make what they needed. George Somers did carry a small chest, crafted in Italy of cypress wood with a detailed rendering of Artemis, the Greek goddess of the hunt, engraved on the inside lid. Like furniture, livestock required a lot of space and thus expense, so usually only a few breeding animals were shipped. Somers's fleet carried at least six mares and two horses, but not on the *Sea Venture*. It did transport a few pigs, a dog, and perhaps some sheep. Archaeological excavations have uncovered sheep bones, and while ships often carried salted pork and fish, mutton did not keep well.[10]

So thoroughgoing was the recovery effort that Somers regretted "all our bread was wet and lost"—a luxurious lament given their bleak outlook just the day before. Whether at the direction of Gates and Somers or through their own foresight, the seamen also salvaged the rigging of the boat and most of the iron, down to the bolts.[11]

By sunset on the 28th, the crew carried the last of the salvageable supplies to shore; little remained of the *Sea Venture* "but bared ribs."[12] And in a matter of days, that last link to the world beyond Bermuda sunk beneath the waves. One hundred and fifty English subjects, sent on a grand mission—to save Jamestown, enrich Virginia Company investors, promote the glory of England and the Christian God—now found themselves stranded 3,000 miles from England, 1,000 miles from any Caribbean island, and nearly 600 miles from the closest spot on mainland North America. Bermuda's notorious reputation made rescue by a passing ship all but impossible. Unless a captain from the scattered fleet returned to search for them—unlikely since Somers gave strict directions to the contrary before leaving England—they would have to fend for themselves.

Before the colonists could begin to imagine how they might live on the island and how they might escape it, the castaways, led by Rev. Buck, gathered to pray. In their first act together, the castaways "all humbly thanked God for his great mercy, in so preserving them from destruction."[13]

Although grateful to have escaped with their lives, the men and women of the *Sea Venture* now found themselves living the ultimate nightmare in the age of sail: shipwrecked. The prospect of being lost at sea understandably fueled fears of isolation and death. But shipwrecks also imperiled the very foundations of English civilization. The early modern English fairly obsessed about order; they held their society together and barbarism at bay by insisting on a rigid social hierarchy that reached into every aspect of life. Congregants, for example, participated in church services according to rank, with gentlemen and their families entering last and sitting in the forward pews. Sartorial laws dictated what cloth and colors people wore, with artisans and farmers forbidden from dressing in the rich colors (such as purple and red) and soft fabrics (including silk and velvet) reserved for elites. A shipwreck destroyed this order by washing away the artifacts of social rank and trapping castaways in a corruptive wilderness that subverted civilization. The English believed that without vigilant attention to religious instruction and the rule of law, men and women would regress to their wicked natures, and savagery would triumph over godliness and civilization. So as England expanded its involvement in transoceanic trading and colonization, fears about being lost on a voyage multiplied. Shipwrecks became a popular trope for playwrights, who found maritime catastrophes alluring to morbidly curious audiences and an ideal metaphor for exploring human nature "in extremis."[14]

Sir Thomas Gates intended to ensure that order, not fear, prevailed on Bermuda. As the next governor of Virginia, he asserted authority over the company after everyone made it safely onto the island. Gates belonged to the velvet-clad gentry of London. As a young man he studied at Gray's Inn but ultimately chose military and diplomatic service over the law. An original member of the Virginia Company, he took very seriously his charge to redeem its American enterprise. Although deferring to Somers and Newport while at sea, he asserted his supremacy once on land—that he wound up on Bermuda rather than in Virginia mattered little to the governor.[15]

As night fell that first night on the island, Gates informed his gathered company that they had landed on the "Isle of Devils." While this would have shocked many of the passengers, as one observer noted, any "skillfull and understandinge marrionour" would have already suspected the truth. Gates quickly reminded the group that Bermuda had saved them from certain death at sea, and he assured them he would deliver them safely to Virginia. Resolved to safeguard the castaways, Gates appointed several night watches to protect the others as they slept. Whether reassured or just exhausted, the castaways lay down on the pink sands to spend the first of many nights on Bermuda.[16]

The stark reality of what they faced greeted the castaways when they awoke on Saturday morning, July 29. They were totally alone. And in this isolation they confronted a very different situation than did the many colonists who preceded them. From the arrival of Columbus on Hispaniola in 1492, Europeans touted their various "discoveries" in what they termed the New World. In reality, they generally collided with established Indian nations, which, predictably, looked none too favorably on intruders claiming their land in the name of strange monarchs. When the English colonists first arrived in the Chesapeake Bay in 1607, it was already home to nearly 20,000 Algonquian-speaking members of the Powhatan confederation. And when the Spanish set foot on the mainland a full century earlier, the Aztec empire stretched throughout central

Mexico, surpassing in size and scope every European kingdom. The capital city of Tenochtitlán (present-day Mexico City) held 200,000 inhabitants, dwarfing Seville's population of 70,000. Even the infamous conquistador Hernán Cortés admitted, "In Spain there is nothing to compare with it."[17]

But in Bermuda everything was different. Amerindians did not build boats capable of traveling to the remote island chain. It remained unknown and untouched by humans before the arrival of Europeans. So, in addition to its secluded location and peculiar coral reefs, Bermuda has the rare distinction of truly being discovered by European colonizers.

Juan de Bermúdez, the first of several unlucky Spanish mariners stranded on the chain around 1503, gave Bermuda its name. By 1511 "la Bermuda" was marked on Spanish maps. Henry May, the first Englishman marooned on Bermuda, wound up there while working on a French ship returning from Hispaniola in 1593. Shortly before their boat sank, the pilots had assured the captain that they were twelve leagues south of the islands and so "out of all danger." They then demanded their "wine of height"—wine given after reaching a certain latitude during the voyage from the Caribbean to Europe. But in their haste to celebrate skirting the "Isle of Devils," the sailors miscalculated. Only twenty-six men survived the wreck, among them May, the only Englishman. He finally made it home from the harrowing ordeal in August 1594.[18]

Like these earlier castaways, the marooned *Sea Venture* voyagers desperately needed water, food, and shelter. A well dug near the promontory above the beach provided a modest amount of safe drinking water. But it could not sustain such a large group for very long. Some men fished in the shallow waters of what had already been named Gates Bay, while others searched the forests for fruit. Men and women worked together building makeshift housing, men felling trees and women arranging palm leaves for thatched roofs. They found the leaves as broad "as an Italian umbrella" and saw that "a man may well defend his whole body under one of them from the greatest storm rain that falls." Women also gathered tree limbs for the fire they tended, ready to prepare meals from whatever the men found. Fewer than a dozen women would be tasked with feeding well over one hundred men.[19]

As everyone went about the first day's work, they saw a small part of the amazing bounty that Bermuda offered. One man later recalled how his opinion of the island changed dramatically over time: "whereas it hath been and is still accounted the most dangerous, infortunate, and most forlorn place of the world, it is in truth the richest, healthfullest, and pleasing land."[20] But that first Saturday the full wonders of Bermuda remained unknown to the lost colonists, as did its real dangers.

Thomas Gates supervised these initial foraging efforts even as he sought to establish the authority his commission as governor granted him. The Virginia Company gave Gates detailed printed instructions for instituting a new government in Virginia, expanding settlements, and getting the upper hand over local Indians. All of that proved utterly irrelevant in Bermuda, but at least Gates found other parts of the directives useful. Religious services reminded believers of God's redemptive power and to keep faith, even in the darkest times. Anglican liturgy served as a central symbol of English civilization, and church worship encouraged community-mindedness and order. Applying the Virginia Company orders to Bermuda, Gates set Rev. Buck to work. Beginning the second day, Sunday, June 30, and under Buck's guidance the castaways fulfilled the company's charge to honor "the true and reverent worship of God" with regular preaching and observing the sacraments "accordinge to the constitucions of the Church of England."[21]

Gates also paid close attention to his directions advising him to secure all tools and weapons. Company leaders worried that Virginia Indians might steal such precious and dangerous equipment. The uninhabited island of Bermuda posed no such threat, but perhaps Gates feared that other, closer enemies might materialize in the coming days, or his military experience could have inspired the decision. In any event, he made sure to keep all the weapons recovered from the *Sea Venture* under constant guard.[22]

To counter anyone questioning his decisions, Gates could point to the Virginia Company orders, which gave him great latitude in defining and defending the law. He could, in the name of King James, act "as shall in your discrecion seem aptest for you." Gates's power under the second charter knew few bounds and included the right to invoke martial law "in all such cases of necessity."[23] Such wide-ranging authority could help him maintain order and preserve civilization—vital influence given the dangerous, corruptive wilderness that he feared surrounded his countrymen.

The first or second night, as most of the company slept, watches suddenly heard ominous noises coming toward the encampment. As they scrambled to respond to the rumbling and snorting, the guards saw the source of the racket: wild hogs had wandered into camp, drawn by the scent of the pigs brought on the *Sea Venture*. As one account humorously put it: the wild hogs, smelling the "newe comers . . . came presently to see in the darck what newes they had brought with them." Spanish mariners, fearful their countrymen might shipwreck on Bermuda and not find adequate food supplies, had left hogs behind years before. With no natural predators or rivals for food, hundreds roamed Bermuda by 1609.[24]

One of Somers's more ingenious sailors trapped the first wild hog by hiding among the domesticated pigs: "when, the boar being come and groveled by the sows, he put over his hand and rubbed the side gently of the boar, which then lay still; by which means he fastened a rope with a sliding knot to the hinder leg and so took him." The castaways eventually turned to hunting hogs with the ship's dog. William Strachey, who was rarely given to hyperbole, maintained that the hunters became so skillful that they could capture fifty pigs in a single week, "for the dog would fasten on them and hold whilst the huntsmen made in." The *Sea Venture* men eventually built sties and twice daily fed the smaller pigs they caught, guaranteeing a steady supply of meat. When the weather kept them from fishing, they slaughtered their fattened hogs. They also wisely tracked the hogs through the forest, discovering which plants they might safely eat themselves.[25]

Rumors of evil spirits haunting the island at night, then, turned out to have entirely benign origins. The terrifying screams allegedly emanating from the islands' demons likewise came from a natural and fortuitous source: thousands of nocturnal birds, named cahows by their new human neighbors, made the "strange hollo and harsh howling" that frightened so many mariners. Cahows arrived in October or November, and to the amazement of the colonists, knew no fear. Men could pluck them and the hen-sized eggs they laid from burrows in the rocks and on the ground. During a single morning a group of sailors collected a thousand eggs in this manner. The birds even laid eggs as men sat beside the nests, waiting to raid them. Colonists hunted the cahows (if it could be called hunting) simply by "standing on the rocks or sands by the seaside and holloing, laughing, and making the strangest outcry that possibly they could." Unafraid, the cahows flew right up to the men, even alighted on them. Taking the birds in their hands, the men weighed them, "and which weighed heaviest they took for the best and let the others alone." Strachey watched twenty dozen of the largest cahows killed in this fashion in just two hours.[26]

Herons, crows, snipes, hawks, swans, and a myriad of other

birds also inhabited the island chain; along with fish they were the only wildlife native to Bermuda. No other species could survive the passage from the mainland, so nothing threatened the birds—or prepared them for the arrival of humans. In addition to the cahows, the colonists found herons "so familiar and tame that we beat them down from the trees." Men could walk through the forest whistling and birds "will come and gaze on you, so near that you may strike and kill many of them with your stick."[27]

The lost colonists found no dangerous wildlife or poisonous snakes; even the spiders did not appear to be harmful to humans. Spiders and flies were a nuisance, and cockroaches often spread "their ill-sented dung" in the colonists' meager belongings. But otherwise, the castaways' biggest trouble came from poison ivy, which, they quickly discovered, "being but touched, causeth red-nesse, itching, and lastly blisters." Although annoying, the blisters would "after a while passe away of themselves without further harme." As they explored their supposedly perilous environment, many of the castaways instead discovered "ease and pleasure."[28]

Far from abandoned by God, then, the English found themselves delivered to a new Eden—and not the chimera of Virginia, but a real island paradise—"fertile, fruitfull, plentifull, and a safe, se-cure, temperate, rich, sweet, and healthfull habitation for Man." Bermuda's forests would have resembled the Florida Everglades, al-though with less botanical diversity. Wind, ocean currents, and birds carried seeds from the mainland to Bermuda, and less hardy plant species would have perished on the ocean passage. Tall cedar trees filled the landscape, along with mulberry trees, palmettos, mangroves, and "others of unknowen both name and vertue."[29] The palmettos bore berries that sailors mashed, strained, and fermented to produce a tasty drink. They boiled the heads of the palmetto trees and declared the dish better than English cabbage. Prickly pears and mulberries abounded. Fish were even more plentiful than birds. In the first week, George Somers took the lead in fishing, and during his first outing it took him less than half an hour to catch enough fish to feed everyone. Using gigs, nets, and hooks, while fishing in shallow water from a small boat that Somers's men crafted, the colonists gathered "angelfish, salmon peal, bonitos, sting ray, cabally snappers, hogfish, sharks, dogfish, pilchards, mullets, and rockfish." On the rocky shoreline, they also found crayfish (bigger than English lobster), crabs, and oysters. Amazed at the vast numbers he saw, Strachey speculated that, "no island in the world may have greater store or better fish."[30]

Giant sea turtles waded onto the beaches in February—just as "the palm berries began to be scant or dry" and "the hogs grew poor."[31] The tortoises awed and delighted the stranded English. Their eggs, which men collected by the bushel, tasted delicious, as did the sweet roasted turtle meat. Women boiled the fat to make cooking oil as rich as butter. Like the birds and fish, the "turkles" made effortless prey: they could be killed on shore while the males and females were "cooting," or as the females laid their eggs, or in the shallow waters as they swam. Silvester Jourdain recalled taking up to forty in a single day. They grew so large that it took three or four men to carry a turtle, and just one went further at mealtime than three hogs, feeding upward of fifty men and women.[32]

Regular, sometimes violent storms struck Bermuda during the castaways' stay there, with thunder and lightning more fearsome than ever known in England, but these passed quickly and without hurting anyone. The castaways never endured snow or sleet or even frost, and avoided the blistering summer heat common in the Caribbean and coastal Virginia. While it was quite warm and humid in August and September, the rest of their time on Bermuda felt like "a continuall Spring." During summer months, Bermuda experiences an average high temperature of 85°F, and its highest recording ever is 92°F. The temperature has never fallen below

45°F and only rarely reaches into the 50s. This idyllic climate only added to the stranded travelers' "ease and pleasure."[33]

As days stretched into weeks and then into months, the growing allure of Bermuda, particularly for the "lesser sorts" of the company, would not have been lost on Sir Thomas Gates. The sailors and servants enjoyed better meals and a safer climate than they had known in England and that awaited them in Virginia. The meager diet of bread and boiled beef that sufficed for most of England's laboring classes could not compare to the abundant fare in Bermuda. Within days, everyone saw that hogs, fish, fruit, and birds abounded "as dust of the earth," and no one ever went hungry.[34] There was no plague or consumption, no scurvy or flux. They could even slip away from camp to swim in cool ponds in Bermuda's underground limestone caverns. For destitute people who had fled the plague-ridden slums of London to take a gamble in the slaughterhouse of Virginia, Bermuda seemed a happy accident, if not a providential gift.

Gates, however, came from another world, the privileged, learned class that congregated at the Middle Temple and attended masques at Whitehall. Gentlemen of his rank routinely feasted from trays laden with roasted mutton, boar, and fish, accompanied by rich puddings and fine wine. A knight and a gentleman in service of the Virginia Company of London under the authority of the king of England, Gates had fundamentally different—and, he undoubtedly believed, superior—concerns than those of the great majority of the people in his care. His future and glory lay not in chasing hogs on Bermuda but in redeeming Virginia. So he steadily focused on two goals: maintaining order by keeping the castaways at work and planning their escape from Bermuda.

In the first few weeks, Gates ran the company with remarkable efficiency. He set some men to crafting nets from the deer toils they had planned to use in Virginia. The largest stretched across a dock the colonists built at Frobisher's Bay, named after Richard Frobisher, a skilled shipwright and *Sea Venture* passenger. There, Gates's men could catch several thousand small fish in a single haul. He made groups of two to three men work in round-the-clock shifts boiling seawater down to salt. Others dried and salted fish, preserving them for a rainy day—and, as Gates imagined, the passage to Virginia. Gates appointed Robert Walsingham, a member of the crew, and Henry Shelley, a gentleman passenger, the most skilled hunters, to supervise the hog-hunting detail. And, to solve their greatest need, a large group of men dug pits to collect rainwater. Explorations of the forest never revealed any rivers or springs but eventually uncovered pools of standing water. By carrying water from the interior and collecting rainwater in their wells, the castaways found plenty to drink. No one questioned Gates's authority; rather "every man disposed and applied himself to search for and to seek out such relief and sustentation as the country afforded."[35] At least during August.

From the outset, however, George Somers did not seem to share the governor's priorities. Gates necessarily deferred to Admiral Somers while at sea, but immediately on making land asserted his superiority. Somers never overtly challenged Gates's authority, but he did not exactly submit to him, either. Instead, he carefully explored the island, taking special note of its rich potential. In early August he laid out a garden, planting melons, peas, lettuce, and herbs from seeds carried on the ship. In just over a week, small plants appeared. They did not reach maturity, most likely eaten by birds, but nonetheless proved that English plants could grow in Bermudian soil. Somers and his men also built a small boat that they used for fishing and transporting hogs back to camp. Not coincidentally, all of this private exploration helped

Somers avoid Gates and the tension between them that lurked beneath the surface.[36]

Like Somers, Christopher Newport would have found it hard to yield to the self-declared authority of Governor Gates; he was used to giving, not taking, orders. Celebrated throughout England as a first-rate captain and fearless soldier, Newport had been the voice of reason in the unruly Jamestown settlement. Everyone from the first governor, Edward Maria Wingfield, to indentured servants praised Newport's constancy and integrity, and they sought his counsel above other men. With good reason, Newport had grown accustomed to playing the role of esteemed leader to respectful followers.[37]

But that would not happen on Bermuda. While credited by the castaways with keeping the ship afloat in the hurricane and grounding it so they might survive, Newport thereafter moved to the periphery of their story. Perhaps some blamed him for taking the route that carried them near Bermuda. More likely, however, it was his disability. After losing his right arm during a battle off the coast of Cuba in 1590, Newport continued his privateering for another decade before going to work for the Virginia Company.[38] Clearly, having only one arm did not handicap his career as a ship's captain. But it is easy to see how that might have compromised his ability to fell trees or net fish. In an environment where physical strength and sheer survival skills mattered most, Newport commanded less authority than either Somers or Gates.

Governor Gates wasted no time in designing the escape from Bermuda. In August he directed a team of men to refit their longboat for an ocean voyage: a small party would sail to Virginia and come back in larger boats for the others. Carpenters added sails and used the hatches salvaged from the *Sea Venture* to create a makeshift deck. The men, probably under the direction of Richard Frobisher, did their best to make the craft seaworthy, aware that the lives of some of their friends would depend on their work. It is a powerful commentary on the stranded sailors' courage and sense of duty that eight men agreed—exactly a month after very nearly drowning in a fierce hurricane—once again to take to the sea.[39]

In the last weeks of August, as Gates supervised the final construction of the rescue boat, Somers began to survey Bermuda and draw an illustrated map of the islands. It was a revealing divergence: Gates looking for a way to save Virginia and Somers seeing Bermuda's rich potential.[40]

As he sailed along the coast of Bermuda, George Somers witnessed the full magnitude of the natural gifts the island chain offered. Beautiful weather and bounteous food were only the most obvious of Bermuda's many pleasures. For anyone aware of England's colonial ambitions—and Somers definitely was—Bermuda held many other attractions. Whales seasonally appeared off the coast, which augured well for that lucrative trade and the possibility of finding ambergris, a waxy excretion from whales used to make expensive perfumes. Pearls also might be harvested in large numbers. There were important international implications as well. Bermuda sat alone in the Atlantic, in the middle of the quickest passage from England to Virginia. With rumors of demonic possession discredited, the island appeared as a strategically ideal location to police traffic to and from America. The coral reefs certainly posed a grave danger to unsuspecting ships' captains, but close study revealed two—and only two—entry routes. Both could be easily fortified. No wonder the English would, in time, brag "how Almighty God by his gracious providence; in their first creation did fit them with two goodly and large harbours" which allowed English colonists "(by the helpe of God) to sinke all Ships of Enemies that shall offer to come in."[41]

The English saw the hand of God everywhere in Bermuda. How else could one explain everyone surviving the hurricane *and* the shipwreck? What besides "the speciall Mercy, and divine providence of almighty God" held the boat up until all the supplies could be recovered? He provided the birds and fish and water that sustained the castaways, and He kept special watch over them. When word of their adventure ultimately reached England, the castaways were likened to the Israelites that God had redeemed from their wilderness. And one of London's devout ministers proclaimed: "The King of Kings hath kept these islands from the King of Spain and all other Kings in the world; till now, that it hath pleased his holy Majesty to bestow them upon the King of England."[42]

Thomas Gates always believed that his duty lay in reaching Virginia, but he could not risk leaving his company in Bermuda or losing his life at sea. So with the makeshift pinnace complete at the end of August, he needed his most trusted men to sail the six hundred miles. Henry Ravens, an experienced mariner who often worked out of Plymouth and had testified against Christopher Newport in the *Susan Constant* lawsuit, was "easily won" to the challenge of commanding the small boat to Virginia. Six other unnamed sailors agreed to go with him, as did Thomas Wittingham. Wittingham seemed an especially trustworthy man. After the crash, he served as cape merchant—the person who kept records of the storehouse. The job required him to closely monitor the group's precious supplies, protect their weapons, and evenly divide their food. Having earned Gates's respect by honorably executing this duty, Wittingham carried his written directions to the Virginia colony.[43]

Gates had no way of knowing the full extent of the political chaos that had erupted in Jamestown after he failed to show up. But experience taught him that confusion and disorder bred rebellion, and he suspected that opportunists might seize on the power vacuum his absence generated. So Wittingham brought Gates's official decree on board the pinnace: Peter Winne was to act as lieutenant governor of Virginia until Gates arrived. Gates also named council members, "gentlemen of quality and . . . lovers of goodness," to assist Winne in implementing a governmental plan that Gates described at length, clearly relying on directions given him by the Virginia Company.[44]

The choice of Peter Winne to lead the colony during Gates's absence indicates that Gates had decided to open the sealed, secret instructions from the Virginia Company. The identities of the colonial council members had been unknown to him and were supposed to be revealed only after he arrived in Virginia. Nine men's names appear in the instructions, including the new secretary for the colony, and it is easy to imagine Gates studying the list as he designated a successor. George Somers's name came first, but he was trapped on Bermuda. John Smith came next, but Gates knew him to be a divisive force that the Virginia Company Council no longer wanted in charge. John Ratcliffe was third, but Gates probably suspected he was lost at sea, since his *Diamond* had sailed into the hurricane along with the *Sea Venture*. Gates also knew of Ratcliffe's long feud with John Smith and the trouble those two had already caused in Virginia. Which brings us to Peter Winne: fourth on the list and named as sergeant major of the Jamestown fort. Winne was also the first man on the list of colonial councilors, excepting John Smith, whom Gates could be reasonably sure was actually in Virginia. The newly appointed secretary of the colony, Matthew Scrivener's name appeared next, followed by two other captains of ships in the *Sea Venture* fleet, with two Virginia residents rounding out the group. If Gates was thinking conservatively—which he doubtless was—he saw few good options. Three men, the fleet captains, might be delayed or lost. Somers was stranded, Smith was unacceptable, Scrivener was secretary. That left Gates

with really only three men to choose from, and Peter Winne out-
ranked the other two. While no record exists of the names of the
men Gates appointed to the colonial council, logic dictates that
they too came from the unsealed instructions. With Somers in
Bermuda, Winne as acting governor, and Scrivener as secretary,
that left six men. Gates named six councilors in the letter he sent
to Virginia.[45]

Gates also handed the rescue team a letter he wrote to the
Council of the Virginia Company, to be forwarded by Peter Winne.
Unwavering in his dedication to Virginia, Gates explained as best
he could the likely situation there, and he begged the council to
send Lord De La Warr's fleet as soon as possible. To be sure, Gates
also asked company leaders to send someone "to redeem us from
hence." But he really counted on Ravens's team to do that, ideally
before his letter even reached England.[46]

Henry Ravens, Thomas Wittingham, and the six sailors set out
on Monday, August 28. They carried plenty of food and water, a
compass, and other navigational equipment. Besides Gates's official correspondence, they took letters the castaways wrote their
loved ones. The men calculated that Bermuda lay around 140
leagues (around 485 miles) from coastal Virginia, and Ravens believed he could make it to Jamestown and back by "the next new
moon," or in a month.[47]

In fact, they returned to camp two days later, frustrated by their
inability to get clear of the island from the northeast, which they
believed to be the safest passage. Ravens feared leaving the way
they came in, from the southeast, but by September 1 he had been
convinced to try. He "made to sea" that Friday, promising on his
life to return for the others.[48]

In the days and weeks that followed, Gates organized a constant
vigil for Ravens's party. He directed several men to attend the fires
that served as beacons for the rescue team. Lookouts sat on the

highest hillside around the clock searching the ocean for any sign of Ravens. They kept a faithful watch for two months. They never let their signal fire die out, and at night they listened for the flap of sails. During that time, according to William Strachey, the lost colonists "gave many a long and wished look round about the horizon . . . but in vain, discovering nothing all the while, which way soever we turned our eye, but air and sea."[49]

Life did not wait for Ravens to return to Bermuda. In November, Elizabeth Persons, the maid of Mistress Horton, married George Somers's cook, Thomas Powell. Their union confirmed that the castaways continued to respect Anglican rituals and England's social order. Both came from the servant class, and Rev. Buck consecrated the marriage before what was no longer simply a random assortment of castaways but an emerging community. John Rolfe's 1614 marriage to his second wife, Pocahontas (also officiated by Rev. Buck), would cement his place in American history. But in 1609, Rolfe was an undistinguished farmer heading to Virginia with his first wife. In early February, she delivered the first of two children born on Bermuda. Mistress Horton, William Strachey, and Christopher Newport, perhaps no longer so powerful but certainly still popular, served as witnesses at the baptism. Signifying the communal bonds of the group as well as their growing affinity for the island, Strachey noted that "we" named her Bermuda. Mrs. Rolfe's name is lost in the historical record, as is the name of the other new mother on Bermuda, the wife of Edward Eason. She bore her son in late March, and as with the Rolfe baby, "we" again named the child in honor of the island, this time Bermudas. Again Strachey and Newport stood for the christening.[50]

Unfortunately, we know nothing from the perspective of any of the women stranded in Bermuda. Often we do not even know their full names. Horton, Rolfe, and Eason were identified, as was customary at the time, only by their relationships to men. In fact, the only female given names on the passenger list or in any contemporary writing belonged to servants like Elizabeth Persons. No woman wrote of her experiences on Bermuda, so we cannot know how Rolfe coped with pregnancy and childbirth. We can only imagine how she felt when her daughter died just a few weeks later.[51]

Bermuda Rolfe was one of six people the castaways had to bury. Three men, Jeffrey Briars, Richard Lewis, and William Hitchman, died of natural causes—an amazingly low number. One sailor murdered another, and Gates executed a man for sedition. Excepting the last of these, Rev. Buck led his congregation in observing funeral rites for the deceased.[52]

Buck worked hard to foster a sense of community and promote the order that Governor Gates so desperately sought. With the aid of Stephen Hopkins, Buck held two church services every Sunday. Hopkins, who carried his Bible wherever he went, read the lessons and the psalms, and Buck delivered the sermons, which mostly emphasized, not surprisingly, "thankfulness and unity." Furthermore, every morning and evening, Buck called the group to prayer by ringing bells. Names were called, and those absent "were duly punished" by Gates. As the days and weeks rolled on without any sign of Ravens's party, Buck and Gates insisted on the importance of faith and order. On October 1 and again on Christmas Eve the community gathered to celebrate the Eucharist; how Buck managed to find bread and wine to consecrate is unclear, but nearly everyone, starting with Governor Gates, took communion.[53]

Gates's good example and Buck's Good Book could not keep everyone from being seduced by Bermuda, however, particularly after two months passed with no sign of Henry Ravens. As Gates grew ever more determined to escape the island, many of his men had become quite comfortable there. It did not require a gentleman's education to know that oysters made pearls and that whales produced ambergris. It was plain for all to see that there was great potential wealth to be made in Bermuda. Servants and soldiers who had heard rumors about the fierce Indians and hard labor that awaited them in Virginia could easily measure that world against Bermuda. Some of the more ingenious (or calculating) among the community even began to wonder: did Gates have any legitimate authority in Bermuda? Or did the shipwreck invalidate his commission—which was, after all, for Virginia—and their obligations to the company? To William Strachey and others, the "major part of the common sort" seemed more than willing "to settle a foundation of ever inhabiting there." As one observer explained, "By reason of the pleasure of the place the most of the company began to growe into such a content" that they started "to neglect the cares due to a future returne and remoue."[54]

Bermuda offered up a rich irony: the "Isle of Devils," once the most terrifying spot in the Atlantic, in a few short months had become an island paradise full of "ease and pleasure." It fell to Gates, Somers, and their diminishing number of followers to remind the others that their future—and the glory of England—lay not in the comforts around them, but in reaching Virginia.

After two months, it seemed clear that Henry Ravens was not coming back—certainly not soon and probably not ever. Gates resolved to keep the wilderness of Bermuda from captivating the colonists and thwarting his dreams. If no one from England or America could rescue them, they would rescue themselves. With an enormous amount of work and a bit of God's help, Thomas Gates might yet save England's claim in America.

CHAPTER 6

TROUBLE IN
PARADISE

The small boat carrying Henry Ravens and seven other souls to Virginia that September represented more than a search for help in Jamestown; it also sent a powerful signal to those on Bermuda that their island home was only temporary. Despite their present life of comfort and plenty, the castaways would have to focus on their future—which lay six hundred miles west in a place where their countrymen were struggling just to stay alive. So as Ravens's party disappeared over the horizon, those who had grown content on Bermuda faced a disturbing reality: Gates would leave no stone unturned in completing his mission of getting everyone to Virginia.

At first many were too caught up in their island paradise to worry. A comfortable life in Bermuda had "caused many of them vtterly to forget or desire euer to returne from thence, they liued in such plenty, peace and ease."[1] Having survived for over a month in Bermuda, the lost colonists grew adept at turning primitive conditions into hopeful results. What once frightened them now seemed providential; the strange howling cahows, for instance, provided an easy and desirable source of food. Palmetto trees made livable island huts, and the islands offered countless caves for cooling off and dreaming about a life of abundance. After all, the marooned colonists had stumbled on unexpected riches—pearls in oysters, silk spiders from mulberry trees, and ambergris. They discovered a stand of tobacco on a distant hill and learned to brew strong drink from ripe palmetto berries. Little wonder that many felt seduced by this paradise.

A few worried castaways, though, saw in the Ravens rescue effort the unraveling of their island paradise. And they were not happy. Initially, they responded with a work stoppage. Six laborers and seamen ordered to help build the small pinnace for Ravens banded together and refused to work. The leader of the scheme was John Want, one of Newport's men, who coaxed five others to join him in pledging "each unto the other not to set their hands to any travail or endeavor which might expedite or forward this pinnace."[2]

Want tapped into a restless group of men growing increasingly anxious about what lay ahead in Virginia. He and the "disquieted pools" knew about Jamestown's terrible reputation and forbidding prospects, especially for poor laborers. It was one thing to risk going to Virginia, where, it was widely rumored, "many wants" beset colonists and "nothing but wretchedness and labor must be expected," when the only alternative was to remain in the plague-ridden slums of London.[3] But Bermuda offered another, far better option.

The September conspirators ultimately envisioned far more than work stoppage. They dreamed of creating their own private world on Bermuda—without the poverty of England or the perils of Virginia—and appealed to their companions to join them. Among those linked to Want in the plot was Christopher Carter, a dissident laborer fast becoming enamored with a future in Bermuda. Want and Carter's desire to jettison their commitment to the Virginia Company had disturbing, dangerous consequences. Such talk could only breed violence. "Some dangerous and secret discontents nourished amongst us," one survivor remembered, "had like to have been the parents of bloody issues and mischiefs."[4]

The plotters, in seeking a life of abundance on the island, employed a strong antiauthoritarian religious message. Want made quite a show of his faith ("in his own prayers much devout and frequent"). But he did not fool everyone. Rev. Buck suspected him and several others on the island of embracing religious radicalism antagonistic to all authority figures, civil or religious. The priest's fears were soon borne out. Want lured the carpenter Nicholas Bennett into his plot by reminding him of the ease of life in Bermuda and by invoking God's will—had He not delivered them there? Like Want, Bennett "made much profession of Scripture" but was seen by company leaders as "a mutinous and dissembling impostor." Through "false baits" Want worked the religion and comfort angles to entice others to join the rebels in striking out for a separate settlement on their own island—removed from Gates's authority and the prospect of carrying on to America.[5]

Virginia's reputation made a great ally for these men. They "preached and published each to other" how dangerous life in Virginia would be. Company loyalists complained that the stories of hardship and deprivation in the colony were spread by men who had never even been to Virginia, and who exaggerated the problems there to shirk their duties to the company. But if only half the rumors were true, that was enough to convince some men that they were not about to go to Jamestown and find out the full story. Strachey further argued that Want and his seditious group could only attract "the idle, untoward, and wretched" castaways who were seduced by the "liberty and fullness of sensuality" that Bermuda offered. But what leaders saw as character flaws seemed only logical to some of the poor laborers, who simply wanted to make a new, peaceful life with the abundance they found.[6]

John Want's peace was Thomas Gates's mutiny. On the very day that Ravens's boat sailed toward Virginia, the conspiracy revealed itself: the six men broke from the rest of the company "and like outlaws retired into the woods to make a settlement and habitation there, on their party, with whom they purposed to leave our quarter and possess another island by themselves."[7]

So small and ill-equipped a group had little chance of success. Gates's men promptly discovered the "outlaws" and exacted swift punishment. And it was punishment of the "be careful what you wish for" variety: Gates granted them their desire to separate themselves on their own island, but *he* chose it. Gates ordered the plotters dropped off on a barren, faraway isle "without smith or carpenter" or provisions. While the larger islands in the chain offered great plenty, many distant and small outcroppings dot the Bermuda coastline, and they would have been covered in scrub, without hogs or birds, and lacking water and shelter. Soon the plotters "missed comfort." According to one castaway, a few of the rebels also developed a sense of guilt and sadness for their offense, but this could have easily been a disguise for hunger. As they grew weary of their outlaw condition, the marooned dissenters sent "many humble petitions" to Gates, "fraught full of their seeming sorrow and repentance and earnest vows to redeem the former trespass, with examples of duties [services]" to the rest of the castaways. Although a man "not easy to admit any accusation and hard to remit an offense," Gates finally gave in and let the conspirators back onto the main island. His actions demonstrated both his resolve and his compassion.[8]

Company promoters, anticipating troubles of this sort, sought to inspire obedience among the passengers and crew. Before they left for Plymouth, the colonists and crew had listened to launch sermons in London preaching the necessity of "love and concord" for their mission, since "by discord great things soone come to nothing." Everyone knew, as Rev. William Crashaw put it, that some of the "vulgar and viler sort" would find their way to Virginia, in all likelihood making the trip only for "ease and idlenesse, for profit and pleasure." A premium had to be placed on order and swift punishment for violators. As Robert Gray observed, "if any mutinous or seditious person dare adventure to move any matter which may tend to the breech of concord and unitie, he is presently to be suppressed as a most dangerous enemy to the state and government there established."[9]

Given the prospects for conflict and chaos in an overseas venture to unknown territory with a ship full of diverse passengers and crew—some deeply committed to the Virginia Company, others simply looking out for themselves—the establishment of authority took the highest priority. Loyalty to the king of England reinforced Christian duty and civil law, which was why, before they could board the *Sea Venture* and the other ships in the fleet, all six hundred passengers and crew had been required to take an oath of allegiance to King James.[10] The question of loyalty was no small matter, especially in the case of a group of shipwreck survivors on an island paradise. As Gates and the other leaders discovered soon after they dealt with the John Want matter, challenges to their authority were far from over.

Though he hoped that Ravens would return with a boat that could rescue his men from the island, Gates hardly sat on his hands waiting for good news. Instead, he ordered Richard Frobisher, a "well-experienced shipwright and skillful workman," to get busy. Frobisher assembled a team that used materials salvaged from the

Sea Venture and the abundant supply of cedar trees on the island to build a boat they eventually named the *Deliverance*. Despite the summer heat, Gates put his men to work felling trees and sawing timber.[11] Sailors had salvaged tools and the rigging from the sinking *Sea Venture*, so the task was not impossible. It did, however, make for lengthy and exhausting work. Even if they succeeded in crafting a vessel, skeptical men would have every reason to question whether it would be seaworthy.

As he commenced the shipbuilding project that fall, Gates understood that morale would be a difficult issue. Doing this sort of hard labor was not something any of his men had expected from the venture, so he knew to be on guard against rebellious sailors and soldiers. Gates's military experience made him skillful at "foreseeing and fearing what innovation [mutiny] and tumult might . . . arise amongst the younger and ambitious spirits" under his charge. To guard against "ambitious spirits" resentful of all the backbreaking work, Gates made a point of working alongside the other men, trying to lead by example to persuade "an ill-qualified parcel of people" to stick to the task at hand. As his directions from the Virginia Company stipulated, he also crafted a precise schedule, setting clear working hours as well as time for leisure. To foster camaraderie, they all ate dinner together every day, and some castaways continued to hunt and fish so that everyone stayed well fed.[12]

At first, his plans seemed to work. Strachey saw how "readier men are to be led by eyes than ears." Deeply impressed by Gates's powerful example, Strachey marveled that Gates's "solicitous and careful" approach to leadership kept the company focused on its mission, even though "so willing were the major part of the common sort (especially when they found such a plenty of victuals) to settle a foundation of ever inhabiting there."[13]

Gates did not rely simply on the force of personality to inspire his men to work on the boat—far from it. He ran the operation like the military commander he was, and he used the full weight of his authority under the Virginia Company charter to ensure the castaways' obedience. Gates's directions from the company gave him explicit advice about managing the American settlement and disciplining the colonists. Upon reaching Virginia, he intended to divide the colonists into three settlements under the command of three leaders. In each settlement work teams would build a church, a storehouse, and an area for growing corn. Finding himself in Bermuda rather than Virginia, Gates simply altered the game plan. Rather than fortifying a colony, the castaways built a boat.[14]

Company directives clearly envisioned the need for a near-militaristic routine and constant supervision of potentially unruly settlers. Gates was instructed to divide his people into teams of ten or twenty or whatever number was necessary to complete a given task, appoint overseers to supervise and keep track of the work hours for each person, and report back to him, especially noting all provisions and goods that had been used: "And thus you shall both knowe howe your men are imployed, what they gett & where it is, as also the measure of your provision and wealth." Nothing was left to chance or individual whim. Workers were called to work and worship by a bell, ate together, allowed a specific amount of free time, and watched to make sure they stayed on schedule.[15]

While Gates ran his disciplined boatbuilding operation, George Somers coasted the islands, fishing, hunting, and mapping. In carrying out this more casual set of duties, Somers stayed close to his own men, who shared his genuine curiosity about the island chain. One can imagine that Somers's light touch, especially now that they were away from the demands of the sea, contrasted sharply with the more authoritarian bearing of Gates. Somers, after all, was known for being a "lamb on the land, so patient that few could anger him . . . but a lion at sea, so passionate that few could please him."[16] Sailing was his and his men's forte; no one was asked to master a new, difficult task, so fewer questions about work and authority would have arisen. So long as they took regular soundings, they faced no dangers—no pirates on the water, no predators on land, no storms they could not escape by simply landing, no shortage of food.

In mapping the islands, Somers was clearly acquiring knowledge immediately useful to the castaways. It is also probable that his exploration offered a sense of calm reassurance to the stranded colonists, doubtless worried that they might never see their families and friends again and fearing that England had already given them up for dead. If no one back home knew where they were, at least they knew about their surroundings and that they had nothing to fear. Making a map also suggested hope and a belief in the future—conveying the sense that others would come to know Bermuda, and so, by implication, that the castaways would get home. And Somers's scouting trips clearly indicated that he saw great prospects in Bermuda, as a place to live and for English colonial investments.[17]

But despite all this, Somers was certainly not ready to make Bermuda his permanent home. Whatever he may have intuited about the long-term potential of Bermuda, Somers, like Gates, knew that his duty and glory lay in saving Jamestown. So when Ravens failed to return, even the mild-mannered Somers took sober stock of the castaways' increasingly disturbing reality. On November 27, "well perceiving that we were not likely to hear from Virginia," and seeing that the vessel Richard Frobisher's crew was building could not possibly carry everyone to Virginia, Somers approached Gates with an important plan. Somers asked the governor for two carpenters (of the four total) and twenty men he could supervise on another part of the island chain. (No contemporary sources pinpoint the exact location of Somers's work site.) With

In sketching his map George Somers clearly saw the great economic potential of the Bermuda islands. Note the whale just off shore and figures chasing hogs. (COURTESY OF BRITISH LIBRARY)

that number of men, he believed he could "quickly frame up another little bark."[18]

Somers made his request in part because some castaways outside Gates's circle suspected Gates was building his boat to save only the soldiers and settlers most loyal to him. Rumor held that Gates intended to leave everyone else behind, in effect giving them up "like savages."[19] Even men and women enjoying life in Bermuda and reluctant to return to the sea would have bristled at such duplicity.

Gates *had* planned to sail to Virginia on the *Deliverance* with a smaller group. But he insisted he intended to return for all the others, and dismissed rumors to the contrary. Still, he saw the wisdom in Somers's idea. With two boats they could carry everyone to America at the same time. It was risky, particularly if another storm hit or if the carpentry failed. But leaving half the company behind held its own set of dangers: without Gates they might fight among themselves, not gather enough food and water, or give in to the lure of the wilderness and degenerate into savagery. Better that all take the gamble together. Gates gave Somers some provisions and tools (only the ones his men were not using), along with twenty "of the ablest and stoutest" of the company and "the best of our men to hew and square timber."[20]

Although he accepted Somers's plan, Gates refused to slow his own efforts by sharing many of the scarce resources with the second group. He claimed he could spare only a single bolt, and that was the only metal that went into building the second ship. Without nails, Somers's crew made dowels and fitted them into sawed and planed planks from cedar trees his men cut. With no oakum available (the limited supply all went to the *Deliverance*), Somers had to be creative with the caulking. He and his men found wax washed ashore from a wreck and mixed it with crushed coral rock and turtle oil. In this imaginative way, they eventually crafted the boat they aptly called the *Patience*.[21]

Among the many happy coincidences enjoyed by the *Sea Venture* castaways—and later touted as part of God's great design on behalf of English America—was the wood available for building the *Patience* and the *Deliverance*. Bermuda cedars were ideal for shipbuilding. Cedar made for a light hull and, unlike many other woods, required no seasoning. It does not shrink or warp, and it requires little caulk, which is particularly amazing since the castaways had very little tar and oakum. Had the winds from Florida carried other seeds, the lost colonists might never have escaped Bermuda. Instead, they built their two vessels from wood that lasted four times longer than oak.[22]

In December, as they continued the backbreaking work of felling those precious cedars, Somers's men probably felt shortchanged. Gates's crew built the *Deliverance* in part from salvaged timbers from the *Sea Venture*, wood that Somers's men had worked hard to retrieve. Now they saw that none of those timbers was set aside for them, but instead reserved for the boat Gates supervised—a boat they still feared would be filled only with soldiers and settlers working under Gates. Given only one iron bolt, twenty men, and leftover tools, the sailors under Somers labored even harder than Gates's men, and doubtless resented the preferential treatment enjoyed at the other work site.

On the surface, the boatbuilding efforts that winter and spring suggested hope and a common purpose. Doing such physically demanding work doubtless reminded everyone of their shared mission. And it kept people busy—not only those building the boats, but the men and women charged with feeding them as well. Idle hands, the leaders knew, were the devil's workshop. Keeping everyone engaged in purposeful work, well fed, and closely monitored left fewer opportunities for the "lesser sorts" to conspire against the men in authority.

Lurking beneath the apparent unity, though, was a widening rift into two rival camps: the soldiers and settlers laboring under Gates and the sailors working for Somers. The division had deep roots in tradition and individual egos. Friction between sea and land commanders had long been commonplace among the English. Distrust and jealousy, after all, lay behind the decision of the three leaders to sail from Plymouth together on the same ship. Fear of the possible advantage one or another might have gained had they traveled on separate boats was how all the leadership managed to get stranded in the first place. In his compiled history of English colonization, John Smith—no stranger to conflicts—reported that because of "the malice of envy or ambition . . . a great difference fell amongst their Commanders" in Bermuda. The factions "lived asunder in this distresse, rather as meere strangers then distressed friends."[23]

The longer Somers and his men worked on their separate part of the island chain building their ship, the more estranged the two camps became. Gates himself took note of the growing division and saw that it was breeding jealousy and anger. Tensions over who would first be rescued would not go away. As one man remembered, "true it was at their first arrival upon this island when it was feared that our means would not extend to the making of this vessel capable and large enough to transport all of our countrymen at once."[24] Gates understood how saving his men first in a ship that would hold only half the castaways could appear to everyone else as abandonment. But he insisted that he never intended "to forsake them." Instead, he had planned to "leave them all things fitting to defend them from want and wretchedness . . . for one whole year or more" until ships could be sent for them. He even took Somers aside and did his best to convince him not to leap to the wrong conclusion. According to one source, he "entreated Sir George to remember unto his company . . . how he had vowed unto him . . . how far it was from him to let them remain abandoned and neglected without their redemption so long."[25] What Somers thought of this exchange is lost in history—but his response was to keep working on the *Patience*.

It would have been trouble enough if the castaways were divided simply over who got preferential treatment. But the pleasures of Bermuda contrasted with the miserable conditions in Virginia conspired to raise profound and troubling questions about the entire enterprise. It was as if the devastating hurricane that shipwrecked the *Sea Venture* on Bermuda had also blurred the normal lines of authority; the torrent of water that poured into the boat not only sank the *Sea Venture* but also cast adrift some men from their leaders.

In January, the dissenting Puritan Stephen Hopkins offered an even stronger challenge to authority than had John Want. Hopkins led a second mutiny, another attempt "to shake the foundation of our quiet safety." This time the rebellion presented a far more fundamental test of authority to Gates and the other leaders. Ever since the *Sea Venture* had wrecked, Hopkins had worked for Rev. Buck as his clerk. Many of his fellow castaways respected him as "a fellow who had much knowledge in the Scriptures and could reason well therein."[26]

But the wild waters crashing the voyagers into Bermuda eventually pushed Hopkins over the edge. Like the mutineers in Want's conspiracy, Hopkins worried about the scarcity he believed lay ahead for them in Virginia. After the *Sea Venture* sank, he became increasingly convinced that no one possessed legitimate authority over the marooned voyagers. In Hopkins's view, while on the ship Captain Newport and George Somers had to be obeyed; upon arrival in Virginia, Thomas Gates would be the governor with full authority. But after the shipwreck, Hopkins reasoned, a new life commenced on Bermuda, one that none of the leaders rightfully controlled.[27]

By early January, Hopkins was speaking with others, including Samuel Sharp and Humphrey Reed, about his beliefs. All God-fearing men, Hopkins insisted, had the right "to decline from the obedience of the governor or refuse to go any further led by his authority (except it so pleased themselves), since the authority ceased when the wreck was committed." The power of the individual conscience Hopkins invoked was sweeping in scope. After the *Sea Venture* went down, he believed, "they were all then freed from the government of any man, and for a matter of conscience it was not unknown to the meanest how much we were therein bound each one to provide for himself and his own family."[28]

Hopkins made two demands: First, that he and his followers acknowledge only God as the true authority—not Gates, Somers, or anyone else. Second, he insisted that he and those who shared his convictions be allowed to remain in Bermuda rather than forced to go to Virginia. He and his followers wanted to stay on the island and enjoy the "abundance by God's providence of all manner of good food." They also expected that in time, after growing "weary of the place," they would "build a small bark" and sail away—but only when they saw fit. A key element in this part of Hopkins's plan involved recruiting the previously "mutinous" carpenter Nicholas Bennett "to be of the conspiracy." Bennett's construction skills would allow those who stayed behind to build their boat and "get clear from hence at their own pleasures." And, with his involvement in the John Want plot, Bennett had shown himself to be open to resisting arbitrary power. Unfortunately for Hopkins, Bennett was kept hard at work and under close watch at the Somers work site.[29]

Hopkins's desire to stay on Bermuda was both principled and self-serving. Being required to continue on the mission to Virginia violated his new sense of legitimate authority. Disregarding the solemn oath he took in Plymouth, Hopkins insisted that God had never instructed him to follow the orders of Gates, Somers, and Newport. His refusal to go to Virginia was also grounded in the realistic fear that he would not be safe in Jamestown. Having challenged Gates's authority in Bermuda, Hopkins reasoned that Gates would surely exact revenge on him when they reached Virginia. And, like others pondering their future in Jamestown, he worried that his punishment would be to suffer through life as a servant for the Virginia Company.[30]

To the authorities around him, Hopkins's dissent, like Want's before him, was instantly recognizable as being rooted in the despised radical Puritan strain known as "Brownism." Named after the intransigent separatist leader Robert Browne during Elizabeth's reign, this branch of extreme Protestantism rejected any church or civil authority beyond the individual believer. There was no true church, according to Browne and his followers, certainly not the tainted Church of England, and men like Hopkins professed allegiance only to God and fellow true believers, not to ministers or political leaders. Radical Protestants like Hopkins made conscience the highest law, trusting an individual's private judgment above that of a magistrate and church government.[31]

All of which may have scared off the very men Hopkins hoped to enlist in his rebellion. Far from persuaded by Hopkins, Sharp and Reed immediately reported his plans to Gates. Gates's response was swift and angry: having been so tolerant of John Want and his co-conspirators' sedition, he now determined to make an example out of Hopkins and his more direct threat to authority. Gates summoned all the castaways by tolling a bell, then guards dragged a manacled Hopkins before the gathered crowd. Hopkins's two former confidants and now witnesses, Sharp and Reed, repeated for the entire company Hopkins's scheme.

For the crime of "mutiny and rebellion," Gates immediately passed sentence on Hopkins: execution. It was an unusually harsh punishment for unruly subjects. Mutiny was not considered a felony under English law. But, as Virginia Company instructions allowed, Gates decided to follow martial, not common law. For bloodless mutinies such as what Hopkins envisioned, captains usually dealt out punishment of a lesser sort, such as fines, ducking, and whipping. Gates's severity simply underlines the overriding concern of the Virginia Company and its leaders for establishing order and authority.[32]

By dramatically calling for the death penalty, Gates may have assumed he would have the last word. But he was wrong. Upon receiving the sentence, Hopkins unleashed a torrent of weepy remorse, especially over the terrible fate that would now befall his wife and children back in England. "So penitent he was," Strachey recalled, "and made so much moan, alleging the ruin of his wife and children in this his trespass," that he touched the hearts "of all the better sort of the company," among them Newport and Strachey himself, who successfully pressed Gates for a pardon.[33]

Clearly, finding sympathy among leading men such as Newport and Strachey made a big difference for Hopkins. Both Strachey and Hopkins were ambitious young fathers with families back home. Strachey recorded how he felt genuinely moved by Hopkins's "sorrow and tears," as was Newport. The two "never left him until we had got his pardon." And no doubt Hopkins had found favor among some castaways who recalled his comforting voice on board the *Sea Venture* and in reading the Bible for Rev. Buck during their many months on Bermuda.

William Strachey saw Gates's compassion in pardoning Hopkins as emblematic of his inherent wisdom. Amid all "these dangers and devilish disquiets," Strachey marveled that Gates managed to maintain social order. And he wondered, "thus enraged amongst ourselves to the destruction each of other, into what a mischief and misery had we been given up had we not had a governor with his authority to have suppressed the same?"

"Mischief and misery" not only confronted Thomas Gates. George Somers, while not under the same kind of assault, also had to contend with unhappy, violent people. Indeed, just after "first landing upon the island" Somers was forced to deal with a murder. Here, too, the conflict centered on disgruntled sailors. And the outcome underlined the importance of Somers's sympathy for and protection of the men who worked for him.

Shortly after the castaways first made land, two sailors, Robert Waters (no relation to Edward Waters, George Somers's faithful assistant) and Edward Samuel, got into an argument. Waters grabbed a shovel and slammed it into Samuel's head, killing him. Waters was arrested and condemned to hang the next day. To dramatize his fate, he was tied alongside the corpse of his victim to a tree during the night "with many ropes and a guard of five or six to attend him." But Waters's comradeship with his fellow sailors trumped any sort of justice: when the guards fell asleep, several of his sailor friends cut the ropes and secreted Waters off to a hiding place in the woods where they fed him every night. Search parties looked for him, but came back empty-handed. Finally, Somers interceded on the sailors' behalf and asked Gates for leniency. "Upon many conditions" Gates relented, and Waters "had his trial respited by our governor."

Tolerant treatment of first Robert Waters, then the John Want group, and then Stephen Hopkins may have been practical, and it temporarily placated many of the castaways, but it certainly did not ensure peace and order. Those loath to head to Virginia continued to seethe about their future. As both the *Deliverance* and the *Patience* neared completion in the early spring of 1610, yet another mutinous storm broke out. In March, resentment reached a boiling point among a group of Somers's men. This time the uprising posed an ominous danger to authority, taking direct aim at Gates himself. It was, as Strachey noted, a "deadly and bloody [scheme], in which the life of our governor, with many others, were threatened." In a well-calculated plot, a large group of men working under Somers, along with a few from Gates's own camp, conspired to break into the storeroom, steal supplies, including weapons—swords, axes, hatchets and mallets "or what else it pleased God that we had recovered from the wreck"—and kill Gates and his supporters. Leading the conspiracy were none other than the murderer Robert Waters and second-time rebel Christopher Carter.

Early on, though, a few members of the "association" of conspirators got cold feet; they "brake from the plot itself" and disclosed it to Gates. The designing "confederates" were not immediately apprehended, as they were spread out over the island between both Gates's and Somers's camps. Gates decided this time not to make any precipitous arrests. Instead, he quietly doubled the night watches and ordered every trusted man to wear a sword and remain vigilant. The walking paths between the *Patience* and *Deliverance* camps were closely watched for several nights. For a while, the increased vigilance seemed to create a sense of calm.

That is, until the night of March 13, when Henry Paine entered the picture. The eccentric gentleman Paine was due to carry out his turn at the night watch. He refused and proceeded to "give his said commander evil language." Then Paine struck him and "doubled his blows." When a nearby guard restrained Paine from killing the commander, Paine erupted in language that would "offend the modest ear too much to express it in his own phrase." Upon being told that Gates would deal harshly with "his insolency," Paine responded in "bitter violence and in such unreverent terms" arguing that "the governor had no authority" and "therefore let the governor (said he) kiss, etc."

With his company on the brink of total mutiny, Gates took immediate action. Once again he assembled the entire group and had Paine brought before him. This time he would not choose compassion. The captain, the watch, and other witnesses testified against Paine. Then Gates, determined to get control of the group and "who had now the eyes of the whole colony fixed upon him, condemned him to be instantly hanged." Paine, like other rebels before him, pleaded—but this time only to die as he had lived: "after he had made many confessions he earnestly desired, being a gentleman, that he might be shot to death, and toward the evening he had his desire, the sun and his life setting together."

Upon hearing of Paine's execution, his co-conspirators rushed to the woods to hide out, fearing that Paine had given them up. He had not. Keenly aware that the two ships under construction were nearly ready for departure to Virginia, the mutineers "sent an auda-cious and formal petition" to Gates demanding two suits of clothes for every man and enough food for a year. While perhaps born out of "mere rage and greediness," the men clearly considered making a go of it alone on Bermuda against the dire prospects that lay ahead in Jamestown. To Gates, there was nothing to negotiate. He reminded the men that even the least among them cost the Vir-ginia Company twenty pounds and that he was duty bound to de-liver them to Jamestown.

Just as importantly, Gates reminded Somers of the long list of obligations they both shared as commanders—"first to His Majesty for so many of his subjects; next to the adventurers," and finally, he insisted, to their own personal honor. Having the au-thority "to compel the adversant and irregular multitude" to "be obedient and honest," and refusing to do so would destroy their reputations. If they failed here, Gates pointed out to Somers, "the blame would not lie upon the people (at all times wavering and insolent) but upon themselves, so weak and unworthy in their command."

Somers stepped into the impasse between the plotters and Gates, offering to mediate. With Gates's approval, Somers ap-proached the conspirators about returning to their duty. Somers made the attempt, using his own reasonable terms rather than the threat of force. He spoke reassuringly with the men, saying that they would not be penalized for their mutiny. He managed to con-vince all but two to return to the company. Christopher Carter and Robert Waters, already rebels twice over, declined to risk testing Gates's wrath in Virginia.

Ironically, then, it was Somers's calm words as much as Gates's assertions of authority that held the fractious colonists together. And when it came to Waters and Carter, Somers may not have needed to be persuasive: as we shall see, they all shared a common interest in the future of Bermuda that may well have transcended the mission to Virginia.

By March, the ultimate goal of getting to Virginia finally lay within reach. The odyssey in Bermuda appeared as a "redemption" to William Strachey. Divine providence, he believed, could be seen everywhere—from their survival of the shipwreck to the turtles and cahows that fed them to the cedar trees that made their new ships.

Yet redemption was not the only way to view the castaways' experiences since crashing into Bermuda. After all, there had been four mutinies in ten months. None had been successful, and, except for Robert Waters and Christopher Carter, the commitment to rescuing Virginia had prevailed. But while the shipwreck and the early days on the island had showcased a moving spirit of cooperation among the castaways, Bermuda, with all its "pleasure and plenty," had revealed that the English were peopling America with men and women whose loyalties did not necessarily transcend their own personal desires. Although they were able to come together for this remarkable overseas enterprise, the sailors and soldiers and settlers who survived the wreck of the *Sea Venture* saw the future in sometimes wildly different, even antagonistic terms. Although miles apart in terms of class and worldview, the gentleman Henry Paine and the religious radical Stephen Hopkins gave voice to a sense of individual liberty that would both bedevil and enrich English America—nowhere more so than in Jamestown.

By the end of March, the boat Richard Frobisher designed for Gates, the *Deliverance*, was fully assembled. It was half the size of the *Sea Venture*; its beams and some of the planking covering its ribs were constructed from oak salvaged from the wrecked ship. The rest came from the island's cedar trees. To ensure that the *Deliver-*

Built from Bermuda's cedar trees and materials salvaged from the shipwreck, the Deliverance, *shown here as a modern-day replica, along with the* Patience *carried the castaways safely to Virginia.* (COLLECTION OF THE AUTHORS)

ance did not suffer from leaks like the *Sea Venture*, Frobisher's crew filled in the cracks between the planks using oakum made from old ropes, and they coated the bottom of the new ship with pitch and tar salvaged from the wreck. A month later George Somers and his crew completed work on the *Patience* and sailed it into the channel where Frobisher and his men's *Deliverance* stood waiting. With both ships ready, the settlers packed their meager clothing and tools and loaded the two ships with salted pork, fish, and casks of fresh water.

While waiting for favorable winds, Gates erected a memorial in the garden where Somers had planted English seeds. He selected a tall cedar tree, made a cross of wood from the *Sea Venture*, and nailed to it a silver coin stamped with a portrait of King James. He engraved an inscription on a copper piece, in Latin and English: "In memory of our great deliverance, both from a mighty storm and leak we have set up this to the honor of God. It is the spoil of an English ship (of three hundred ton) called the *Sea Venture*, bound with seven ships more (from which the storm divided us) to Virginia, or Nova Britannia in America."

On May 10, 1610, strong winds finally blew. Admiral Somers and Captain Newport took rowboats out to mark the narrow path out to sea with buoys and prevent the sailing ships from crashing against the coral reefs. Finally, by midmorning the ships set sail, carefully making their way through the narrow channel. Then came a horrifying sound—the *Deliverance* struck a rock. Everyone waited, no doubt in anguished silence, expecting water to pour in through the torn hull. For a moment, it appeared they might be in for a longer stay on Bermuda. But, as Strachey remembered it, "God was more merciful unto us." A wave rose and the ship glided harmlessly over the rock, then moved smoothly out into the open sea.

As the *Deliverance* and the *Patience* sailed away from Bermuda, one can imagine that Robert Waters and Christopher Carter stood on a hill watching the company head toward Virginia. Having chosen solitude on Bermuda over the mission to Virginia, they must have wondered if they would survive for long, and if they would ever see a familiar face again.

Piloting the *Patience*, George Somers must have glanced back at the island paradise he was leaving behind, a place of plenty he had mapped and fished and hunted for ten months. He was certainly committed to completing the voyage to Jamestown, but the allure of the island had made an indelible impression on him. He would soon be back.

Riding on the *Deliverance*, Gates looked only to Jamestown. After a three-hundred-day delay, he was finally again pursuing the business of the Virginia Company and, he believed, God's will.

It was just as well that neither man knew what lay ahead.

CHAPTER 7

JAMESTOWN STARVING

Soon after the passengers and crew of the *Sea Venture* sailed into a hurricane in the western Atlantic in late July 1609, their mysterious fate conjured up a host of grave questions to those awaiting them in Virginia: Could the ship and those on board have survived such a violent storm? If so, would they somehow make it to Virginia? If not, what did such a loss suggest about English— and God's—plans for Virginia?

Virginia's volatile but effective leader, Captain John Smith, who departed from Jamestown for good in October 1609, believed that, despite the feared loss of the new governor, Thomas Gates, he left behind a colony in decent condition. Thanks to the new arrivals from the *Sea Venture* fleet, Virginia's total population had grown to nearly five hundred settlers. Under Smith's dispersal plan they had scattered over several different settlements, optimizing the availability of food for each group of colonists while reducing tensions in Jamestown. In the previous spring, Smith had stocked Hog Island with more than sixty pigs to be used as a backup food source.

And he had cultivated an effective, if sometimes harsh, policy of strong-arming Indians into bartering for valuable corn and food supplies. By the time Smith left in October, Jamestown was "strongly Pallizadoed," with ten weeks' worth of provisions, twenty-four pieces of ordnance, three hundred muskets, shot, powder, pikes, swords, helmets, and "an hundred well trayned and expert Souldiers; Nets for fishing; Tooles of all sorts to worke; apparell to supply our wants; six Mares and a Horse; five or sixe hundred Swine; as many Hennes and Chickens; some Goats; some sheep."[1]

But behind every bit of hope lurked worry and doubt, including in letters sent on the same voyage as John Smith. John Ratcliffe, who had piloted the *Diamond* in the ill-fated *Sea Venture* fleet, wrote a letter to Robert Cecil of the Virginia Company Council, painting a very different picture of Smith's leadership and the colony's circumstances. Although he boasted that as part of the dispersal plan, he was "raysing a fortification upon Point Comfort," Ratcliffe's letter was largely a plea for help. The *Sea Venture*, Ratcliffe lamented, appeared to be lost and so was its critical cargo: additional food supplies and Virginia's new leader, Thomas Gates. Thanks to the successful arrival of nearly four hundred new settlers from the rest of the *Sea Venture* fleet, Virginia's population had expanded greatly, but without the flagship and Gates, Jamestown was teetering on the edge of disaster. Everyone in Virginia, he conceded, had "exceedinge much need" of victuals "for the country people set no more than sufficeth each familye a yeare." And because the woods were "so thick" and the labor necessary for clearing and planting "so much ground as would be to any purpose is more than we can afford" in their dispersed state, Ratcliffe asked for a full year's food supply from London.[2]

Insufficient provisions were only half the problem; inadequate leadership in the colony deepened the dilemma. With Gates apparently lost at sea, John Smith, Ratcliffe reported, had refused to surrender his authority to any of the newcomers. Smith was consequently being *"sent home to answere some misdeamenors."* (Ratcliffe never mentioned Smith's severe injuries or his near murder.) And while Ratcliffe boasted that, along with George Percy, Francis West, John Martin, and himself, the "best and worthyest" men in Jamestown now worked together, it was clear that effective, respectable leadership was a rare commodity in Virginia.[3]

Having conspired against Smith, apparently including a failed attempt to murder him, Ratcliffe, along with John Martin and Gabriel Archer, took over the colonial council in the fall of 1609. They decided in their wisdom to elect George Percy as president. It was a decision they and the settlers would all soon regret. A twenty-nine-year-old nobleman, a younger son of an earl, Percy came to Virginia to find what he was never going to acquire in England: a landed estate and political prominence. Classically trained at Oxford and the Middle Temple, Percy was the virtual opposite of his bumptious predecessor, John Smith, whom Percy openly disdained, calling him "an ambitious, unworthy and vainglorious fellow." If Smith prided himself on brash confrontations with the Indians and immense curiosity about Virginia's environs, Percy fancied himself belonging to a class of elegant "gentlemen of fashion," and he wished to re-create civilized London amid the brutality of Jamestown. And so President Percy requested from England—asking his elder brother to cover the expenses—a refined new wardrobe appropriate for his elevated position: five suits, decorated in taffeta, a dozen pairs of new shoes, stockings, and socks, ribbons for shoestrings, six pairs of boots, nine pairs of gloves, twelve shirts from Holland, a dozen handkerchiefs, six nightcaps, six pairs of garters, and a sword "hatched with goulde."[4] If he intended to stand out as a genteel aristocrat in a frontier outpost, he no doubt succeeded. But, as events would quickly reveal, he was out of his element in every other way—which in early Jamestown became a formula for disaster.

Percy was smart enough to appreciate the irony that all the settlers who arrived in the late summer on the *Sea Venture* fleet had not helped sustain the colony as expected but in fact inadvertently endangered it. There were many more mouths to feed and a dwindling supply of food, in terms of crops that could be safely cultivated or bartered from the Indians. And with the plague and other diseases the newcomers had brought with them, many of Jamestown's settlers had grown too weak to labor effectively for their own survival. Even nature conspired against the settlers: a severe drought that fall hampered efforts to raise crops.[5]

To make matters worse, Powhatan could easily see that with John Smith gone and the colonists scattered in small, poorly fortified settlements, the English had become extremely vulnerable. Powhatan seized on this opportunity to threaten and make war on the colony in ways he had rarely done when John Smith ran things. Powhatan's men began instigating surprise attacks on numerous settlements. In short order, the assaults panicked the settlers and even some of the leaders. "[F]earing to be surprised by the Indians," John Martin abandoned his post at Nansemond, leaving a lieutenant named Sicklemore (no relation to John Ratcliffe, whose alias was also Sicklemore) in charge of the increasingly rebellious men at the fort. Martin arrived in Jamestown "pretending some occasions of business," but President Percy was not fooled; he saw that Martin's concern for "his own safety" lay behind his flight from Nansemond. Martin departed just in time: within days seventeen men at Nansemond mutinied and stole a boat, claiming they were taking off on a trading expedition with the Indians at a nearby village. In fact, they were running away. They did not get far before the Indians killed them. Percy decided "they were served according to their deserts, for not any of them were heard of after."[6]

Meanwhile, Lieutenant Sicklemore desperately tried to save the famished men at his partly abandoned settlement by taking a group on a mission to trade with the Indians for food. A few days later, their bodies were found murdered in a dramatic and chilling fashion: "their mouths stopped full of bread." Percy read the meaning: "that others might expect the like when they should come to seek for bread and relief amongst them." It was a grisly scene that struck Percy as eerily reminiscent of a story he heard about Spanish colonists in Central America: natives angry at all the Spanish gold-hunting captured the colonists and poured "melted gold" down their throats, while yelling, "Now glut thyself with gold!"[7]

In the wake of these attacks, all the remaining settlers in Nansemond rushed to Jamestown for safety, as did Francis West and his colonists at the falls after he lost eleven men and a boat during Indian attacks. Jamestown was safer than the outlying settlements due to its stronger fortifications and narrow entry point at the neck of a peninsula. By early November everyone, except for the settlers at Point Comfort, crowded into Jamestown with "our store decreasing."[8]

As best is known from the limited surviving evidence, Jamestown was a very modest triangular-shaped fort, about an acre in size, near the southwestern end of Jamestown Island. It was enclosed, with watchtowers or bulwarks at each of the three angles. In time, the enclosure held a church, storehouses, and a variety of dwellings, but it was makeshift at best in the early days. While occasionally residents spoke fondly of the town's "handsome form" with "fair rows of houses, all of framed timber," most were far less generous in their assessments. Some, such as a Spanish prisoner, Don Diego de Molina, held at Jamestown in 1613, ridiculed Jamestown's fortifications as "so fragile that a kick would destroy them." Molina scoffed that the gap-filled palisade walls left enemies on the outside safer than defenders inside.[9]

It was on such a poorly fortified site that most of the Virginia enterprise now hinged. Even a dandy like Percy could grasp the critical question those huddled inside the fort were facing: how was an ill-provisioned colony, rife with fear and sickness, going to feed itself in the approaching winter? As late as November, Percy had done nothing to prepare for the coming winter. All fourteen of the colony's fishing nets lay useless, having rotted in the water. The harvest, such as it was, had already been consumed. Percy appointed the colony's cape merchant, Daniel Tucker, to see what could be done by way of rationing provisions. Tucker's dismal report underscored the severity of the problem: with well over three hundred men and women now crowded into the fort, the settlers could not last more than three months on a meager ration of about half a cup of meal per person per day. They would be out of food by February, still in the winter, with no expectation of help arriving from London.[10]

Just as Percy was pondering his next move, Powhatan intervened, ostensibly to save the floundering colonists. He sent the English teenager turned Indian interpreter, Henry Spelman, to make contact with the English and proffer a friendly invitation to resume trade. Spelman told the hungry colonists that Powhatan promised "if they would bring their ship and some copper, he would fraught her back with corn." Percy jumped at the opportunity "to procure victuals and corn." He sent John Ratcliffe with a large party of men to trade with the Powhatans. At last, Percy had a game plan.[11]

Unfortunately, it would quickly become a disastrous one. At first, Powhatan, "the subtle old fox," played along as the benevolent, generous trading partner, "although his intent was otherways." Powhatan steered Ratcliffe and his party to a storehouse a half-mile from the river where their boat was anchored. There the English began successfully to barter copper and beads for corn. And then, through a combination of naive mistakes by Ratcliffe and Powhatan's likely entrapment of the English visitors, what began as a productive negotiating session for food soon turned violent. Ratcliffe's first misstep came in his excessively generous offer of trade goods to the Indians—a tactic that signaled weakness rather than the strength that John Smith always suggested by his bullying and bluffing. Indeed, this time it was the Indians who were doing the bluffing: they were apparently cheating by pushing up the bottoms of baskets so a smaller amount of corn would fill them. English accusations of Indian deceit sparked angry denials among the Powhatans. And then Ratcliffe made his second misstep: he allowed his men, lured by Indian women and food, to "straggle into the savages' houses," where they were ambushed and slain. Percy later blamed Ratcliffe's "credulity" in failing to exchange hostages first and in letting Powhatan, "the sly old king," bide his time until Ratcliffe's men were scattered and could be surprised.[12]

No one, though, was more tragically surprised than Ratcliffe himself. Before he could make it back to his pinnace, where Captain William Phetiplace and a few other men waited helplessly, Ratcliffe was captured by the Powhatans, stripped naked, and tied to a tree. As a fire raged before him, Indian women using mussel shells scraped his flesh from his bones and "before his face, [it was] thrown into the fire." "And so for want of circumspection," Percy noted, "[he] miserably perished." A few of Ratcliffe's men managed to escape, but not until after a bloody assault on the waiting pinnace. The Powhatans wiped out all but sixteen of the original fifty men under Ratcliffe's command, along with the food they had loaded onto their boat.[13]

Captain Phetiplace and his largely decimated crew straggled back to Jamestown. Upon learning of the tragic fate of Ratcliffe and his men, Percy decided to put Captain James Davis in charge of Point Comfort, the last settlement outside of Jamestown. Meanwhile, he sent Francis West, the brother of Lord De La Warr, with a company of thirty-six men on board the *Swallow* to sail up the Potomac to barter for food with some friendly Patawomecks. Perhaps a more peaceful approach would work. When it did not, West applied some brutal pressure: using "some harsh and cruel dealing," including cutting off two Indians' heads "and other extremities," he got their attention. In short order the Patawomecks filled the *Swallow* with corn and grain.[14]

But the triumphant, if cruel, trading venture would do nothing to lessen Jamestown's woes. When West's ship sailed out of the mouth of the Potomac River and came upon Captain Davis at Point Comfort, Davis yelled out to West, reminding him of the "great wants" of Jamestown and "to make all the speed they could" to get the ship full of provisions to the famished settlers. Much to Davis's horror, West's men rebelled on the spot; Davis watched in dismay as the *Swallow* turned not up the James but out to sea, "directly for England."[15]

It is unclear how much Francis West actually opposed this abandonment of Virginia, but the consequences for the settlers in Jamestown were the same, regardless of his motives. As the *Swallow* stole away for England, the dreams of the thirty-six rebellious men on board became a nightmare for everyone in Jamestown, waiting on a ship full of corn that would never arrive. West's departure left them all "in that extreme misery and want."[16]

It was an "extreme misery" that Powhatan was only too willing to exploit. Realizing the vulnerable position of the English settlers, especially with Smith gone and their food supplies dwindling, Powhatan decided to starve out the colonists. He had some of the English boats at Jamestown cut loose from their moorings, thus limiting the colonists' travel and fishing expeditions. His men also attacked Hog Island and slaughtered all the animals. Scattered attacks by Powhatans throughout the late fall effectively sealed off the colonists, confining them to the fort. Crowded inside Jamestown, increasingly desperate for food, and fearful of Indians all around them, English settlers would somehow try to survive the winter. Powhatan's people would wait them out. By November a perfect storm of incompetence, bad luck, rebellious spirits, and growing Indian confidence had converged on Jamestown, imperiling the entire English adventure in America.[17]

"Now all of us at James Town," Percy lamented, began "to feel that sharp prick of hunger, which no man truly describe but he which hath tasted the bitterness thereof." He in no way exaggerated when he added: "A world of miseries ensued."[18]

The starving time, as this "world of miseries" came to be known, began with criminal behavior and ended in unspeakable acts of desperation. With meager food rations of eight ounces of meal and a half pint of peas a day—"the one and the other moldy, rotten, full of cobwebs, and maggots, loathsome to man and not fit for beasts"—settlers were quickly driven to extremes. At first, "forced by famine to filch for their bellies," some men robbed the colony's storehouse. Percy promptly "caused them to be executed." Even Percy admitted the colonists stole only "to satisfy their hunger," but he nonetheless dispensed with the thieves, sometimes in vivid, symbolic fashion.[19] One man caught stealing a couple of pints of oatmeal had a needle thrust through his tongue and was chained to a tree until he starved. Many others, "adventuring to seek relief in the woods," abandoned Jamestown and "put themselves into the Indians' hands." Sadly, they found little relief and instead "were by them slain." As his settlement fell apart, President Percy, helpless to feed his people, watched as "To eat, many of our men this starving time did run away unto the savages, whom we never heard of after."[20]

Struck with famine in the "depth of winter" and unable "to satisfy our hungry stomachs" in any other way, the colonists soon found themselves compelled to eat dogs and horses, then rats, mice, snakes, "or what vermin or carrion soever we could light on." Settlers devoured whatever looked remotely edible: toadstools, tree fungus, anything "growing upon the ground that would fill either mouth or belly."[21] Desperate hunger drove them to bizarre behavior: the famished settlers ate shoe and boot leather and even boiled their starchy collars into a "gluey porridge." With starvation "beginning to look ghastly and pale in every face . . . nothing was spared to maintain life and to do those things which seem incredible."[22]

In the wretched winter of 1609–10, "incredible" meant that men and women resorted to cannibalism. The English had long imagined "barbaric" Indians engaged in that "savage" behavior, but in fact English settlers were the ones who surrendered to "eat those things which nature most abhorred: the flesh and excrements of man." Some Jamestown residents, desperate to stay alive, raided graves and ate the corpses, while others "have licked up the blood which hath fallen from their weak fellows." Even their Indian enemies became suitable prey. An Indian killed in a raid was dug up "after he had lain buried three days, and wholly devoured." Others, "envying the better state of body" of those few settlers "whom hunger had not yet so much wasted . . . lay wait and threatened to kill and eat them."[23]

In the most ghoulish example of starving-time desperation, a man identified only as "Collines" (Collins) murdered his pregnant wife while she slept, "cut her in pieces," salted her, "and fed upon her till he had clean devoured all parts saving her head." He did not eat his own child, but instead ripped the fetus out of the mother's womb and tossed it in the river. Once President Percy discovered the "cruel and unhuman fact," he ordered Collins hung by his thumbs with weights on his feet until he confessed to the atrocity. Then Collins was "for so barbarous a fact and cruelty justly executed."[24]

Months later, when word of the colonists' horrendous suffering and descent into cannibalism reached London, this incident threw the Virginia Company into a public relations nightmare. Company insiders tried to downplay the Collins story by claiming that marital discord led to the murder, and that Collins cut up his wife's body to hide his crime. Officials even went so far as to claim that a search of Collins's house confirmed that he could not have been starving but in fact had "a good quantitie of meale, oatmeale, beanes and pease." The contrived story was both implausible and pointless, given the many other appalling, tragic reports that testified to Virginia's starving time.[25]

In a heartbreaking sign of the colonists' plight, some "being weary of life" dug their own graves "and there hid themselves till they famished."[26]

Others lashed out at God. Percy witnessed one famine-crazed settler, Hughe Pryse, "in a furious distracted mood," rushing around the fort "crying out that there was no God, alleging that if there were a God He would not suffer His creatures, whom He made and framed, to endure those miseries, and to perish for want of food and sustenance." Pryse wandered into the woods later that day with the colony's butcher, "a corpulent fat man," looking for something to eat. Both were found killed by the Indians. But Percy saw God's wrath visited upon Pryse for his blasphemy. His body had not only been riddled with arrows, but Pryse, despite being a "lean, spare man," had also been ripped apart and disemboweled by wolves. In contrast, the rotund butcher, "not lying above six yards from him," though shot dead by the Indians, otherwise appeared "altogether untouched."[27]

Sadly, much of this suffering and death need not have happened.

When the Indians lifted their siege in early May 1610 to begin their own spring planting, Percy, who himself had been sick all winter from the famine, finally traveled to Point Comfort to check on Captain Davis and his settlers. What he discovered there left him shocked and angry: a fort well-stocked with fish and crabs (with enough surplus to fatten the settlers' hogs!) and "Our people . . . in good case and well liking." All winter Davis and his men had "concealed their plenty" from the starving settlers in Jamestown, apparently so they could prepare themselves for a return to England. Percy lashed out at Davis for "not regarding our miseries and wants at all." And, he reminded Davis, that though they could always build "another town or fort . . . men's lives once lost could never be recovered."[28]

Percy told Davis he would be bringing half of Jamestown's survivors to the better-provisioned Point Comfort. Ready yourselves to receive a large number of sick and starving people, Percy instructed Davis. And when that half of the Jamestown residents recovered, the second half would arrive "to be sustained there also."[29] Percy never implemented this plan, for fate would shortly intervene.

George Percy provided a remarkably candid and full commentary on the starving times, but he never explained in his "True Relation" why he did not do more to save his people. Why did he let the winter of 1609–10 pass without checking on the Point Comfort residents or removing the starving Jamestown settlers there? It is unclear why Percy apparently failed even to consider the potential relief that relocating to Point Comfort would have offered the Jamestown settlers. Maybe it would have simply required too much effort to pick up and move. Weakened by disease and famine, most settlers perhaps lacked the strength to relocate. The reluctance or inability to leave Jamestown may also have been due to the presence of so many sick women and children in Jamestown, whom the men were unwilling to leave behind.[30] It is equally plausible that the inept and sick Percy lacked the leadership to conceive of the move. Fear of being killed by the Powhatans if settlers stepped outside the fort also no doubt played a role. And Davis did his part by keeping the food supplies at Point Comfort a secret from his countrymen at the Jamestown fort.

Whatever *might* have been done, nothing was. So in its vulnerable isolation Jamestown turned into a charnel house. The death rates reveal the magnitude of the disaster. When John Smith departed from Virginia for England in October 1609, he left behind about 420 colonists. (Nearly 80 people, including 40 to 50 sailors and "thirty of those unruly youths . . . not wanted in Virginia" sailed on the fleet with Smith.) Subtracting those who died from Indian attacks at the falls and Nansemond and others who had moved to Point Comfort, as many as 350 settlers remained at the Jamestown fort that winter to endure the starving time. By March 1610, just six months after John Smith had left the colony, only 60, the "most miserable and poore creatures," remained alive. The gruesome result: a mortality rate of over 80 percent.[31]

Who and what should have been blamed for the suffering in Jamestown that winter? Captain John Smith pointed a finger at his incompetent successors, including John Ratcliffe, John Martin, and Gabriel Archer, even after he knew that, of the three, only John Martin survived the ordeal in Jamestown. Ratcliffe met his grisly demise at the hands of Indians, and Archer died like so many others in the winter of 1609–10.[32]

In the absence of his own strong leadership, Smith charged, the colonists were left at the mercy of the Indians, and "wee had nothing but mortall wounds with clubs and arrowes." Meanwhile, he claimed, "our commanders and officers did daily consume" the livestock and food supplies "till all was devoured." It was not the idea of Virginia that had failed but the inept leaders and improvident settlers: "the occasion was only our owne, for want of providence, industrie, and governement, and not the barrennesse and defect of the countrie."[33]

Back in England, when Rev. William Crashaw, one of the colony's most outspoken supporters, learned of the horrors of the 1609–10 winter, he blamed the starving time on "our want of government—the most disastrous accident that ever befell that business, brought all to nothing, for it hindered the building of houses and planting of corn. Nay, it burnt up the houses and consumed the provisions . . . and which was worse consumed our men, and which was worst of all it lost us the savages, which since hath cost many a man his blood, and to this day is not recovered." Robert Johnson, once a propagandist for Virginia, now saw nothing in Jamestown but "Ambition, sloth and idlenes," a distressful place where "the houses decaied, the Church fell to ruine, the store was spent, the cattell consumed, our people starved, and the poore Indians by wrongs and injuries were made our enemies."[34]

Even Thomas Smythe, the bold entrepreneur behind the Virginia adventure, came in for serious criticism in the wake of Jamestown's suffering. Throughout Smythe's regime, insufficient food supplies and a constant obsession to push settlers to look for gold and other commodities rather than till the soil had compromised the enterprise. Survivors later complained bitterly that "Neither were we for our future and better maintenance permitted to manure or till any ground . . . but were by the direction of Sir Thomas Smith and his officers here wholly employed in cutting down of masts, cedar, black walnut, clapboard, etc., and in digging gold ore . . . which being sent for England proved dirt."[35] And some adamantly insisted, "we were constrained to eat dogs, cats, rats, snakes, toadstools, horsehides, and whatnot" because "our sustenance was to come from England"—but it never did. In time, some men publicly proclaimed their contempt for Smythe: "And indeed so miserable was our estate that the happiest day that ever some of us then hoped to see was when the Indians had killed a mare, they wishing whilst she was a-boiling that Sir Thomas Smith were upon her back in the kettle."[36]

With the colonists overwhelmed with loss and misery, hope had become as scarce as food in Jamestown; even the will to live wavered. But despite all the suffering, there were also reservoirs of faith. Among those who survived the horrific winter into the spring of 1610 were two married women who the year before had launched out of Plymouth with Thomas Gates's rescue fleet. Temperance Yeardley and Joan Pierce sailed aboard the *Falcon* and *Blessing*, respectively, while their husbands, Captain George Yeardley and William Pierce, traveled on a different boat in the fleet: the ill-fated *Sea Venture*. Did Temperance and Joan endure the horrors of the starving time in part because they clung to the hope of some day reuniting with their husbands?[37]

On Wednesday May 23, 1610, George Percy and Captain Davis stood at Point Comfort assessing their grim situation. While acknowledging "Our miseries now being at the highest," something appeared on the horizon: "we espied two pinnaces coming into the bay." Not knowing what awaited them with the approaching boats, Percy and Davis kept their guards close and a "watch all that night."[38] And no doubt they worried and wondered. The morning would bring answers to their questions: Were the ships friend or foe? What news, what provisions might they bring? And did they carry on board what Temperance and Joan and so many others had been hoping for for nearly a year?

CHAPTER 8

REDEMPTION IN VIRGINIA

The *Patience* and the *Deliverance* left Bermuda on Thursday, May 10, around ten in the morning. For a moment, when the *Deliverance* struck a rock on the starboard side, the shipwreck survivors' "hearts failed," for it seemed they might yet again be stranded. But by the coxswain's skill and "God's goodness" the boat passed over the rocks and, with the *Patience* alongside, sailed out into the Atlantic. For two days, "the wind served us easily," so that by late Friday the island chain that had sustained the stranded colonists for nearly ten months disappeared over the horizon. William Strachey later pronounced it "to the no little joy of us all" that the castaways "got clear of the islands."[1] But surely this applied more to the gentlemen seeking glory in America than to the poor laborers leaving a land of plenty for the rumored deathtrap of Jamestown.

Those first two days' easy journey gave way on Saturday to "wind sometimes fair and sometimes scarce and contrary." For a week the two boats struggled along. Twice they got separated, with Somers's *Patience* falling behind the better equipped *Deliverance*. This would have caused terrific anxiety given the passengers' and crewmen's experiences on the Atlantic. Although Thomas Gates had been reluctant to share supplies and equipment during the boatbuilding efforts, once at sea, he was obliged to be more generous. The *Deliverance* crew "spared him [Somers] our main topsail and sometimes our forecourse too" so that the two vessels could keep in close consort.[2]

On May 17, passengers began to see debris floating alongside their ships and noticed changes in the color of the ocean. Even inexperienced voyagers knew what this meant: "we were not far from land." Soundings taken over the next two days confirmed that the two boats were sailing into increasingly shallow waters. Then, around midnight on May 20, the passengers began to detect "a marvelous sweet smell from the shore." But the blackness of night kept everyone from seeing what they smelled. As soon as dawn broke, one of the sailors cried land. One year to the day after the *Sea Venture* fleet gathered at Plymouth, the voyagers from the flagship had at last made it to Virginia.[3]

They weighed anchor at Cape Henry, the westernmost point at the opening of the Chesapeake Bay, named in 1606 for King James's son, Prince Henry. But the *Patience* and the *Deliverance* remained there only a few hours before catching a favorable wind and sailing up the James River. On Monday morning, May 21, the boats came within sight of a fortified outpost where none, as far as Gates knew, was supposed to exist.[4]

As the *Patience* and *Deliverance* approached the fort, the weather turned bad: "a mighty storm of thunder, lightning, and rain gave us a shrewd and fearful welcome." That storm turned out to be a sign of things to come.[5]

The small outpost was Point Comfort, also known as Fort Algernon, and home to some thirty-odd Englishmen. On top of the foul weather, the beleaguered voyagers received a less than gracious reception from their countrymen. Unable to identify the approaching vessels and ever fearful of a Spanish invasion, the men at the fort "discharged a warning piece" above the boats. Somers and Gates anchored their ships and sent ashore a small party to identify themselves as belonging to the long-lost *Sea Venture* and to find out who held the fort.[6]

Once the men at Point Comfort learned the identity of the two ships, Captain Davis and President Percy "hailed them" and beckoned the passengers and crew to join them in the fort. But Gates, "having no knowledge of any fort to be builded there, was doubtful whether we were friends or no," and delayed embarking until he confirmed his people would be safe. Only then did "he and Sir George Somers with divers others come ashore."[7]

The castaways had gone a year without news from home, and well over a year had passed since they last heard anything about Virginia. Beyond sharing the happy news that the rest of the *Sea Venture* fleet had arrived safely in Virginia the prior summer, the men at Point Comfort offered only devastating reports.

Henry Ravens's rescue party did manage to reach coastal Virginia, they learned, but the Powhatan Indians had captured and executed them before they could make contact with the colonists. Powhatan himself "would describe the people and make much scoffing sport thereat." Powhatan's people enjoyed such an advantage over the colonists that he could admit to the killings, and even mock the English deaths, without fear of retribution. This represented a shocking departure from the promises made in Virginia Company literature of Indians converting to English ways and colonists peacefully possessing Indians' lands.[8]

As for the principal settlement at Jamestown, one piece of "unexpected, uncomfortable, and heavy news" followed another. The Point Comfort settlers shared with their countrymen the litany of horrors that had beset Jamestown the prior winter. Upon hearing those appalling reports, a "much grieved" Gates left Point Comfort, and the two ships under his command made their way "sadly up the river."[9]

Nothing they heard at Point Comfort could have prepared Gates and his company for what they saw at Jamestown. They reached the fort on May 24, and could, as George Percy put it, "read a lecture of misery in our people's faces." Five hundred settlers should have greeted the *Patience* and *Deliverance*. But only sixty people had survived the winter, and the great majority of them "were so maugre [meager] and lean that it was lamentable to behold them." Some were bedfast, others deranged from hunger, and all half-starved. When they heard of Gates's arrival, men and women desperate for any relief and "so lean that they looked like anatomies" ran naked from their deathbeds toward him, "crying out WE ARE STARVED! WE ARE STARVED!"[10]

To be certain, there were also joyous reunions. Temperance Yeardley was reunited with her husband, as was Joan Pierce and her daughter, Jane. (Jane Pierce would eventually become the third wife of *Sea Venture* passenger John Rolfe.)[11] To once again be with their beloved relatives, especially after surviving the starving times, must have seemed to these women like a gift from God.

But for all the joy the Virginians felt "to see them who had been held so long in the bottom of the sea . . . their sweet congratulation was sharply sauced" when the famished colonists realized how few provisions the newcomers brought with them.[12]

For the great majority of passengers and crew, seeing the emaciated bodies of their countrymen and the spectacle of Jamestown in shambles—to say nothing of the stories they heard of starvation and cannibalism—could have only been a hellish nightmare. William Strachey was stunned to see "the palisades torn down, the ports open, the gates from off the hinges." Although seldom at a loss for words, Strachey felt overwhelmed by what he witnessed; he saw "many more particularities of their sufferances . . . than I have heart to express."[13]

The principal settlement of the Virginia colony and the foundation for England's claim to America had failed on a colossal scale. Several hundred English men and women died in the winter of 1609–10, from Indian attacks, disease, and starvation. There could be no greater mark of failure.

This was certainly not the colony that Gates had pictured himself leading. Indeed from everything Percy and others told him, it was the exact opposite of the godly, stable, lucrative settlement he had imagined when leaving London the prior summer. Despite the dire situation, he set himself to following the directions from the Virginia Company Council.

At first, Gates, "finding all things so contrary to our expectations, so full of misery and misgovernment," could think of nothing to do but summon the residents of the fort with the church bells. Rev. Buck said "a zealous and sorrowful prayer" before the handful of malnourished settlers and the doubtless appalled and devastated former castaways, who, it now appeared, had fled paradise for an earthly hell. It would have been impossible to avoid comparing the wretchedness of Virginia with the abundance of Bermuda, and more than a few must have wished they had stayed with Robert Waters and Christopher Carter instead of boarding the *Patience* and *Deliverance*.[14]

With President Percy having taken up temporary residence at Point Comfort, there was no government to speak of operating in Jamestown. Gates quickly found out that several of the men named to assist him in his long-delayed administration were dead. Indians had, of course, killed John Ratcliffe. Peter Winne had succumbed to the starving time, and the secretary Matthew Scrivener had drowned. To replace the latter, Gates turned to William Strachey, who had ingratiated himself with the leadership and won the favor of many of the castaways during their exile in Bermuda. As his first act, and following the instructions given Gates by the Virginia Company Council, Secretary Strachey read Gates's commission before the gathered settlers. Percy, again according to company directives, immediately "delivered up unto him his commission, the old patent, and the council seal."[15]

The long-delayed installation of Governor Gates did nothing to change the fact that the two hundred or so colonists now under his command lived like hostages inside the Jamestown fort. The Powhatans attacked "any boat upon the river or straggler out of the fort." Anyone who stepped "into the woods a stone's cast off" took his life in his hands. Two people survived the hurricane, being marooned on Bermuda, and the passage to America only to be shot and killed by Indians after just five days in Virginia.[16]

The arrival of the *Patience* and *Deliverance* did nothing to deter the Indians from their determination—and ability—to starve out the English. Powhatan had forbidden all trade with the colonists, a policy he continued that May. Either ignoring those directions or, as Strachey surmised, sent "as spies to discover our strength," a party did come to the fort to propose to trade shortly after Gates reached Jamestown. But the terms the Indians demanded seemed unbearably high to the colonists; Strachey complained about their "subtlety" and "contempt" in "trucking with us upon such hard conditions." Governor Gates grew so frustrated with the exploitative terms that he "neither could well endure nor would continue it" and cut off negotiations. In any event, the Powhatans lacked an adequate supply of corn, to say nothing of the will, to feed all the Jamestown residents. And the colonists could not feed themselves. They had not planted that spring because most of the sixty survivors were too weak to work. Their nets had rotted, so the newcomers could not even fish.[17]

It did not help matters that the *Patience* and *Deliverance* carried from Bermuda "no greater store of provision . . . than might well serve 150 for a sea voyage." Before sailing from Bermuda, Gates and Somers had been careful to load their boats with "powdred Porke" as well as salted fish and birds—plenty to feed the voyagers during their crossing to Virginia. But they left the bounteous island chain completely unaware of the "desolation and misery" destroying Jamestown, so that the meager provisions remaining after the trip could not possibly feed for more than a few days the two hundred settlers now residing in Jamestown.[18]

Determined to effect unity, Gates called the company together and admitted to the dire straits confronting them and then promised: "what provision he had they should equally share with him." He also issued "orders and instructions"—laws designed to secure order—which he had nailed on a post at the church. In time, those instructions would be expanded into the infamous *Lawes Divine, Morall and Martiall*, which would militarize life in Virginia.[19]

But that June, measures to uphold Gates's authority and promote stability did little to remedy the crisis in Jamestown: there was simply nothing to eat and no prospects of that changing. Gates "entered into the consultation with Sir George Somers and Captain Newport," along with George Percy and the other "gentlemen of the town," to try and craft a plan of action.[20] It would have been personally humiliating and financially devastating for Gates and Somers to accept that they could not salvage the Virginia Company's American investment. So they and the leading men of the colony wracked their brains for any solution short of failure. They gathered all the provisions from the fort, along with the supplies aboard the *Patience* and *Deliverance*, to see exactly where they stood. Reluctantly, "after much debating it could not appear how possibly they might preserve themselves" on the meager supplies they possessed. Gates and his advisers calculated that even if they carefully rationed all the remaining food, as Somers put it, "our meanes would not continewe above 14 daies." Gates felt devastated by the situation, and even more grievous "was the impossibilitie which he conceived (*and conceived truly*) how to amend any one whitt of this."[21]

While the leaders weighed their options, the survivors of the starving times, "most famished and at point of death, of whom many soon after died," begged to leave America. Their "lamentable outcries" soon "moved the hearts of these worthies, not being in any sort able long to relieve their wants."[22]

From the outset, Gates had promised the settlers that "if he should find it not possible and easy to supply them with something from the country by the endeavors of his able men, he would make ready and transport them all into their native country." Within a matter of days, Gates and the other leaders admitted they had no way to save their people from starvation other than abandoning the colony. And so, with a heavy heart, Gates accepted the inevitable and agreed "with all speed to return for England." Gates later told his friends that he much preferred to starve to death in Virginia than admit defeat and leave. But "carried by voices, he would not overrule" he accepted "there was no human help left on earth but with all speed to hasten for England."[23]

While the gentlemen leaders of the colony considered the concession that Virginia could no longer survive a devastating failure of their duty to England, the laboring classes greeted the announcement that they were heading home with "a general acclamation and shout of joy." Those lucky enough to survive the winter of 1609–10 celebrated the prospect of being delivered from their nightmare. And the newcomers shared in their relief: "for even our own men began to be disheartened and faint when they saw this misery amongst the others." The Bermuda castaways apparently recognized that they would shortly find themselves in the same sorry state if they lingered in America.[24]

As soon as Gates announced the plan to abandon Virginia, the colonists set about readying themselves for a final ocean voyage that would end their misery—along with England's presence in America. Only two small boats remained in Virginia that summer, the rest of the 1609 fleet having long since returned to England. Gates decided the best hope for the colonists' survival lay with sailing those pinnaces, the *Virginia* and the *Discovery*, along with the *Patience* and *Deliverance*, to Newfoundland. There he hoped they could "relieve their wants" and catch a ride back home on some of the English fishing vessels that worked the North Atlantic.[25]

Somehow the starving colonists found the energy to work: "some to make pitch and tar for trimming of our ships, others to bake bread, and few or none not employed in one occasion or another." Colonists later insisted that "Every man glad of this resolution labored his utmost to further it." In three weeks' time, they were ready to take to the sea.[26]

Gates ordered all small arms loaded onto the boats. The heavy ordnance they buried just inside the fort gate, facing the James River. Every last scrap of food was equally divided among the four ships. Ever mindful of the Virginia Company's investment in America and apparently desperate to recover some money from the failed colony, Gates directed his men to strip the fort of anything "which might to the adventurers make some commodity upon the sale thereof at home."[27]

A drumbeat ushered the settlers on board their boats. All that remained of England's dreams for America that June of 1610 were a few ramshackle buildings inside the walls of a crumbling fort.

But this would have been no maudlin procession. The great majority of the colonists gladly left "the poor buildings in it to the spoil of the Indians, hoping never to return."[28] A few wanted to take more drastic actions.

Some "intemperate and malicious people"—at least in the opinions of the gentlemen leaders—decided they would burn down Jamestown. Gates appealed to them to "let the town stand," and pointed out, "We know not but that as honest men as ourselves may come and inhabit here." But reason did not work; it required military force to keep the group from razing the fort. Gates's men guarded the settlement as the colonists made their way to the waiting boats, and Gates "was himself the last of them" to step from the shores of Virginia. As when he left Bermuda, Governor Gates commanded the *Deliverance*, and George Somers sailed on the *Patience*. George Percy was on the *Discovery*, and Captain James Davis, former commander of Point Comfort, led the *Virginia*.[29]

Around noon, on June 7, with "not an English soul left in James Town," the boats, "giving by their peal of shot their last and woeful farewell" headed down the James River.[30] The hope of saving America for Protestant Christianity seemed lost. Jamestown had limped along for three years, never turning a profit and rightly earning the reputation of a death trap. And now Gates faced the painful duty of returning home to report the ignominious ending to London's grand dreams.

It is easy to imagine the mix of jubilation, trepidation, and heartbreak that filled the four boats as they slowly made their way along the James River. Although at last escaping Jamestown, the voyagers still faced a perilous ocean voyage in four small, ill-equipped boats. The laborers who lived through Jamestown's brutal winter of 1609–10 would have been the most elated. The *Sea Venture* survivors most likely had their relief tempered by their dearly bought experience with the Atlantic's awesome summer storms. And the colony's leaders, none more so than Thomas Gates, doubtless dreaded the humiliation of conceding their failures to Thomas Smythe and Virginia Company insiders. As night fell, the boats weighed anchor at Hog Island. The passengers and crew slept, unaware that this first night of their voyage from Virginia would also be their last.

Thomas Gates's adventures in America were not ending, but only beginning.

The four escape boats were anchored at the small island midway down the James River when, in the early afternoon of June 8, some of the crew noticed a longboat making its way in their direction. The boats soon buzzed with speculation: who was on board the approaching vessel and what news might they bring? An hour passed from the time the longboat was first spotted until the pilot made contact with the anxious, waiting colonists, so there was plenty of time to wonder and gossip.[31]

When at last the man piloting the longboat, Captain Edward Brewster, reached the *Deliverance*, he handed Gates a letter, which rerouted the governor's course and that of American history. Word of the letter's content ran like wildfire through the boats: the Lord De La Warr was at Point Comfort with 150 colonists and three ships full of supplies.

Silvester Jourdain believed that God had preserved him and the other passengers of the *Sea Venture* when they sailed into the hurricane in 1609. Now, in the news brought by Captain Brewster, he saw again God interceding on his countrymen's behalf. Although he and the two-hundred-some-odd colonists intended to abandon Virginia for Newfoundland and then England, Jourdain decided that "it pleased God to dispose otherwise of us and to give us better means." Certainly the letter to Gates indicated that De La Warr would "dispose otherwise" of the evacuating settlers, who soon learned the full story behind De La Warr's coincidental arrival in America.[32]

In response to reports of the upsetting loss of the *Sea Venture* and the pandemonium that erupted in Jamestown in the fall of 1609, the Virginia Company had scrambled to send another rescue mission, this time headed by Thomas West, the third Lord De La Warr. But the 1609 fund-raising campaign, including efforts at shaming Londoners into paying their subscriptions, floundered. De La Warr could not gather nearly as many men and supplies as quickly as he wanted, so he was delayed in leaving England until April 1, 1610. His fleet of three ships put in at Point Comfort on June 6—just one day before Gates ordered the evacuation of Jamestown.[33]

Lord De La Warr was not quite thirty-four when he sailed to America. Educated at Oxford as a young man, he fought against the Spanish in the Netherlands. He became a devoted promoter of the Virginia Company in the years before his 1610 mission and a powerful figure in London, serving on King James's privy council. He had only inherited his title a few years before the voyage, but was widely revered by his countrymen as a paragon of "courage, temper, and experience."[34]

De La Warr arrived at Point Comfort only to be greeted with news of Gates's "resolution to depart the country." The men at the fort were in fact waiting for the boats to come down from Jamestown and collect them when they saw De La Warr's ship sailing up the river. De La Warr, like Gates and Somers just two weeks before, listened in horror as the men at Point Comfort recounted the dreadful story of Jamestown's last year. De La Warr later confessed it "brooke my hart" to hear about the inconceivable suffering. The only relief he felt came when he found out that Gates was alive and finally in Virginia.[35] But then this was blunted by learning that Gates had been forced to give up on the colony. It was also no doubt personally embarrassing to find out that his younger brother, Francis West, had been a prime contributor to the factionalism of the prior fall and then had run away to England.

Upon hearing about the imminent evacuation of Virginia, De La Warr quickly wrote the letter to Gates and dispatched Edward Brewster, himself an investor in the Virginia Company, to deliver it to Jamestown. Brewster covered around half the James River before he saw a convoy in the distance; about an hour later, he greeted Gates.[36]

After Gates read De La Warr's letter, he immediately turned the *Deliverance* around and directed Somers, Davis, and Percy to follow his lead. De La Warr had brought men, supplies, and, most important, confidence—they were all going back to reclaim Jamestown.

The wind blew so favorably that by nightfall on June 8, Gates "relanded all his men at the fort again." For the gentlemen who had invested their money and reputations in Virginia, the return brought sweet relief. Gates would not have to go back to London in disgrace, but could instead stay in America and see the venture through. Somers shared in Gates's excitement at the news of De La Warr's arrival and the knowledge that Virginia might last after all. Reclaiming Jamestown, he declared, "made our heartes very glad." Robert Rich, another gentleman invested in English America, echoed Gates's and Somers's enthusiasm. In his poem celebrating the *Sea Venture* story, he insisted that the return to Jamestown "cheeres their hearts, that they abound with joy." Company promoters later claimed that the colonists shared in this elation. Rev. William Crashaw maintained that the colonists "all with as much joy returned as with sorrow they had come away."[37] But this was not how most of the settlers remembered feeling.

Far from being joyful, some of the colonists forced to return to Jamestown that June confessed that, when Gates turned the *Deliverance* around and headed back up the river, it caused "the great grief of all his company." The settlers had celebrated the abandonment of Virginia just a day before, and many dreaded the very idea of returning to "those poor ruinated habitations at James Town." It is hard to believe claims by Virginia Company insiders that the colonists happily dug up the ordnance they had buried just days before and greeted the prospect of another year in Jamestown "with all joy and applause."[38]

But even the most reluctant of settlers would have understood just how profoundly different their situation was after June 8 than it had been before. What a turnaround a day brought! De La Warr had plenty of provisions, so for the first time in over nine months the long-suffering residents of Jamestown would have plenty to eat. The 150 colonists sailing with De La Warr nearly doubled the size of the settlement. And for the first time in the colony's brief history, the government was fully staffed with cooperative leaders.

For true believers, De La Warr's propitious arrival, especially after Gates's and Somers's remarkable redemption the prior month, provided compelling evidence that God stood on the side of the English and that He intended their Virginia colony to survive. What else could possibly account for all that happened in 1609 and 1610? For many, including Captain John Smith, the only explanation for the confluence of events was that "God would not have it so abandoned." Expanding on the convictions of men and women who, like Silvester Jourdain, lived through that summer, Rev. Crashaw proclaimed, "the Hand of Heaven from above at the very instant sent in the Right Honorable La-war to meet them even at the river's mouth with provision and comforts of all kind." And he calculated that if De La Warr "had stayed but two tides longer had come into Virginia and not found *one Englishman*." All of which convinced Crashaw that "If ever the hand of God appeared in action of man, it was here most evident."[39]

What Lord De La Warr saw when he got to Jamestown on June 10, 1610, seemed the exact opposite of God's country. In a letter to the Earl of Salisbury, he described the town as "a verie noysome [stinking] and unholsome place." As for the people, they seemed "never so weake and so farr out of order as nowe I found them." To make matters worse, De La Warr immediately fell ill, "welcommed," he complained, "by a hot and violent Ague."[40]

Gates had hastily organized a proper English welcome for his successor. Armed soldiers stood at attention along the shoreline just outside the fort walls. William Strachey carried the flag, and all the colonists gathered to honor their incoming governor. For all the brutality and chaos the English had endured in Virginia, they still clung to the rituals that symbolized their respectability and order.[41]

Continuing the ceremony, De La Warr disembarked from his ship and immediately—and no doubt with great dramatic effect—"fell upon his knees and before us all made a long and silent prayer." He then marched at the head of his delegation toward the fort. As De La Warr crossed the gate doors, Strachey "bowed with the colors and let them fall at His Lordship's feet." It was exactly the way an English aristocrat of Lord De La Warr's standing would expect to be greeted. But the peculiarity of enacting this courtly ritual in the wake of eating snakes, boot leather, and then their dead neighbors just a few months before could not have been lost on the poor colonists. The procession headed next to the chapel and listened to Rev. Buck deliver a sermon. After the service, one of De La Warr's assistants rose to read his commission. Gates then stepped forward and "rendered up unto His Lordship his own commission, both patents, and the council seal."[42]

Deferential displays notwithstanding, De La Warr remained horrified by the "many miseries and calamities" his countrymen had, as he saw it, not simply endured but rather caused themselves. He quickly decided that "no story, I believe, ever presented the wrath and curse of the eternall offended Majestie in a greater measure."[43]

Governor De La Warr wasted little time in "laying many blames" upon the gathered colonists. He found the state of affairs in Jamestown revolting, and he held the settlers responsible. In a self-congratulatory letter back to the Virginia Company he admitted that he rebuked them "for many vanities and their idlenes" as soon as his commission was read. In his initial address he also promised the residents that, if they continued in their debauched ways, he would not hesitate "to drawe the sworde of Justice, to cut of such delinquents."[44]

This was hardly the pep talk the exhausted Virginians needed to hear, but it was a faithful predictor of what lay ahead for them under the De La Warr regime. On Monday morning, June 11, the first full day of his governorship, De La Warr put everyone to work. His sailors unloaded supplies from the three boats in his convoy while the colonists cleaned up their despicably filthy, dilapidated fort. Carpenters busied themselves repairing buildings, fishermen went out fishing. After seeing how the colonists responded to his commands, De La Warr felt confident that he would "verie short-lie . . . returne something valuable unto the adventurers."[45]

While Silvester Jourdain perhaps exaggerated when he said the food De La Warr brought "revived all the company and gave them great content," there could be little question that being able to eat regularly sustained this new work regime. In short order the settlers repaired their houses and fortified the walls of the fort so that it could "assure the Inhabitants, and frustrate all assaylants." And within a month of his arrival, the new governor was able to send back to London a ship laden with walnuts, cedar, and clapboard the colonists had harvested in the forests. While it was not the gold and silver London investors dreamed of, at least something of value went home.[46]

De La Warr also understood that a proper working government was essential, and he turned his attention toward that task on his second day in office. His directions from the Virginia Company called for him, if he found Gates and Somers alive in Virginia, to appoint Gates lieutenant governor and Somers admiral. The council wanted Thomas Dale to serve as marshal and Christopher Newport as vice admiral to Somers. On Tuesday, June 12, De La Warr followed those directions. He also retained William Strachey as colonial secretary. As with Gates, the Council of the Virginia Company did not wish "to tie your Lordship to the stricte perfourmance of theis newe instructions" but instead granted him wide latitude to "doe therein as shall seeme best in your owne discretion." And that part of his directions he followed as well.[47]

De La Warr presided over a more highly militarized settlement than the Virginians had yet known. The colonists worked according to a precise routine and under armed guard. Each day began with church services and then a morning meal. From 6 a.m. until 10 a.m. and then again from 2 p.m. until 4 p.m. the settlers all labored for the common good, repairing buildings, preparing food, and fishing. Contemporary accounts pointed out that De La Warr and Gates succeeded where prior leaders had all failed in coercing the settlers to work together: "Those that knew not the way to goodnesse before, but cherished singularitie and faction, can now chalke out the path of all respective dutie and service . . . every man knoweth his charge, and dischargeth the same with alacritie."[48] Unlike their fractious predecessors, Gates and the other colonial officers stood squarely behind De La Warr. With fewer squabbles among the leadership, the laborers experienced fewer op-

portunities to slack off. And it did not hurt that De La Warr's soldiers policed the work detail. The settlers apparently believed him
when he said he would "drawe the sworde of Justice" against any
insurrectionary.

Gates and then De La Warr had arrived in Jamestown to find
the chapel "ruined and unfrequented." Both men found this unacceptable and commanded the settlers to repair it. Strachey reported
that "at this instant many hands are about it." The building measured sixty by twenty-four feet, and housed a communion table
made from Virginia walnut. The pews and pulpit were crafted out
of cedar, and the carpenters who built the church made sure to include plenty of windows "so cast as it be very light within." Gates
and De La Warr required the interior continually decorated with
"divers flowers" (which made it look good and helped mask the
odor when dozens of unwashed people crowded inside a small
space) and mandated attendance at sermons each Thursday and
twice on Sunday, as well as at morning prayers.[49] Rev. Buck found
himself far busier in Jamestown than he had ever been on Bermuda.
In addition to running the services, he officiated at the funerals for
the colonists who died after De La Warr's arrival.

Holding services inside a proper church mattered not only in
terms of meeting spiritual needs but also because it promoted
community stability. Religious rituals afforded the gentlemen
leaders of Virginia a venue for affirming their authority by daily reminding the colonists of their duty to God and country. The services also reinforced the social order De La Warr, Gates, and their
advisers presided over. Every Sunday, the governor and lieutenant
governor attended church "accompanied with all the councilors,
captains, other officers, and all the gentlemen." No fewer than fifty
guards lined either side of the path this procession took toward the
modest chapel. De La Warr listened to Rev. Buck's sermons from a
special chair upholstered in green velvet, and he kneeled to pray on

a matching velvet cushion. He sat at the head of the church, surrounded by his entourage, just the way the English liked: "each in
their place."[50]

Despite these initial signs of accomplishment, the problem of
feeding the colonists would not go away. De La Warr, like Gates before him, knew that the colony could not survive if the settlers were
not adequately provisioned; none of his rebuilding efforts would
matter if another famine occurred. And while De La Warr's ships carried enough oatmeal and peas to last as long as a year, they brought
no meat. No one in England had imagined the colonists would
slaughter even their breeding stock, so they did not waste precious
space on the ships sending salted meat or live animals. But then no
one imagined the colonists would resort to cannibalism, either.
When De La Warr arrived he saw "there was not above one sow . . .
not a henn nor chick in the forte (and our horses and mares they had
eaten with the first)." The settlers had devoured all their livestock
the prior winter, and the Powhatans had killed the hogs they let for-
age in the woods as part of the campaign to starve out the colonists.
Efforts at hunting failed, as did trading for deer with the Indians.
Fishing was not going well, either. De La Warr brought new nets,
and he immediately sent men out on the James. They came back day
after day with next to nothing. According to De La Warr, "every day
and night we hayled our nett sometimes a dozen times once after another, but it pleased not God so to bless our labours."[51]

A solution to the looming food problem came from George Somers.
When the colonial council met on June 13, Somers reminded the
increasingly anxious new governor how "marveilous full and well
stored" Bermuda was with fish, birds, and hogs. He volunteered to
sail to the islands that had intrigued him so and return to Virginia
"with six moneths provision of flesh, and with live Hogges."[52]

De La Warr promptly agreed to Somers's excellent plan. It was an easy decision. The colonists needed meat, and Bermuda provided the only likely source. Somers was the man "best acquainted with the place," and so the most logical choice to sail back. And he had the courage to volunteer for this "dangerous adventure for the good of the Colonie."[53] Silvester Jourdain, who got to know Somers during their months stranded on Bermuda, praised his "worthy and valiant mind" and willingness to risk the trip to help his countrymen with no concern for "his own private gain." De La Warr felt the same, describing in a letter to the Earl of Salisbury how Somers's "love and zeale" for English America inspired him to volunteer without the slightest hesitation "to performe so Dangerous a Voiage." At the same time, it was lost on neither Jourdain nor De La Warr how old Somers was to head such a risky excursion. The thirty-three-year-old governor respectfully referred to Somers as a "good old gentleman," and Jourdain pointed out his "being of threescore years of age at the least."[54]

De La Warr decided it best to send two boats on the mission, and he selected Captain Samuel Argall to go along with Somers. Argall had scouted the shorter, northern route just weeks before the *Sea Venture* fleet departed from England in 1609, and he returned to America as captain of De La Warr's ship in 1610. In addition to his experience, he was a kinsman and a favorite of De La Warr, sent perhaps to ensure that Somers's interest in Bermuda dovetailed with the governor's.[55]

As he prepared for the voyage, Somers wrote his own letter to the Earl of Salisbury explaining, "I am goinge to the Bermooda for fishe and hogge." He felt confident he could "be back againe before the Indians doe gather their harvest" with a ship full of meat. After all, as he explained to Salisbury, Bermuda "is the most plentifull place, that ever I came to."[56]

Somers and Argall departed Jamestown on June 19, Somers in

the lead aboard his trusty *Patience*. The colonists watched from the shoreline, and some prayed: "that God will send a pillar of fire to direct his journey" to Bermuda and that "He will protect him and send him well back again."[57]

It took several days for Somers and Argall to make their way down the James, so that they arrived at Cape Henry on June 22; they needed "to take more balast" before they headed out to sea. Heavy rains that day delayed their departure for several hours—a sign of things to come. For more than three weeks after leaving Cape Henry, Somers and Argall fought the winds and "weather very stormy, with many sudden gusts of wind and raine." At six in the evening, on July 16, in the midst of another storm, Argall brought his *Discovery* alongside the *Patience*, close enough to hear Somers who, in Argall's words "when I hayled him, told me that he . . . was not able to keepe the sea any longer." Somers said he was aborting the mission to Bermuda and sailing for Cape Cod instead and that Argall should follow. As they headed north, Argall struggled to keep up with Somers. At one point a heavy fog blanketed the sea, so that only by "hallowing and making a noyse one to another all the night" were they able to stay together. The two boats eventually made their way to the Sagadahoc River where they found good luck fishing; they caught "neere one hundred Cods" in a single day.[58]

On July 26, Somers announced "that he would set saile" again, and this time Argall lost him in fog "so thicke, that we could not see a Cables length from our ship." Argall repeatedly called out to Somers, then fired a shot, and "kept an hollowing and a noise to try whether I could find him againe." But the admiral never responded. Argall fished some more along the coast of New England and then returned to Jamestown in late August, unsure of Somers's whereabouts and doubtless curious about why he had not returned to Virginia to unload his fish.[59]

When Argall got back to the fort, De La Warr dispatched him on an expedition to trade for corn with the Indians. Much to Argall's shock, when he arrived in the Indian town he saw "an English boy, one Henry Spilman"—the teenager in the *Sea Venture* fleet whom John Smith had traded to the Powhatans a year earlier. Spelman had the good fortune to spend the winter of 1609–10 not in the death trap of Jamestown but among the Powhatan Indians. Argall found him in fine health and having formed a close enough attachment to the leaders of the village that they "fraughted his [Argall's] ship with Corne, wherewith he returned to James towne."[60]

While Argall and others worked to supply the settlement, Governor De La Warr continued to feel the effects of living in the swamps of Virginia. In a July letter back home he explained that he was sick but believed that God would soon "restore me to health."[61] As his health deteriorated, so, too, did relations with the Powhatan Indians.

Both during his brief governorship and in the early weeks of his service as lieutenant governor to De La Warr, Thomas Gates rejected violence against the Indians: "since his first landing in the country (how justly soever provoked) would not by any means be wrought to a violent proceeding against them." Gates was a no-nonsense man, and his motives were strictly practical. He believed it "possible by a more tractable course to win them to a better condition." He rejected the harsh tactics of John Smith, pursuing instead the Virginia Company's preferences: that the Indians be won over to English ways.[62]

But attempts to negotiate with the Indians faltered when De La Warr insisted that Powhatan (Wahunsonacock) subordinate himself to the English. Powhatan reasonably considered demands from inside Jamestown at best presumptuous if not laughable. He replied that De La Warr and his people should confine themselves to their fort; if they strayed into Powhatan's forests and rivers, he promised to kill them. Adding insult to injury, Powhatan directed De La Warr never again to send emissaries "unlesse they brought him a Coach and three Horses" so they he, too, might travel in the style of English leaders.[63]

For Gates, the turning point was more personal and more visceral. On July 6, he and several of his men were sailing down to Point Comfort in heavy winds. They spotted a longboat along the shoreline, and supposing it lost from Point Comfort in the high winds, sent one man, Humphrey Blunt, to retrieve it. When he went ashore, Indians seized him "and led him up into the woods and sacrificed him." The unprovoked violence "did not a little trouble the lieutenant governor." In that moment, Gates saw that the Indians had no intention of welcoming or aiding the English, and he abandoned his policy of conciliation. Now, "he well perceived how little a fair and noble entreaty works upon a barbarous disposition and therefore in some measure purposed to be revenged." If negotiations would not work, maybe force would.[64]

In the wake of that episode, the commanders at Jamestown unleashed a series of vicious raids into Indian country. Gates led one of the earliest assaults, just three days after the murder of Humphrey Blunt. According to George Percy, Gates, "being desirous for to be revenged unto the Indians," sent a musician to "play and dance thereby to allure the Indians to come upon him." Soldiers then attacked the Indians, killing many and forcing the survivors to flee into the woods. Gates assailed the town and ordered his soldiers to occupy it. In Percy's words "having well ordered all things" Gates then returned to Jamestown.[65]

The raids did not end there; Percy participated in the next one, which was even more violent. On August 9 he and two boatloads of soldiers laid siege to another Indian town. Like Gates's soldiers, his party killed many of the men in the village and chased the remainder into the forest. Percy also commanded "my soldiers to burn their houses and to cut down their corn growing about the town." This time, unlike in Gates's incursion, the forces took hostages, including a woman and her children. By Percy's own account, once the soldiers reboarded their boats and headed back to Jamestown, they began to complain about the hostages being spared from death. So, he conferred with his men and all agreed "to put the children to death, the which was effected by throwing them overboard and shooting out their brains in the water." The mother they kept alive.[66]

When Percy's outfit made it back to Jamestown, De La Warr let Percy know "it was my lord's pleasure that we should see her dispatched." Percy and James Davis discussed the method of execution, with Davis preferring to burn the woman alive. According to Percy, he then "replied that having seen so much bloodshed that day . . . I desired to see no more." So Davis took the woman "and in the woods put her to the sword" instead.[67]

Samuel Argall led another assault, and when all the villagers fled he "could have [no] other revenge than by cutting down their corn, burning their houses, and suchlike." All the while De La Warr, despite repeated illnesses, personally oversaw the brutality inside the fort. For instance, when a group of Indians came to the fort, perhaps to trade or negotiate for peace, De La Warr rejected anything other than a violent response. He "caused one to have his hand cut off, and so sent unto his fellows to give them warning for attempting the like."[68]

As the violence escalated, the harsh Virginia environment continued to exact a toll on the governor. Unlike Gates and Somers, De La Warr did not take well to what long-term residents called "the seasoning"—the months getting acclimated to, and usually sickened by, the local environs. After his first fever, he contracted dysentery and then scurvy, evidence that food and water remained inadequate inside the fort, even for the leaders. And the colonists suffered as well, although certainly nothing like they had in the winter of 1609–10. Critics of De La Warr's authoritarian leadership complained that their fellow settlers continued to die in the early weeks of his government, "chiefly for want of means to comfort them in their weak estates." Under his regime, settlers still faced great hardships and spent their days, as they later recalled, "doing little but enduring much." While it seemed in the fall of 1610 that Virginia had stepped back from the brink of collapse, it appeared equally evident that the men and women living there would endure—and create—a world of misery and violence.[69]

Sir Thomas Gates was not in Virginia to hear about Percy's cruelties or to witness De La Warr's declining health and the colonists' mounting resentments. Shortly after his own raid, he sailed from Virginia, along with Christopher Newport. He arrived in England in September, carrying a letter from De La Warr that explained his safe arrival and ongoing (and, as De La Warr told it, valiant) efforts to turn Virginia around. But, of course, the most exciting news Gates did not have to report at all—it was his very arrival, when all of London thought him dead.[70]

In the fall of 1610, Gates would reveal to England the wondrous story of his miraculous redemption and convince Thomas Smythe and the Virginia Company Council that, despite the long troubles with Jamestown, they should stick by their American enterprise. The 140 people that Gates transported from Bermuda, along with the 150 colonists De La Warr brought after the feared loss of the *Sea Venture*, made the colony large enough and strong enough to survive another year. And the chance convergence in

Virginia of Gates and Somers with De La Warr inspired great numbers of English men and women to believe that God wanted them in America. Powhatan and Ambassador Zúñiga's shared fear was fast becoming reality: the English seemed to be in America to stay.

CHAPTER 9

GOD IS ENGLISH

In the spring of 1610, a new Spanish ambassador, Don Alonso de Velasco, arrived in London to replace Don Pedro de Zúñiga. Just a few months into his service, Velasco heard all about the horrors at Jamestown, apparently from the men under Francis West's command who stole the *Swallow* and fled Virginia in the height of the famine. In a June 14 letter back to Madrid, Velasco reported how the Powhatans had surrounded the colonists' fort and that the settlers "were left so entirely without provisions that . . . the survivors eat the dead." The men who escaped confessed to "having eaten dogs, cat skins and other vile stuff." Velasco observed, with considerable understatement, that "it looks as if the zeal for this enterprise was cooling off." While he did not match Zúñiga's passionate language, Velasco shared his predecessor's convictions about Virginia, and pointed out that now was an ideal time for Spain to strike: "it would . . . *be very easy to make an end of it altogether by sending out a few ships to finish what might be left in that place.*" Apparently De La Warr's modest fleet, which had left

London in April to fortify the colony, did not impress Velasco. Key advisers to Philip III held even lower opinions of the Virginians than their ambassador in England; they convinced the king of Spain that letting the English continue to squander their money and lives in the wasteland of North America, while sending occasional reconnaissance missions to frighten them into spending even more, remained the cleverest policy.[1]

Although Velasco had no way of knowing it, even as he wrote, the Virginia colony was enjoying an amazing reversal of fortune. As had been the case since 1607, information available to curious London observers lagged far behind events on the ground in America. De La Warr was already in Virginia on June 14, having arrived less than a week earlier. He and Gates were busy feeding and sheltering the sixty famished souls left in Jamestown and trying to bring some semblance of order to the settlement. The same June day Velasco wrote his letter, Somers was preparing to leave Virginia and return to Bermuda. As Velasco's letter made its way to Madrid, Somers headed down the James River.

Admiral Somers had volunteered for the mission to Bermuda strictly for altruistic reasons—or at least so it appeared to the Virginians deeply impressed with his willingness to risk his life to bring them food. Weather altered his course, however, and after a month-long delay in leaving the coast of America, Somers finally departed for the island chain on July 26—without Captain Samuel Argall. While the exact date of his arrival in Bermuda is not known, even with a slow crossing, he would have made the islands within a month. He was, after all, supposed to speed there and back again. The hungry Virginians were waiting for his supply of meat, and they must have wondered what happened to Somers and his foraging trip, especially after Argall returned to Jamestown alone. As it turned out, Somers was still in Bermuda in November, over four months after leaving Jamestown.[2]

Some of Somers's contemporaries believed that helping the Virginians was not his only motivation for returning to Bermuda. It was later rumored that a "promise to thoes two left behind"—Robert Waters and Christopher Carter—that he would return to scout a colony drew Somers back to the islands. Certainly his mapmaking and agricultural experimentation while on Bermuda testified to "an affection he carryed to the place it selfe."[3] Then there was the matter of his immediately volunteering to return to Bermuda to gather provisions. While most celebrated his "dangerous adventure for the good of the Colonie," others believed that he used "a pretence of fetchinge newe reliefe" to leave Virginia for Bermuda. His behavior with Argall during the mission to Bermuda adds to the suspicions; even though Lord De La Warr directed them to travel to Bermuda together, Somers inexplicably failed to rendezvous with Argall, so that he wound up sailing alone. And as the castaways had readied to depart Bermuda in May 1610, it was Somers who convinced all the rebellious men to join the voyage to Virginia—except Carter and Waters. So while there is no direct proof that Somers encouraged Carter and Waters to stay in Bermuda to protect a claim to the islands when the *Patience* and *Deliverance* left, a good deal of circumstantial evidence supports the suspicion that he had been "meditating a returne into thes ilands" for some time.[4] Certainly a man of his vast experience could not have failed to see the advantages, for his colleagues back in England and for himself, of starting a colony in Bermuda.

Waters and Carter met Somers and his men, including his nephew Matthew Somers and faithful assistant Edward Waters, shortly after they made land. Both men appeared healthy, none the worse for having lived alone on the islands for several months. Somers "receiued farther light of the commodities of the soyle" from the two men, and he learned even more about the abundant environment. If Somers did not have designs on colonizing

Bermuda before his return, he certainly did after he talked to Carter and Waters. What they told him about their time on the island "so inflamed him" and confirmed "his first inclination . . . [that] he resolued vpon a plantation."[5]

Somers never saw this dream reach fruition. He died in early November, some said while chasing hogs through the forest, others claimed while enjoying the fruits of his labor: "of a surfeit in eating of a pig."[6] Both stories may be apocryphal—they certainly seem poetic.

As he lay dying, Somers directed his nephew to "returne into Virginia" with what supplies the *Patience* could carry. But Matthew had different ideas. After his uncle died, he and "the greatest part" of the crew, "longing to be at home againe," did leave Bermuda, but rather than sailing west to Virginia, they headed east for England.[7]

Robert Waters had had enough of Bermuda by this time and certainly did not want to face Gates in Virginia; he leapt at the chance to return to England. Carter, however, decided to stay. He did not want the islands "left desolate," for he believed that Somers's friends in England would see the wisdom of starting a colony on Bermuda. He "would by noe meanes be induced to a returne with the rest," and resolved to stay on the island alone if no one volunteered to join him. Edward Waters also wanted to preserve the claim and legacy of George Somers, so he, along with Edward Chard, agreed "to be the compagnions of his [Carter's] fortunes." When the *Patience* left Bermuda under Matthew Somers's command, Carter, Chard, and Waters, who later became known as "the three kings of Bermuda," watched from the shore. They had no way of knowing they would not see another soul for almost two years.[8]

By early 1610, Sir Thomas Smythe desperately needed some good news from his Virginia enterprise. But he had scarcely launched the

De La Warr fleet when he and all of London heard from the mutinous men on board the stolen *Swallow* that George Percy was presiding over a failure of colossal proportions. When the *Swallow* left Virginia, Powhatan had already trapped the settlers inside the Jamestown fort, and men and women were raiding graves for food.[9] Somers and Gates were still believed dead, and it was feared that soon all the settlers would meet their same fate: a cruel death in service to the folly of an American colony. Smythe and Virginia Company insiders could do little in the summer of 1610 except wait and hope against hope that De La Warr might somehow salvage their investment. History was not on Smythe's side, however, for the past three years had been a study in failure, each more crushing than the next.

Then, in September 1610, the most astonishing thing happened: none other than Sir Thomas Gates, along with Christopher Newport, arrived home. Met by the great joy of everyone associated with the Virginia Company, they broke the news of their remarkable odyssey on Bermuda.[10]

Gates's arrival back in London and the amazing account he told of his past year brought new life to the Virginia Company and its American colony at precisely the moment when great numbers of investors had resigned themselves to failure. Word of the survival of the *Sea Venture*'s passengers and crew ran through London like wildfire. De La Warr had been wise in sending Gates and Newport to tell the tale themselves. Conveyed by others, the story of how the castaways survived the hurricane and shipwreck, discovered a bountiful paradise on the island chain of Bermuda, and safely made their way to Virginia might have been discounted as too incredible to believe. But there was no questioning the physical presence of these two esteemed men. Their rousing tale of the *Sea Venture*'s deliverance overshadowed, for once, the dreadful news from Virginia.

The *Sea Venture* story seemed to many seventeenth-century

Protestants—particularly those who lived through it—as nothing short of a miracle. Survivors of the *Sea Venture* wreck spread the word that God had saved them and wanted America for England. Gates and Newport transported to England the first of these providential texts: Robert Rich's poem, *The Lost Flocke Triumphant*, and Silvester Jourdain's narrative, *A Discovery of the Bermudas, Otherwise Called the Isle of Devils*. Rich vowed that "God will not let vs [us] fall" and charged "He that would crosse so good a worke, to God can be no friend." Jourdain, far more expansive than Rich, similarly attributed the safety of the *Sea Venture* passengers and crew to God's "most gracious and merciful providence." At every turn— the spotting of land, the ship not sinking, the bounty of Bermuda, the passage to Virginia, the serendipitous meeting with De La Warr—Jourdain credited God who "showed Himself still merciful unto us." Their story made it seem that company promoters and the ministers at St. Paul's Cross had been right all along: colonizing Virginia was "the cause of God."[11]

The nation was enthralled by this remarkable tale. The Virginia Company rushed Rich's and Jourdain's works into print in the fall of 1610. A third manuscript, much longer and much more evocatively written, made its way around London; William Strachey's *A True Reportory of the Wreck and Redemption of Sir Thomas Gates* was not published for several years, most likely because it recounted the mutinies on Bermuda and other unflattering tales that the Virginia Company would have found detrimental to their interests. But many influential people read Strachey's work, including William Shakespeare. All three first-person accounts of the *Sea Venture* wreck fueled the conviction that the ship—and the English nation—had been chosen by God for greatness.[12]

Virginia Company promoters and Protestant ministers quickly picked up on the providential explanation of the shipwreck survivors. A flurry of publications saturated London in late 1610. The tracts shared a powerful common premise: God did not want English America abandoned. While the Virginia Company did not self-servingly invent the idea of divine intervention—Jourdain, Rich, and Strachey wrote first and from Virginia, after all—they certainly played it up to great effect.

Ministers on both sides of the Atlantic proclaimed, "If ever the hand of God appeared in action of man, it was here most evident," and "assuredly God Himself is the founder and favorer of this plantation." Writing from Virginia, Rev. Alexander Whitaker believed with an unshakable faith that "the finger of God hath been the only true worker here. That God first showed the place, God first called us hither, and here God by his special providence hath maintained us." Whitaker claimed that the deliverance of the *Sea Venture* castaways "could proceed from none other but the singular providence of God." Even Captain John Smith, no longer affiliated with the Virginia enterprise, viewed events in the same light. "God that would not it should bee unplanted," Smith wrote, and so sent Gates and Somers to Virginia in time "to preserue us." He added, "Strange it is to say how miraculously they were preserved."[13]

Company tracts and ministers' sermons cataloged the myriad ways in which God interceded in the *Sea Venture* voyagers' fate. That everyone survived the hurricane seemed a wonder in itself. "Gods divine providence" not only kept the damaged *Sea Venture* afloat during the storm, but also pushed the ship onto the coral reef, which allowed the passengers and crew to save themselves and their supplies. Then, God revealed to the English that Bermuda, long thought of "rather a habitation of Diuells, then fit for men to dwell in," was in fact "one of the sweetest Paradises that be vpon the earth." Rev. William Crashaw raved, "The *Barmuda* Ilands are not only accessible and habitable, but also fertile, frutifull, plentifull, and a safe, secure, temperate, rich, sweet, and healthfull habitation for Man, and especially for English bodies."[14]

In the providential retelling of the *Sea Venture* story, God fed the castaways with the island chain's birds, fish, and hogs; He left the cedar trees from which they built their boats; and "by Gods great mercy" they finally made their way to Virginia "when all Englishmen deemed them to be utterly cast away."[15]

The divine intercession continued as the survivors reached Virginia. If Gates and Somers had been delayed only one week longer in Bermuda, writers speculated, "the famine, which had by that time devoured the most of our countrymen here, would have consumed the rest." When Gates saw no option other than abandoning Virginia, God whispered in his ear to save Jamestown from the evacuating colonists who wanted to burn it down. And, finally, as the beleaguered settlers sailed down the James River, "the Hand of Heaven from above at the very instant sent in the Right Honorable La-war to meet them even at the river's mouth with provision and comforts of all kind." God had delivered De La Warr precisely in time to intercept the boats and return to Jamestown before the Indians destroyed the settlement. How to explain all these remarkable coincidences? There seemed only one plausible answer: "This was the arme of the Lord of Hosts."[16]

But it would take more than faith in God's favor to convince the leaders of the Virginia Company to continue to pour resources and time into their disappointing American investment. After all, their best efforts over four years had hardly produced an inspiring financial success. The company had never turned a profit, and investors remained justifiably skittish about giving away any more of their money. So, the Virginia Company Council "finding the smalnesse of that returne which they hoped should have defrayed the charge of a new supply, entred into a deep consultation." Even after hearing the remarkable tale of Gates's shipwreck and salvation, they still debated whether to try to raise yet more funds or "to send for them home, and give over the action"—in other words to abandon Virginia entirely.[17]

Council members turned to Gates, imploring him "to deale plainly with them." His answer would be key to the future of the American colony. Gates "with a solemne and a sacred oath" assured the council that Virginia would turn a profit.[18]

Although not in the way that he had imagined back in the summer of 1609, Thomas Gates had, with that promise, saved Virginia after all. On his word the Virginia Company Councilors rededicated themselves to the colony, and they never again seriously debated giving up on their New World empire.

With Gates's assurance, Thomas Smythe and the Virginia Company Council in the winter of 1610–11 set themselves to the practical matter of fortifying their colony. Gates gave them cause to think that Virginia had already turned a corner. As Smythe noted in a letter to a likely contributor, "we haue the hopes of good successe." Gates, in addition to his own positive appraisal, brought home private letters from George Somers and Lord De La Warr, as well as an official report from the new governor and his colonial council. All told a similar tale of the prior year, culminating in their shared conviction that "wee are in a good hope to plant and abide" in Virginia. De La Warr's report began by refuting "the aspersions . . . which have bin scattered by malignant and ill-disposed people." While admitting the horrors of the past winter, he assured the Virginia Company Council that their colony still offered great potential, that he had already set it on a right course, and that they could shortly expect a return on their investment.[19]

Of course making money required money. To that end, the heartfelt assurances by *Sea Venture* survivors and company promoters that God stood on the side of English America helped the Virginia Company raise the money essential to their colony's survival. In his preface to the tract *Good News from Virginia*, for example,

Rev. Crashaw pointed out four clear signs that God stood behind English America: the salvation of Somers and Gates; their discovery of the Bermudas; the coincidental arrival of De La Warr in Virginia; and, most strategically, the willingness of investors to continue to fund the colony. Crashaw argued that God called men to invest: "This to do willingly and voluntarily . . . cannot be but the working of God to some higher end than ordinary." Rev. Alexander Whitaker, the author of *Good News from Virginia*, went even further, promising investors, "I dare affirm that by God's assistance your profitable returns shall be of more certainty and much shorter expectation."[20]

Just as they had done in the 1609 fund-raising campaign—but with even more conviction and force—writers working on behalf of the Virginia Company argued that financially supporting Virginia was the duty of good Christians. *A True Declaration of the estate of the Colonie in Virginia*, published by the Virginia Company in 1610, forcefully reminded English subjects of the "dutie of christianitie, to behold the imprinted footsteps of Gods glorie, in every region under heaven." According to *A True Declaration*, while God intended the English to possess America, He required earthly partners. Men and women of faith needed to work hard to bring God's plan to fruition: "Doubt ye not but God hath determined, and demonstrated (by the wondrous preservation of those principal persons which fell upon the Bermudos) that he will raise our state, and build his Church in that excellent climate, if the action be seconded with resolution and Religion." The tract cautioned investors that they should anticipate further sacrifice: after all, what noble achievement "is not sauced with some contingent miserie"?[21] But as publications of the Virginia Company in the coming months and years consistently explained, it remained the inviolable responsibility of English Christians to adventure their money and lives in America, for if they did, "then will God assuredly maintain

His own cause." God had preserved Virginia for the English and "we should so in judgement remember mercy, as to give Virginia againe to God."[22]

After 1610, ministers and promoters depicted the prior set-backs in Virginia as divine tests; faithful Christians should perse-vere in periods of tribulation and would, in the fullness of time, be rewarded by God. God, the promotional writers pointed out, had never abandoned the *Sea Venture*, and so never abandoned Virginia, although English men and women in Bermuda and America in 1609 and 1610 were sorely tested. Even the names of the boats the castaways built to escape Bermuda seemed to con-vey the partnership between man, who showed "patience" in the face of suffering, and God, who, on behalf of a chosen people, of-fered "deliverance."

If London's preachers had been unable in 1609 and 1610 to ex-plain why God would test His chosen people so, the answer seemed clear after the September return of Gates and Newport: God had rescued them against all odds to mark them as His own people, and to show His favor for their mission. Colonial promoters pointed out Biblical precedent for these hard trials. God delivered the English in America just like the Israelites; God "would have his people passe the red Sea and Wildernesse, and then to possesse the land of Canaan." And for those who wanted a speedy resolution to all Vir-ginia's problems came a reminder that God "*makes euery thing beau-tifull in his time.*" Only "the foolishnesse of men" led doubters to ask "why was this so soone, and that so late?"—the clear implica-tion being that skeptics of Virginia questioned God's will.[23] Indeed in the post-1610 propaganda campaign, opponents of the Virginia enterprise were often depicted as in league with the devil. Alexander Whitaker beseeched his countrymen to "be not discour-aged with those many lamentable assaults that the devil hath made against us." And William Crashaw assured his readers that "God will tread Satan under your feet shortly . . . and the ages to come will eternize your names as the 'Apostles of Virginia.' "[24]

In language more often associated with the Puritan colony of Massachusetts Bay, founded years later, ministers and investors wrote passionately of the English people called to a divine mission in America. And they believed that nothing less than the future of their faith and their nation hung on fulfilling that duty: "The eyes of all Europe are looking upon our endeavours to spread the Gospell among the Heathen people of Virginia, to plant an English nation there, and to settle a trade in those parts."[25]

The Virginia Company Council turned to Gates to make this happen. After his triumphant return to London, Gates was celebrated throughout the city as a hero. Sir Ralph Winwood captured the popular sentiment when he proclaimed: "Among the many who have worked hard to carry out this design, there is no one who has done more to advance this business, than . . . Thomas Gates." No one, therefore, seemed better qualified to lead a new expedition to America, "both for his own qualities and for the practical knowledge of those regions which he possesses." And it certainly did not hurt that many Londoners believed Gates had been led through his ordeal "by the Providence of God."[26]

Gates agreed to return to Virginia, and Sir Thomas Dale, who befriended Gates when they fought in Ireland and then served with Gates in the Netherlands, signed on as well. Born into a yeoman family, Dale distinguished himself on the battlefield and then in the eyes of influential men in London, including the Earl of Southampton. He was knighted in 1606. Dale was an ambitious, hard man, who brought to Virginia a rigid military discipline that was equal parts effective and unrelenting.[27]

The efforts that winter to recruit colonists emphasized the exemplary leadership of Gates and Dale. In January, the company distributed a broadside calling for "many honest and industrious men" to join Gates and Dale on their new mission to Virginia. The broadside conceded the colony had endured "such hard successe and the manifold impediments knowne to the World." (The stories about Virginia were such common knowledge that they did not even attempt a refutation.) But the company also promised potential colonists that it still "pleased God . . . [that] the state and businesse of the English Plantation there succeedeth with hope of a most prosperous event." In soliciting shareholders, Virginia Company Council members likewise admitted the colony had endured "manifold disasters" but promised investors that "now, under the government of noble and worthie leaders" Gates and Dale, the colony was being revived and "we trust ere long shall flourish."[28]

The Virginia Company needed to raise thirty thousand pounds for the 1611 expedition; they managed to secure pledges for only eighteen thousand pounds (some paid in installments). This allowed them to send six hundred colonists to Virginia in two waves. Three hundred settlers left with Thomas Dale in March 1611, and the remainder followed in May under the command of Thomas Gates.[29]

Unfortunately, the Virginia Company's troubles hardly disappeared once Dale and Gates launched their fleets. Barely a month after Gates sailed—and with subscriptions still to collect from chary investors—Lord De La Warr unexpectedly showed up in London. De La Warr had never adjusted to the Virginia climate, and he stayed sick the whole time he lived there. He left Virginia on March 28, 1611, only, he insisted, because his health had deteriorated so much that, "I was upon the point to leave the World." He arrived home in June to the disgust of council members. De La Warr immediately began apologizing. On June 22, he wrote the Earl of Salisbury maintaining that only numerous grave illnesses compelled him to sail for home. Now a "perfectly recovered" De La Warr professed his continued devotion to the Virginia enterprise:

"This long and painful sickness of mine hath no whit discouraged me to proceed with the business I have undertaken." He followed up such private apologies by publishing a long "relation" in which he explained his illness and expressed his contrition. But the damage was already done.[30]

Virginia Company leaders felt so frustrated by De La Warr's return because they immediately understood that his abandonment of Virginia would undermine their fund-raising efforts. Sure enough, even De La Warr publicly admitted that "since my comming into England, such a coldnesse and irresolution is bred in many of the Adventurers, that some of them seeke to withdraw those payments, which they have subscribed towards the Charge of the Plantation." Company insiders tried to pitch De La Warr's leaving Virginia as yet another divine test: "God minding to make us know that our arme was yet but flesh, even in the front of his enterprize overthrew the Nobleman by laying such a heavie hand of sicknesse and diseases upon him, that . . . he was forced with griefe of heart . . . and for remedie to save his life, after eight moneths sicknesse to returne for England againe." But his abrupt return nonetheless crippled the company's ability to collect subscriptions. In the fall the company began suing investors, with mixed success. One thing was clear: the days of soliciting subscriptions in London were over. By the summer of 1611, Matthew Somers also arrived home, bearing his famous uncle's body. While Matthew Somers confirmed all the glowing reports about Bermuda, the death of George Somers dealt another hurtful blow to the Virginia Company.[31]

None of this bad news deterred Thomas Smythe and the Virginia Company councilors. In fact, they sought a new charter in early 1612. The third charter expanded the boundaries of their company's holdings to include the Bermuda Islands, which Smythe was already planning to develop as a second colony. The charter stipulated that the extended boundaries included "divers islandes lying desolate and uninhabited, some of which are already made knowne and discovered by the industry, travell, and expences of the said Company." That would, of course, be Bermuda. The Virginia Company assumed ownership of all "landes, groundes, havens, ports, rivers, waters, fishinges, mines and mineralls, . . . gold and silver . . . perles, precious stones, quarries, and all and singuler other commodities, jurisdiccions, royalties, priviledges, franchises and preheminences, both within the said tract of lande uppon the maine and allso within the said iselandes and seas adjoyning." By March 1612, the Virginia Company owned a second colony.[32]

To remedy the problem of raising funds for their first, still badly floundering colony, the council secured rights to run a lottery. Smythe seized on the idea mostly out of desperation. As it turned out, while Londoners no longer wanted to invest their hard-earned money in Virginia, they did like the idea of gambling. A London tailor won the first grand prize of one thousand pounds. Ministers tolerated the gambling, and to everyone's surprise two churches finished as runners-up in the first drawing. In 1615, the game transitioned into "running lotteries" that traveled from town to town across England. King James, who never cared much for them, eventually put a stop to the lotteries in 1621. But for those crucial years, lotteries kept the Virginia Company and its first colony afloat.[33]

Smythe's resolve and imaginative fund-raising did not translate into quick success in America. The Virginia colony's troubles abounded, despite the widely touted leadership of Dale and Gates. Christopher Newport carried Dale to Virginia, arriving on May 10, 1611. Dale immediately replaced George Percy, who had acted as governor since De La Warr's departure. Dale's ascendancy marked the beginning of a new era for the colony and the end of Newport's involvement. Dale and Newport quarreled after Newport criticized Smythe's handling of the company; Governor Dale pulled Newport's beard—apparently an insulting act of aggression—and threatened to hang him. Newport returned to England and was rewarded for his long service to the Virginia enterprise with thirty-two shares in the company. He did not long linger on land, however, and shortly began working for the East India Company. He never again returned to America.[34]

Dale, meanwhile, confronted more of the same old troubles with the colonists. He arrived to find them "growing againe to their former estate of penurie, being so improvident as not to put Corne in the ground." He wrote home complaining about this failure to plant and the settlers' "many omissions of necessary duties." The church, storehouse, stables, and guard house all needed repairs, but the residents spent their days "bowling in the streetes." It seemed clear to Dale that the Jamestown settlers had fallen yet again into idleness, and the entire enterprise suffered as a consequence. He refused to tolerate such ineptitude.[35]

The three hundred settlers and "great store of armor, munition, victuals, and other provision" that Dale brought to Virginia that May helped to stabilize the colony somewhat. Far more importantly, Dale governed according to a new legal system that allowed him to coerce labor. Under threat of violence, "all our men being set to work: some to plant, some to sow corn, and others to build boats and houses."[36]

Presiding over a compulsory labor system was just the first of Dale's many powers. He fully implemented a legal code that essentially put Virginia under martial law. The new regulations originated in the 1610 governorships of Thomas Gates and Lord De La Warr; Dale finalized the laws in 1611. William Strachey, secretary to all three governors, edited and published the code, known as the *Lawes Divine, Morall and Martiall*, when he returned to England in

1612. The strict laws remained in operation in Virginia through 1618.[37]

Discipline and order were the main priorities of the *Lawes Divine, Morall and Martiall*. Disorderly colonists would pay dearly for any insubordination, with public whippings and even executions. Killing livestock became a capital offense, and any person participating in a mutiny or attempting to flee the colony would be summarily executed "with the Armes which he carrieth." The laws also placed significant emphasis on religious observances, which helped promote order. Blasphemy and taking the name of God in vain were criminal offenses, and recidivists could be executed. No one could "demeane" any preacher, under threat of a public whipping. Soldiers enforced church attendance and searched the town for backsliders before every service.[38]

In the fall of 1611, Governor Dale presided over an increasingly regimented and violent government. He unleashed "more invasions and excursions upon the savages." His men ruthlessly "cut down their corn, burned their houses and, besides those which they had slain, brought some of them prisoners to our fort." Dale did not hesitate to turn the violence on wayward colonists, either. While laboring under the governor's oversight to construct a fort at Henrico, several men fled to live with the Indians. When Dale's soldiers caught the runaways, he ordered them executed: "Some he appointed to be hanged, some burned, some to be broken upon wheels, others to be staked, and some to be shot." As George Percy explained it, Dale used these killings "to terrify the rest for attempting the like."[39]

Fear and force became Dale's favored tactics for governing. Not surprisingly, many settlers abhorred Dale and the fact that he ruled by the "most cruel and tyrannous laws, exceeding the strictest rules of martial discipline." Colonists complained bitterly of being forced to work "as slaves in irons" and watching as their friends "for petty offences!—were daily executed." As for the provisions he brought, some scoffed that the food was "of such quality for the most part as hogs refused to eat."[40]

Thomas Gates arrived back in Virginia in early August 1611 with three hundred more colonists, a hundred head of cattle, and "all other manner of provision." He took over the governor's position from Dale, but while Gates seemed less brutal than Dale, his presence in Virginia did little to alter the violent, dictatorial governmental culture. Settlers later complained that "Under this tyrannous government the colony continued in extreme slavery and misery for the space of five years."[41]

If Gates was not as ruthless as Dale, nor was he the man he had been in Bermuda. Forgiveness came less easily to him, and he acted as if he had decided that negotiation usually failed and that force was a better option when dealing with belligerent underlings. Perhaps the death of his wife during her crossing to Virginia in 1611 left him less compassionate. Most likely, his experiences with rebellious castaways in Bermuda and lazy and suffering colonists in Virginia made him ever more certain that rigid enforcement of rules was the only way to save the colony. In any event, he showed little reservation about presiding over a government that whipped people who showed up late for work or criticized their leaders, and executed adulterers, runaways, and unauthorized traders.[42]

Rigid laws and swift punishments did not make Virginia peaceful. From the administrations of Gates and Dale through 1624, when the Virginia Company collapsed and the colony came under royal authority, Virginia continued to be plagued by a myriad of problems. The company never seemed to send the right sort of colonists—those who would work hard and obey the law. Dale complained that among the three hundred he brought in May 1611, "not many give testimony beside their names that they are Christians." Two years later, a Spanish prisoner in Jamestown observed that the men "are badly disciplined" and the colony "abounds with poor people who abhor peace." Company promoters throughout the 1610s and early 1620s continued blaming the errant colonists for Virginia's difficulties. Samuel Purchas faulted the entitled gentlemen who sought ease and glory in America: "because they found not English Cities, nor such faire houses, nor at their owne wishes any of their accustomed dainties . . . neither such plentie of Gold and Silver and dissolute libertie as they expected, had little or no care of any thing, but to pamper their bellies, to fly away with our Pinnaces, or procure their meanes to returne for England." Such complaints were not far off the mark. Despite the extensive religious rhetoric employed to entice settlers to Virginia, those who chose to sail showed little evidence of religious zeal or restraint. From its founding through 1624, Virginia predominately attracted self-interested, acquisitive settlers, concerned with profit more than piety. Company leaders did not systematically follow through on the religious idealism promoted in their recruitment campaigns, either in vetting emigrants or in evangelizing among Indians.[43]

The swamps of coastal Virginia continued to rob these ambitious settlers of their lives. Jamestown remained "seated in somewhat an unwholesome and sickly air . . . and hath no freshwater springs serving the town." Colonists still drank from wells "fed by the brackish river oozing into it." Although the settlement predated the germ theory, William Strachey rightly intuited this was not healthful: "I verily believe the chief causes have proceeded [from the water] of many diseases and sicknesses which have happened to our people." While the mortality rates never replicated the abysmal numbers of 1609 and 1610, the colony remained a place of chronic sickness and swift death. Between 1607 and 1624, 7,000 to 7,200 English subjects migrated to Virginia. The 1625 census counted only 1,232 residents, so that just over one of every seven migrants survived their "adventure" in America.[44]

Nearly everyone who invested money in Virginia lost everything they wagered. In 1616, John Chamberlain believed that the colony "might in time become commodious," but admitted, "there is no present profit to be expected." That long-anticipated time of profitability never came. When the company dissolved in 1624, most investors had never seen a return.[45]

There were, to be certain, reasons to keep hope alive after 1610. Like most everyone who visited Virginia, Lord De La Warr affirmed, "The Country is wonderfull fertile and very rich." The forests offered endless tall trees for crafting ships' masts, and the waterways teemed with fish. Everything he saw seemed to "encourage every good minde to further so worthy a worke." Whatever failings England had brought to its American colony, the environment offered nearly boundless potential.[46]

With each passing year, the colonists seemed to grow a little more adept at using the Chesapeake's natural resources and providing for themselves. In 1616, the Virginia Company touted the fact that the colonists could "maintaine themselves with food."[47] This was certainly a long way from the boundless riches promised in *Nova Britannia*—at once revealing the company's greatly tempered dreams for Virginia and affirming the colony's real viability.

Despite lingering troubles at Jamestown, in the years after 1610 colonists staked out other settlements in the Chesapeake region, and unlike in 1610, they sustained those communities: at Henrico, Charles City, and Kecoughtan. Many of these newer settlements proved far healthier than Jamestown. William Strachey pointed out that the colonists outside Jamestown did not suffer from the same diseases as those in the central settlement. He therefore asked his London readers to not "lay scandal and imputation upon the country of Virginia because the little quarter wherein we are set down (unadvisedly so chosen) appears to be unwholesome and subject to many ill airs."[48]

Virginia held no gold and no passage to the East, but in the 1610s, a *Sea Venture* survivor, John Rolfe, began experimenting with tobacco seeds. In 1617, Rolfe shipped to England the first cargo of the crop that would define Virginia's economy and society throughout the seventeenth century. The ensuing boom made Virginia tobacco planters rich, desperate for a steady labor source, and, in time, masters over a brutal system of racial slavery.[49]

In 1619, shortly after Rolfe's agricultural experimentation set Virginia on a path toward profitability, the Virginia Company designed a new government for the colony, modeled after the English system. The colonial governor and council continued to be appointed by the company in London, but the dictatorial *Laws Divine, Morall and Martiall* were abolished. A locally elected assembly assumed many lawmaking powers. That body, the House of Burgesses, was the first representative assembly in British America. George Yeardley, another survivor of the *Sea Venture* shipwreck, became the first governor under this new system.[50]

After 1610, then, there were reasons both to keep worrying about Virginia's future and to stay hopeful. Religious zeal that had animated so much of the promotional campaign for the *Sea Venture* enterprise may not have always surfaced in the daily conduct of the often desperate Jamestown settlers, but the commitment to ensuring the survival of the colony had clearly gained strength. Whether cynical or sanguine, the Englishmen who wrote about Virginia in the wake of the *Sea Venture* saga never debated pulling out of America. After 1610, although troubles persisted in Virginia—including staggeringly high mortality rates, a violent and deadly offensive launched by the Powhatans in 1622, and the collapse of the company in 1624—the colony had endured the worst. Never again would the situation in the colony grow so bleak as it had in 1609 and 1610, and never again would the settlers and their English backers seriously contemplate abandoning the enterprise.

Part of that resolve came from the colony's (relative) stability after 1611, part from the discovery of tobacco as a profitable commodity, and part from the dedication of company and colonial leaders.

But for the actual participants—those who invested in Virginia and adventured their lives there—it was still something larger than themselves that made them believe in the colony. Many had decided that English America was simply the will of God, and that Virginia would survive, come what may. When Rev. Crashaw considered his confidence in the colony, he concluded, "this work is of God, and will therefore stand, though men should unfaithfully forsake it." Writing in 1616, after burying his second wife, Pocahontas (known then as Rebecca Rolfe), John Rolfe viewed his life in Virginia as "the good blessings of God." Despite his harrowing ordeal on the *Sea Venture* and the loss of two wives and a child, Rolfe saw no reason to doubt Virginia's future. "God's hand" had preserved the colony thus far and so, Rolfe asked, "What need we then to fear but to go up at once as a peculiar people marked and chosen by the finger of God to possess it?" Having endured much of the worst that Virginia could bring, Rolfe kept faith that "undoubtedly He is with us."[51]

The same faith that led Englishmen to see the hand of God guiding their North American enterprise convinced them that He had used the *Sea Venture* to point them toward building a colony on Bermuda. According to Rev. Lewis Hughes, who migrated to Bermuda to minister to the settlers, God had made sure that "all Navigators and Mariners have been carefull to avoid and shunne" Bermuda before 1610, so that the islands could belong to English Christians. From London, William Crashaw shared Hughes's conviction; he told his followers that God had given England "the rightfull possession . . . of so rich so wholesome, and healthfull Ilands, which may be as nurseries to *Virginia*." For years, the English

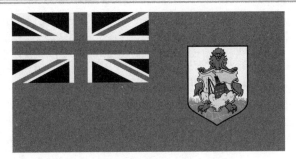

*With their flag, Bermudians commemorate the
shipwreck that gave birth to their country.*

pointed to the "the miraculous delivery" of the *Sea Venture*, which
"by the providence of God miraculously wrack'd and saved upon
the hopeful Sumer Islands," as evidence that God authorized their
presence in the West.[52]

While the *Sea Venture* saga offered up a powerful religious justifi-
cation for staking a claim to Bermuda, the men who considered
funding the enterprise needed to believe that they could profit from
their investment. The stories that the castaways told about Bermuda
echoed the rapturous picture painted by *Nova Britannia*—the islands provided an Edenic environment, ripe for English exploita-
tion. The difference was, with Bermuda the stories were true.
Bermuda did offer "great plentie of woods and loftie Cedars: well-
stored with fowle and great plenty of good fish." The land "would
beare with great encrease, all kind of English grayne, fruites, trees."
Assurances of finding ambergris and pearls, fishing and whaling
commercially, and cultivating lucrative commodities such as sugar,
pineapples, tobacco, and olives all appealed to entrepreneurs anxious to turn a profit in overseas investments. Both London and Virginia buzzed with the exciting prospects of colonizing Bermuda:
"they do not cease praising the good features of this island and its
advantages."[53]

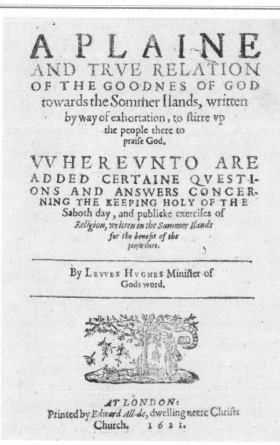

In this 1621 publication, Reverend Lewis Hughes interpreted the wreck of the Sea Venture *as God's design for settling Bermuda.* (COURTESY OF HUNTINGTON LIBRARY)

By the summer of 1611, Londoners had heard so much about Bermuda's idyllic environs that the city's leading businessmen were ready to start a colony there. Because "the place is so opulent fertile and pleasant," many prospective settlers "were willing to go thither."[54]

There were, to be certain, dangerous implications for staking this claim—in particular, antagonizing Spain. By May 1611,

Madrid got word that "many people were minded to go and settle there [Bermuda], and a number had banded together for that very purpose." Spanish officials were outraged by the plans to create a colony on "what is so wholy His Majesty's as that island." King Philip announced his great annoyance "that in all the years since the Indies have been discovered, no one should have thought to make certain of this island." He upbraided his advisers, "clearly, this won't do." The Council of the Indies, which governed Spain's New World colonies, replied to Philip's complaints by explaining, "it was always understood that Bermuda was uninhabitable land," so dangerous that "all have shunned the place. . . . Therefore it was not supposed that any enemy could possibly dare to establish himself there."[55] But the *Sea Venture* wreck had changed all of that: the island chain was safe, bounteous, and quickly becoming English.

Rather than deterring plans for the Bermuda colony, the thought of defying Spain's domination in the Americas seemed to promoters an added incentive, complementing their commercial and religious motivations. "This island," observed John Smith, "is an excellent bit to rule a great horse." Both England and Spain understood that Bermuda lay at the crossroads of the Atlantic. As King Philip's advisers explained, "everything what comes from the Indies must pass to south or north of it." Bermuda was ideally situated to supply English ships making their way to and from America and to raid Spanish vessels, and it provided a potential gateway to further encroachments in the Caribbean. Leaders on the Council of the Indies feared—rightly, it turned out—that if the English established a foothold on Bermuda, "they will continue to spread in those parts . . . from which very grave detriment may result."[56]

Furthermore, once settled and fortified, a Bermudian colony would seem to be unassailable. Like many Londoners, Samuel Purchas heard that Bermuda's coral reefs, with only two narrow

and easily fortified breaks, made the island chain so naturally im-
pregnable "that she would laugh at an Armada, at a World of
Ships." Rev. Lewis Hughes saw the reefs as further evidence of
providential design: "God did then inviron and fortifie them
about, with fearefull Rocks and sholes" that made Bermuda "safe
from forraigne invasion." Regardless of the origins, Bermuda
certainly afforded England a first and tremendous strategic advantage in its nascent rivalry with Spain. In Purchas's mind, Virginia and Bermuda appeared "as two American hands, eares,
feete; two eyes for defence: two keys . . . for offence: two Armes
to get, encompasse, embrace: two Fists to strike."[57]

As Spain weighed their options, London businessmen busied
themselves designing their colony. Thomas Smythe took the lead,
and he wasted little time in preparing to launch this second, more
promising settlement. At first, the Virginia Company Council
thought about calling their newest creation "Virginiola," but then
they thought better of it and settled instead on Somers Island. That
name both conveyed "the continuall temperatayre" of the islands
and honored the memory of George Somers.[58]

Rumors spread through London from time to time that Spain
would send forces "to dismantle the forts of Virginia and of
Bermuda." But Smythe and his compatriots remained undeterred.
Bermuda brought new hope for profits and glory, so that even the
threat of Spanish invasion would not keep them from pursuing
their dreams. Ministers and *Sea Venture* survivors, convinced that
settling Bermuda was divinely ordained, abetted the campaign for
the Somers Island colony. William Crashaw predicted that Bermuda
would "prove a matter of greater consequence than most men think
of, and of more worth than any islands or continent discovered in
our age." Silvester Jourdain promised, "this I say to them that haue
aduentured in Virginia, especially to such as thinke they shall lose
by that worthy action: let them do the like to vs, and I make no

doubt but wee shall in short time giue them satisfaction." And "in short time" Bermuda surely did.[59]

The first voluntary Bermuda colonists left England on April 28, 1612, just a month after the issuance of the third charter of the Virginia Company, which validated the company's claim to the islands. Robert Davis, who sailed with the 1609 *Sea Venture* fleet, commanded the *Plough*. He carried around fifty colonists and Bermuda's first governor, Richard Moore. Governor Moore was a carpenter, not a gentleman, but he had been on board the *Sea Venture* and he knew the islands well. The settlers reached St. George's harbor on Saturday afternoon, July 11, 1612.[60]

"As soone as wee had landed," recalled one colonist, "we went all to prayer, and gaue thankes vnto the Lord for our safe arriuall." But an approaching boat interrupted the settlers' prayers: rowing their way came Christopher Carter, Edward Waters, and Edward Chard. Both the newcomers and three men in the small boat "did much reioyce [rejoice]" at their reunion.[61]

It had been better than a year and a half since Carter, Waters, and Chard had laid eyes on another soul. They joyfully sung a psalm with their countrymen and then shared supper and doubtless hour upon hour of conversation. The "three kings" must have been as anxious to hear news from London as the settlers were to learn about life on Bermuda. Everyone spent Sunday in worship and rest, but on Monday morning the entire company reboarded the *Plough* to visit Carter, Waters, and Chard's settlement. The three had made their home on Smith's Island, located off the coast of St. George's. Using seeds that George Somers had brought from Virginia—still more evidence of his intentions to colonize Bermuda—they grew corn, melons, beans, and tobacco. Having fallen "almost out of hope" of the English ever returning to

Bermuda, they had been in the weeks just prior to the arrival of the *Plough* working on a cedar pinnace they planned to sail to New-foundland. But now they would stay and with the small group of settlers begin to build a colony on Bermuda.[62]

Governor Moore received strict directions from the Virginia Company about leading the colony. "A religious government is to be effected," they charged Moore, and he was to make certain the settlers readied the land for growing crops so as to free the company from "the care and charge of continual supplies from hence." Moore followed through on these expectations. On August 2, he called everyone to his home, where the settlers all signed a compact, pledging to live in Christian harmony and duty to their London backers. The agreement was heavily influenced by convictions of providential destiny, and began with a vow to follow faithfully the "true and euer-liuing God" and the Church of England. All residents of Bermuda would also "set a-part all our owne labours and imploiments" on the Sabbath "and apply our selues to the hearing of Gods word, Prayer, and all other exercises of Religion." They would never take God's name in vain and follow all His laws.[63]

In a strong communitarian ethic that would mark much of Bermuda's early history, the colonists also promised "to the vttermost of our power we will liue together in doing that which is iust [just], both towards God and Man." They mutually pledged "also to liue together without stealing one from another, or quarrelling one with another, or slandering one of another." They affirmed their loyalty to King James and vowed "neuer to reuolt from him . . . but euermore to acknowledge his Supreme Gouernment," and promised to be diligent in meeting their obligations to the investors in London. Finally, if ever invaded by a foreign enemy, they would "fight as true English men, for the defence of the Commonwealth we liue in, and Gospell wee professe, and that whiles we haue breath we will not yeeld to any." Moore sent the compact to

England. Like all of Moore's official correspondence, it would have been marked with his seal: a ring engraved with Sir Thomas Smythe's coat of arms.[64]

But before Moore's seal had even dried, those promises of living together in harmony and for the collective good were already being broken, and by Bermuda's longest residents. Unbeknownst to Governor Moore, Carter, Waters, and Chard had, during their long solitary occupation of Bermuda, found an enormous chunk of ambergris—weighing well over one hundred pounds. Since the substance excreted from sperm whales and used in manufacturing perfume brought £3 per ounce in England, it was worth a fortune, and the "three kings" knew it. They also understood that finders-keepers did not apply to colonial enterprises. The Virginia Company, not them, rightfully owned the ambergris. In fact, the company anticipated that some ambergris might be discovered and their directions to Governor Moore stipulated that he should administer "due punishment" to anyone hiding such a find.[65]

Carter, Waters, and Chard did not turn over their treasure as the law required. Instead, they approached Captain Davis about sneaking it back to England on the *Plough*. But hiding a hundred-pound rock—especially one so extraordinarily valuable—was no easy feat. Moore soon got wind of the conspiracy and interrogated Chard, who had been named one of the six councilors assisting Moore. He denied everything. Carter eventually broke ranks with the other conspirators, several of whom went to jail. The ambergris arrived in London in October 1613. When the Virginia Company sold it, they made enough to recover all their expenses in the Bermuda enterprise, with handsome earnings to spare. In a year, Bermuda had turned a profit; the Virginia enterprise never did.[66]

With the ambergris controversy behind him and the fear of a Spanish invasion looming, Moore turned his attention to building fortifications around the island chain. He also salvaged two cannons from the *Sea Venture* wreck, which along with his forts proved most fortuitous. In December 1613, Spanish ships appeared on the horizon. When the mariners attempted to reach the shores of Bermuda, Governor Moore ordered them fired upon, and they beat a hasty retreat. It later turned out the ships carried peaceful Spaniards only seeking supplies. But the episode confirmed the belief that a fortified Bermuda could easily fend off threats. And that was the only time Bermudians ever had to defend their home from foreign aggression in their nearly four-hundred-year history.[67]

Moore also moved the principal settlement from Smith's Island to St. George's, which remains the oldest continuously inhabited English town in the Western Hemisphere. He experimented with tobacco cultivation, which soon became the centerpiece of Bermuda's growing economy. With Rev. George Keith, an Anglican priest who traveled on the *Plough*, Moore oversaw the building of a church in St. George's and ensured that the settlers followed their pledge to live as faithful Christians.

Once Bermuda was peopled with English Protestants, ministers in London proclaimed, "Now then let the Christian world rejoyce to see, that God is worshipped in the Deuills Ilands, and that English men liue safelie and sweetly there where neuer any liued before them." But religious life on Bermuda did not always proceed according to Anglican plans. From the beginning, Bermuda attracted large numbers of Puritans, who brought to the island their distinctive, dissenting Christian faith. In 1614, Rev. Lewis Hughes, an outspoken preacher with strongly Puritan leanings, joined Rev. Keith on Bermuda. Whereas Keith had adhered to Anglican practices, Hughes made no secret of his dissent. He even crafted his own substitute for the *Book of Common Prayer* and, "by the helpe of God," designed an independent system of church governance.[68]

Rev. Hughes maintained an unshakable faith that God wanted

Bermuda for England and expected devout Bermudians. Hughes beckoned new migrants to "leave their sins behinde them, and come hither as it were into a new world, to lead a new life." But he showed no tolerance for sinners who spurned that advice. Disgusted with a group of "whorish women," Hughes had them dragged behind a boat in St. George's harbor, "to coole them a little." Hughes was quite popular among the laity, but that did not translate into official approval. He twice went to jail, and he repeatedly quarreled—during church services—with Governor Moore's successor, Daniel Tucker.[69] But even with Hughes's escapades and Bermuda's growing reputation as a Puritan haven, settlers in these early years lived in a generally pious, peaceful Christian community, in sharp contrast to their countrymen on the mainland of America.

Certainly the Bermudians confronted, some might even say partly created, their share of problems. Governor Moore's demands that the colonists devote so much of their time to building fortifications meant that they did not farm as much as they should have, and they consequently endured periods of deprivation. A Spanish ship full of grain, seized by English privateers in 1614, solved that problem but created an even worse one. Rats escaped the ship's hold and, lacking any predators whatsoever, soon overran the islands. The rodents devoured the colonists' meager crops, even eating the seed corn as soon as it was put in the ground, and raided their storehouses. Poor Rev. Hughes found they even nibbled on his clothes and shoes.[70]

Political conflicts beset the colony as well as the London companies overseeing it. After three years, Governor Moore ended his service to the Virginia Company with each side feeling "mutuall discontent and distast." The men Moore put in charge when he abruptly left his post proved at best incompetent and quite often corrupt. In early 1616, the newly independent Somers Island Company appointed Daniel Tucker, a five-year resident of Virginia who had survived the starving times, to serve as Bermuda's second governor. Tucker shared Thomas Dale's exacting temperament and instituted many of Dale's draconian laws, which soon earned him the enmity of many Bermudians.[71]

Meanwhile in London, relations among the leading entrepreneurs running the Bermuda colony turned sour. On top of the predictable business conflicts, Thomas Smythe's son, against his father's wishes, married the daughter of Robert Rich, the Earl of Warwick. Smythe and Rich's personal tensions exacerbated their professional rivalry. Within a few years of the founding of the Bermuda colony, factionalism within and between the Somers Island Company and the Virginia Company had "grown so violent," one Londoner reported, the leading men "seldome meet upon the Exchange or in the streets but they brabble and quarrell, so that yf that societie be not dissolved the sooner, or cast in a new mould, worse effects may follow then the whole business is worth."[72]

Yet all these difficulties paled in comparison to the tribulation the Virginians endured. In the 1610s and 1620s, Bermuda emerged as a religiously centered, stable, healthy, fertile, profitable colony— everything that Virginia was not. Between 1612 and 1615, the Virginia Company sent upward of 600 settlers to secure their claim to Bermuda. Nearly all survived. Meanwhile, barely 350 of 1,200 who immigrated to Virginia from 1607 to 1615 still clung to life in the older settlement. In 1615, the Somers Island Company was fully separated from the Virginia Company, and between 1615 and 1622 nearly a thousand more colonists arrived on the islands. The settlers enjoyed a healthy climate and diet and lower mortality rates than their English counterparts. By 1625, nine forts and a militia were in place, ministers led services at six churches, and 2,500 residents were governed in part by an elected assembly. Bermuda, in short, had become a model English colony. The contrast to Virginia could not have been starker. In 1622, the Virginians endured a massive offensive by the Powhatans that killed a fourth of the 1,200 colonists. The Virginia Company collapsed in 1624 under the weight of corruption and infighting, eighteen years of ceaseless economic disappointments, and the deaths of thousands who adventured their lives in America.[73]

One thing England's two colonies, otherwise so intensely different, shared in common was a future wrought by the *Sea Venture*. The *Sea Venture*—both the events surrounding the shipwreck and their providential retelling—paved the way for England's continued commitment to a transatlantic empire: the English would, despite continuing doubts and setbacks, stick by their New World interests, in both Virginia and Bermuda, and weather whatever storms that came. Englishmen who traveled between the worlds of England, Virginia, and Bermuda often marveled at the remarkable confluence of events that unfolded in those three wildly different places in 1609 and 1610. Many decided "that Almighty God . . . hath some great worke of wonder" planned for their nation, and so they kept faith that they and their children and their children's children "*shal say, Blessed bee God that suffered Sir* Thomas Gates *and Sir* George Sommers *to be cast away upon these Ilands.*"[74]

CHAPTER 10

"O BRAVE
NEW WORLD"

The story of the safe deliverance of the shipwrecked *Sea Venture* swept through London in the fall of 1610 with the force of providential truth. For the passengers and crew to have survived the horrific hurricane in the western Atlantic and ten months on an uninhabited "isle of devils," and then to safely arrive in Jamestown to help save the colony after its "starving times" winter—such a journey could only be explained by divine providence. And so the supporters of the Virginia Company in London happily spread the word not only that God was English but also that He had actively intervened to preserve the English presence in the New World.

At first, the public got just the sanitized version of what happened to the *Sea Venture*. Only those portions of the accounts written by William Strachey, Robert Rich, and Sylvester Jourdain that supported this providential perspective were repeated in the company's *True Declaration of the Estate of the Colonie in Virginia*, printed in 1610. The mutinies on Bermuda were conveniently removed and the horrors of Jamestown downplayed in the Virginia Company's version of events. But as much as Strachey liked endearing himself to the high officials of the Virginia Company, he wanted even more to get his story into print. Long before he returned to London in the fall of 1611, presumably because he fell ill from the swampy, disease-ridden environment in Jamestown, Strachey made sure that his *True Reportory* found an audience. He clearly had literary ambitions for the work, which was originally addressed as a letter to an "Excellent Lady" (most likely Dame Sara Smythe, the third wife of Sir Thomas Smythe).[1]

Well before his fateful voyage on the *Sea Venture*, Strachey had developed strong ties to London's theater community. For years he had been a shareholder in the acting company, the Children of the Queen's Revels, which occupied the Blackfriars Theatre. Strachey frequently visited the Blackfriars, and he knew many of the players, playwright Ben Jonson, and quite possibly Shakespeare himself. It was here, among an intimate circle of literary and theater friends—a group whose support and validation he clearly sought—that Strachey likely revealed his escapades on the *Sea Venture* and circulated his written tale of the voyage.[2] Even though he would be thwarted in his literary ambitions—*True Reportory* was not published until 1625, five years after his own death—Strachey's vivid account of the *Sea Venture* odyssey worked its way into London's (and ultimately, the world's) consciousness in an entirely different but unforgettable way: through the imagination of William Shakespeare.

On November 1, 1611, at the spectacular Whitehall Palace, King James sat with an audience to watch the opening production of a new play by Shakespeare, as performed by his troupe of actors, the King's Men. It was called *The Tempest,* Shakespeare's last play that he wrote alone.[3] Shakespeare almost certainly read—or learned the substance of—Strachey's (as well as Jourdain's) graphic story of the horrendous hurricane and near-fatal sinking of the *Sea*

Venture and the wondrous "ease and plenty" the castaways found in Bermuda. While *The Tempest* touched on many other themes related to power and magic, art and nature, the remarkable story of the *Sea Venture* and the castaways' odyssey in Bermuda offered unmistakable inspiration for Shakespeare's enchanted play.

At the level of plot, *The Tempest* may not immediately suggest the world of the *Sea Venture*. Simply put, the play revolves around the magical ruler Prospero, whose throne has been unjustly usurped by his brother; Prospero has been sent into exile with his daughter, Miranda. Suffused in spectacle and the supernatural, *The Tempest* tells the tale of Prospero's quest, while stranded on a strange, distant island, to reestablish justice by restoring himself to power. Most interesting is the location and nature of Prospero's exile where the magical story plays out. *The Tempest* opens, just as with the dramatic odyssey of the *Sea Venture*, in the middle of a torrential storm, when a ship crashes and wrecks on a mysterious island. The powerful opening shipwreck scene amid a wild hurricane, the scenarios of providential deliverance, the very title of the play—all clearly allude to the *Sea Venture* wreck. Parallels between the play and the shipwrecked castaways abound. Both in the play and in Bermuda, no one drowned. ("But are they, Ariel, safe?" Prospero asks. "Not a hair perished," he replies.) We later learn that the storm had been conjured up by Ariel, a spirit under Prospero's command who haunted the ship in the form of the very same St. Elmo's fire that Strachey witnessed in the middle of the fateful hurricane. And, as in the ship's near-tragic ending, in *The Tempest,* the mariner Stephano and his companions find solace in a liquor supply.[4]

Although presumably set in the Mediterranean, *The Tempest* ultimately becomes Atlantic in meaning. The island is inhabited by a "brutish" native, Caliban, and the spirit Ariel. The play clearly evokes the landscape and issues of England's American colony, including the master-servant relationship between Prospero and Caliban.[5]

One can imagine that members of the Virginia Company of London in the audience at Whitehall would have found many familiar New World allusions in the words, phrases, and locations Shakespeare invoked throughout play. Most notable of the Bermuda references comes when Ariel refers to their island home as the "still-vexed Bermoothes." Gonzalo, the faithful counsel to King Alonso in the play, uses the colonial word "plantation"—the only time that word is ever used in Shakespeare's work. Shakespeare was clearly interested in the Bermuda experiences of Strachey and Jourdain; in *The Tempest* he made creative use of their obsession with tempests, shipwrecks, and mutinies, as well as in descriptions of exotic fish and fowl, native peoples, manners, and music.[6]

While romantic and theatrical issues surface throughout *The Tempest,* we should not forget the importance of the timing of the play's production. It was first staged in 1611, a significant moment when England was encountering "other" peoples and struggling to determine the boundary between "civilized" and "savage"—both in Ireland and America. Imperial power was clearly in the wind, both in England's emerging American empire and in the play's conceits.[7] Sebastian tells the audience at one point: "I think he [Prospero] will carry this island home in his pocket and give it to his son for an apple." Prospero, like the English nation itself, was getting into the colonizing business. He possesses the island and enslaves the primitive native, Caliban, who is seen as a "thing most brutish" belonging to a "vile race." Indeed, as many scholars have noted, the very name, Caliban, seems to be a play on the word "cannibal." To be sure, Shakespeare drew on other texts, such as Michel de Montaigne's 1603 essay, "Of the Cannibals," that likely influenced his thinking, but many Shakespeare experts maintain that Caliban's character marks the first American Indian depicted on an English stage.[8]

Near the end of the play, Miranda, upon her triumphant marriage to Ferdinand and her father's victory over his opponents, utters what could well be the play's signature comment on the new and startling human landscape English settlers were encountering: "O, wonder! How many goodly creatures are there here! How beauteous mankind is! O brave new world that has such people in 't!"[9]

Some of the play's appeal lay simply in the exotic world of faraway places. Fanciful accounts of overseas voyages circulated widely in London's literary circles. Both Shakespeare and his audience found common ground in these exploration tales. Ferdinand Magellan's circumnavigation voyages, for example, were full of stories of mutinies and miracles. But few carried the sense of immediacy and special interest for Londoners that could be found in the stirring account of the *Sea Venture* wreck in Bermuda. In combining history and romance, therefore, Shakespeare dramatized what his contemporaries had lived.[10]

Shakespeare was personally well connected to those adventuring in the west. He knew many colonial enthusiasts, such as Sir Humphrey Gilbert and Lord De La Warr; Richard Hakluyt was a personal friend. He also associated with officials of the Virginia Company. His principal patron, the Earl of Southampton, served as a key promoter of Virginia, as did other friends such as the Earl of Pembroke.[11]

Much of what defined the experiences of these enterprising men, Shakespeare's contemporaries, was the crossing itself: the powerful, unpredictable Atlantic. From the opening sequence, *The Tempest* is drenched in sea spray. Watery images pervade the story. The mariners enter "wet" in the first scene; Miranda is reduced to tears worrying over the fate of the sailors caught up in the "wild waters"; Alonso, fearing that his son is dead, decides to drown himself. And then there is the tempest itself, whose ferocious waters not only destroyed the ship but also seem to course through the entire play.

An Atlantic crossing in this era was rife with danger and unpredictability, whether or not it was disrupted by a "tempest." Moving from the Old World to the New not only put lives at risk; such a crossing often proved transformative, freeing men and women from an ordered life to confront in a foreign setting their more primitive, violent, and even rebellious natures. Thus, some of the passengers on the *Sea Venture* after being shipwrecked on Bermuda felt liberated to challenge the authority of Gates and Somers. The mutinies of John Want and Stephen Hopkins, the embrace of solitude of the "three kings of Bermuda"—all these represented but extreme versions of a less restrictive, less ordered, alternative world made possible by an Atlantic crossing.[12] And likewise, men such as Gates and Newport found in the shipwreck and their months on Bermuda a powerful need to deepen their commitment to authority, loyalty, and the mission to Virginia. Stranded between two worlds, one familiar and ordered, the other distant and chaotic, the passengers and crew of the *Sea Venture*, like Miranda, must have marveled—with both alarm and wonder—at the "brave new world" into which they had been tossed "that has such people in 't."

If Shakespeare's fictional tempest presented a special sort of Atlantic crossing, the real experiences of those who funded, promoted, and sailed on board the *Sea Venture* suggest that the actual tempest they encountered transformed their lives in ways every bit as dramatic as Prospero conjured up on stage.

The larger meaning and importance of the *Sea Venture*'s odyssey can be revealed, at least in part, through a glimpse into the arc of the lives of its principal characters. What the *Sea Venture* passengers made of this new, increasingly international Atlantic world—and what it made of them—speaks volumes about how this little-known shipwreck story deeply affected the initial spread of English America.[13]

Many of the *Sea Venture* promoters, passengers, and crew lived expansive, successful lives, while others found themselves, literally and figuratively, at sea. An entrepreneur like few others, Thomas Smythe served as the energetic and resolute link between London's rising merchant community and the English government. Without him, England's overseas empire would never have taken off when it did. As Samuel Purchas noted, it was "our honourable Smith . . . at whose forge and anvill have beene hammer'd so many irons for Neptune."[14]

In the years after the redemption of Jamestown, Smythe remained a powerful force in the emerging English empire. Despite suffering from ill health after 1615 and wishing to retire from most of his positions, he continued his involvement in London's leading merchant companies, holding meetings and keeping records at his house on Philpot Lane. In 1616, he helped finance yet another voyage to search for the Northwest Passage.

Dissension, though, continued to tear at the ranks of the Virginia Company and by 1618, Smythe found himself in a three-way fight that pitted most of the leading gentry under Robert Rich against a faction under Sir Edwin Sandys and Smythe's own group of merchants. Both Rich's and Sandys's parties were jealous over the wealth that Smythe's group had acquired and the control the merchants held over governing England's far-flung empire. So they came together to displace Smythe, making Sandys the new head of the Virginia Company. Smythe's critics complained bitterly of his supposed "foule deallinge" as head of the Virginia Company and charged him with egregious mismanagement: "the business was carryed Unjustly; covertly; without Accompts given." Smythe was ultimately forced to submit to an audit of the company's accounts. As it turned out, Smythe was exonerated while his successor Sandys was condemned for malfeasance.[15]

Though Smythe never set foot in any of the American colonies, he did so much to fund and promote them that he left a permanent legacy for English settlers who made the Atlantic crossing. He not only served as governor of the Somers Island Company from 1615 to 1621, he also gave his name to the island on which the "three kings" built their settlement and one of Bermuda's parishes. Smith's Island, near Cape Charles, Virginia, was also named for Thomas Smythe, as were many other capes and sounds: "His name was justly engrafted on land and water in the highest latitudes reached by man in his day."[16]

Though beset by criticism, Smythe remained a member of the Virginia Company Council until its dissolution in 1624. He died the next year, probably from the plague. Despite the tumult in his final years, Smythe ended his life on a philanthropic note— providing in his will a four-penny loaf of bread apiece for every week to thirty-six of London's most underprivileged citizens along with a winter garment for each, and donating money to educate poor children. He left five hundred pounds to the Muscovy Company and one hundred pounds to build churches in Bermuda and Virginia. He also gave an annual bequest to be distributed by the Skinners' Company, a guild to which he belonged and that had helped finance the voyage of the *Sea Venture* fleet.[17]

A successor to Smythe as treasurer of the Virginia Company and patron to Shakespeare, Henry Wriothesley, the Earl of Southampton, like so many others in London's influential circle of rich merchants and literary types, devoted much of his life to overseas adventures. Part profligate, part leading nobleman, and enormously rich and well connected, Southampton took an early interest in the

Virginia Company. And like many of Virginia's early leaders, Southampton loved both the theater and the military: he spent time in the Netherlands fighting with the Dutch against Spain; in 1609, he not only helped finance the *Sea Venture* voyage but also helped found the East India Company. He contributed to financing Henry Hudson's tragic voyage in 1610 to discover the Northwest Passage. Finally, he joined Smythe and others and became an investor in the Somers Island Company. Upon his death in 1624, Southampton was celebrated for his "singular wisedome providence and care and much Noble paynes and Industrie and with unquestionable integritie."[18]

Like Smythe, Southampton's name lives on both in Bermuda and Virginia: Southampton parish in Bermuda honors him, and in a sort of "mutilated immortality," half of his name is commemorated in the city of Hampton, Virginia. The adjacent harbor of Hampton Roads came originally from what was called in the seventeenth century the Southampton (or Hampton) River.[19]

Closely linked with the literary associates of the London-based Virginia enterprise, William Strachey sought in his post–*Sea Venture* career to make his mark by getting his version of the adventures in Bermuda and Virginia into print. After returning to London in 1611, he began writing *The History of Travel into Virginia Britannia,* a compilation of writing that borrowed from previous authors of popular voyage literature, from Richard Hakluyt's *Voyages* to John Smith's *Map of Virginia*.[20] While he lived in Virginia, Strachey determined to be an honest "Remembrancer of all accidents, occurrences, and undertakings." Unlike his fellow *Sea Venture* survivor Silvester Jourdain, whose propagandistic *A Discovery of the Bermudas* ignored the mutinies on the islands and the horrific conditions in Jamestown, Strachey wrote a colorful description of the country as well as a detailed narrative of explorations and settlement from Raleigh's first voyage in 1584 to the failed effort to settle New England in 1606.

While drawing heavily on Smith's *Map of Virginia*, Strachey nonetheless contributed valuable firsthand reports from his experiences in the colony, especially relating to the Indians.[21]

Despite being one of the most clear-eyed and vivid witnesses to the adventures in Bermuda and early Virginia, Strachey would find his literary ambitions thwarted at nearly every turn. Because his *History* was as critical of Virginia as the *True Reportory* he had composed in 1610, the Virginia Company refused to publish it. He dedicated his first manuscript to the Earl of Northumberland in 1612 and over the next six years produced two additional versions of the work. But his *History* would not make it into print for over two centuries; the Hakluyt Society published it in 1849. As was the case so often in the creation of the foundational story for Virginia, John Smith beat Strachey to the punch. Smith's account of Virginia took root and shaped perceptions about the early years in the colony that last until today. Strachey, our most revealing guide to the odyssey of the *Sea Venture* and so much else in early Virginia, died of unknown causes in Surrey in June 1621, indebted and poor.[22]

Unlike Strachey, some of the leaders of the *Sea Venture* found their crossing brought enormous gain in stature and influence. Sir Thomas Gates and Captain Christopher Newport remained international men of empire to the ends of their lives, and both made their mark as Virginia Company loyalists. A lifelong military man, Gates brought his company from the Netherlands with him on board the *Sea Venture* in 1609. Despite losing his wife on a voyage to Jamestown in 1611, Gates remained committed to the Virginia enterprise. As governor following Sir Thomas Dale, he established the authority of the Church of England and fortified the new settlement at Henrico, named after King James's son Prince Henry. Gates sailed to England in April 1614 and shortly afterward returned to his post in Holland. By 1619, he was again working with the Virginia Company, and the following year he was named to the council establishing the

Plymouth colony in New England. Gates's final years are difficult to document, but he appears to have traveled back to the Low Countries in 1621 and perhaps died there. He was granted five thousand acres in Virginia in honor of his faithful service to the colony.[23]

Several years before Gates died, Sir Edwin Sandys spoke before the Court of the Virginia Company, proclaiming Gates "had the Honour to all Posterity of being the first named in his Majesty's Patent and Grant of Virginia." And in an eloquent commentary on both the trials and triumphs of this most determined leader, Sandys recalled that Gates "was also *the first* that, by his Wisdom, Industry, and Valour, accompanied with exceeding Pains and Patience, in the Midst of Many Difficulties, had laid the foundation of the present prosperous State of the Colony."[24]

Christopher Newport made his last voyage to Virginia in March 1611, carrying Thomas Dale, the new governor. He spent three months building a bridge at Jamestown. But an altercation with Dale abruptly ended Newport's stay. He sailed to England on August 20, 1611, never again to return to America. But as an inveterate ship captain, he spent the rest of his life in the employ of England's expanding overseas empire. From 1612 on, he served the East India Company, making three voyages to Bantam on the isle of Java. He carried ambassadors to Persia and India and, as always, earned respect for the efficiency and profitability of his voyages. In one of his trips to Bantam, in which he carried Ambassador Thomas Roe, we catch a rare glimpse of Newport's command style as something of a benevolent dictator. Though Roe was a former sea commander himself, Newport would not truck with Roe conducting any part of the voyage. Roe complained: "It goes against my stomach (that am very moderate) to be denied a candle, or a draught of beer of a steward, without asking the captain's leave: whom yet, I must say, used me well: but loved that I should know his authority, and then denied me nothing."[25]

Christopher Newport commanded ships that ranged the Atlantic and Pacific oceans. He was one of the first Englishmen to explore the Chesapeake Bay and the James River, the Persian Gulf, and the Sind River in India. Early in 1617, he sailed from London on a third voyage to India, commanding the *Hope*. He arrived safely at Bantam but passed away a few days later, on September 1, 1617. Captain Newport died as he had lived: "The admiral of Virginia," an early historian noted, "lived on the ocean; he died on the ocean; the ocean is his tomb." At a meeting of the Virginia Company of London on November 17, 1619, lands were set aside in Newport's honor on the James River. Newport News bears his name.[26]

If for men such as Smythe and Southampton, Gates and Newport, the adventuring in Bermuda and Virginia enlarged their influence and provided them a valuable legacy, for others the experience seemed to undo them. Men such as George Percy and Lord De La Warr found frustration and failure more than contentment and success.

George Percy had come to Virginia as a well-traveled younger son of a prominent English family. He spent most of his adult life seeking fame in England's far-flung empire. But Virginia all but ruined him. During the horror of the "starving times" and in the treacherous and bloody relations with the Indians, Percy failed as Virginia's governor. Apparently troubled by epilepsy and other ailments as a child, he continued to be enfeebled both as a governor and a man. With his recurring illnesses, he returned to England in April 1612. In 1615, he considered joining a voyage to the Amazon delta, where he thought his health might improve. Meanwhile, his financial fortunes suffered as well: creditors pursued him relentlessly for payment of debts run up years before. The final blow came with Percy's sullied reputation, especially at the hands of John Smith who, since returning from Virginia, busied himself publishing memoirs of his American experiences. Like others,

Percy tried to correct Smith's "many untruths," composing his own account of events in Virginia to counter Smith's self-congratulatory perspective. But Smith's version triumphed over Percy's, just as it did Strachey's. At the end of his life, with dreams of glory fading, Percy turned to the military, commanding a company when war broke out in the Netherlands in 1627. He had a finger shot off in battle and died unmarried in 1632 at the age of fifty-two.[27]

For Thomas West, the Lord De La Warr, Virginia offered at least one shining moment of fame and great achievement. On June 10, 1610, De La Warr's climactic, perfectly timed arrival in Jamestown conjured up a majestic ceremony in assuming office: surrounded by fifty red-cloaked servants and standing before the bedraggled settlers and ruined fort of Jamestown, De La Warr, along with Gates and the survivors of the *Sea Venture*, made a heroic imprint on early Virginia. But that would be the height of De La Warr's glory; he spent only ten months in America, much of it holed up on his ship, sick with fevers, diarrhea, and scurvy. His ailments forced his unplanned return to England in March 1611, which distressed Virginia Company officials and their investors. Without him, various deputy governors—Gates, Dale, and Argall—assumed control of the colony. De La Warr distinguished himself only in some brutal moments with Indians; perhaps fittingly, De La Warr died at sea on June 7, 1618, en route to Virginia to quell yet another political crisis in the colony.[28]

English America unleashed opportunities that for some led to personal destruction. Few men found the "ease and plenty" of Bermuda more alluring and, ultimately, more unsettling, than Robert Waters. Caught up in one of the early mutinies on the island and guilty of killing another sailor in a dispute, Waters had been spared by the humane intervention of George Somers. Fearing the wrath of Gates if he went to Jamestown, Waters chose solitude on Bermuda when the *Patience* and *Deliverance* sailed on to Virginia.

When George Somers died on Bermuda in the fall of 1610, Waters again refused to go to Virginia, instead sailing with Matthew Somers to England. There he worked for the East India Company and died at sea during a voyage to East India in August 1614. Haunted by the murder he committed and homeless but for the sea, Waters found himself "long diseased in bodie . . . [and] in minde by torment of conscience."[29]

Another soul driven to mutiny during the *Sea Venture* odyssey, Stephen Hopkins, the devout Puritan who challenged the authority of Gates on Bermuda, spent two years in Jamestown as a presumably loyal employee of the Virginia Company before returning to England. But, once liberated from authorities, Hopkins determined to keep his liberty. And so when a group of radical English Separatists (known as Pilgrims) organized a venture to New England in 1620, Hopkins, this time with his entire family, including his pregnant wife, Elizabeth, his son Giles, and daughters Constance and Damaris, along with two servants, boarded the *Mayflower*. Hopkins joined a group on board who made "discontented and mutinous speeches" insisting, "when they came ashore they would use their own liberty, for none had power to command them." Although he brought to bear useful experience with the Indians from his days in Virginia, Hopkins distinguished himself early on in the Plymouth Colony as a leader of discontented rabble-rousers. His initial Atlantic crossing that had crashed on Bermuda and erupted in a mutinous search for personal liberty finally found a healing expression a decade later, when as a Pilgrim, Hopkins's diplomatic efforts helped create the first Thanksgiving of peace with the Indians.[30]

Those who wagered their lives in Virginia found that, despite their best intentions, they had not made a wise bet. This was especially true for men like Gabriel Archer and John Ratcliffe. Archer, who had piloted the *Blessing* in the *Sea Venture* fleet, died, as did so many others, during the winter of 1609–10. Ratcliffe fell victim to a more persistent problem in Virginia: angry relations with the Indians. His grisly death by flaying only underlined the dangerous nature of English-Indian encounters.[31]

For a few, living among the Indians offered the ultimate transformation in the New World. Henry Spelman, the teenager whom John Smith sold to the Indians in 1609, stayed with Powhatan for more than a year before returning with De La Warr to England in March 1611. But Virginia beckoned again to Spelman; he returned and worked as an interpreter in 1616. He rose to the rank of captain thanks to his language skills, as he "knew most of the kings of that country, and spake their Languages very understandingly." But Spelman learned the hard way that trying to live between two antagonistic cultures placed him on precarious ground. Shortly after the Virginia colonists inaugurated the first representative assembly in the New World in July 1619, the House of Burgesses tried Henry Spelman for making derogatory comments about Governor Yeardley when negotiating with the new principal chief Opechancanough. Spelman had apparently spoken to Opechancanough "very unreverently and maliciously against this present Governor." Spelman denied the charge but his accuser, a fellow interpreter, testified that he "had in him more of the Savage then of the Christian." Despite "several and sharp punishments . . . pronounced against him by diverse members of the Assembly," he got off with a lenient sentence, losing his rank as captain. Spelman's ultimate punishment, though, came a few years later in March 1623. While trading with Indians living along the Potomac, he was beheaded by them.[32]

As for Powhatan, whom Spelman had served for a time, the arrival of unwelcome English settlers sent him and his people spiraling into a descent. Although initially Powhatan appeared to be winning the battle against the encroaching English—having nearly decimated the Jamestown garrison by starving them out in 1609 and 1610—he in fact lost ground in the early 1610s through attrition and the desertion of key allies. Meanwhile, increasing numbers of white settlers poured into Virginia, and he saw that his men could not expel them. Powhatan agreed to a short-lived peace in 1614 and reluctantly consented to the marriage of his daughter Pocahontas to John Rolfe. By 1617, Powhatan, now in his seventies and disheartened, surrendered power to his more militant kinsman Opechancanough. The next year Powhatan died in seclusion, his world turned upside down. According to his adversary John Smith, Powhatan posed a profound question to the colonists: "What will it availe you to take . . . by force [what] you may quickly have by love, or to destroy them that provide you food. What can you get by warre?"[33]

The *Sea Venture* survivor who in the fateful confrontation with the Indians chose love over war was John Rolfe. Few men lost and gained so much in this momentous Atlantic voyage. In Bermuda he and his first wife welcomed a baby girl, aptly named Bermuda, who died on the island. Then, shortly after arriving in Virginia in May 1610, Rolfe lost his wife. Within a few years he met Powhatan's daughter, Pocahontas, while she was being instructed in the Christian faith and English customs. Rolfe, a deeply religious man of Calvinist leanings, wrote an impassioned letter to Governor Dale outlining the less than romantic justifications for the marriage: "for the good of this plantation, for the honour of our countrie, for the glory of God, for my owne salvation, and for the converting to the true knowledge of God and Jesus Christ, an unbelieving creature, namely Pokahuntas."[34] They were married April 5, 1614. Two years later, at the end of a trip to England exhibiting Pocahontas (now renamed Rebecca) as an exotic Indian princess, she died. Rolfe returned alone to Virginia, leaving behind his young son Thomas, whom he had named in honor of Governor Dale. Back in Virginia, Rolfe served the colony as secretary and member of the governor's council. He married a third and final time; his last wife, Jane, was the daughter of William Pierce who had sailed on the *Blessing* in the *Sea Venture* fleet. Rolfe died in 1621, on the eve of the colony's most vicious Indian war—led by Opechancanough, half brother of the recently deceased Powhatan, Rolfe's former father-in-law. While very little came of Rolfe's attempt to bridge the gulf between settlers and Indians through his marriage to Pocahontas, he undeniably helped launch Virginia's economic future through his successful cultivation of tobacco. And he clung tenaciously to the providential view of his venture to Virginia, always seeing divine intervention at work in keeping himself and the colony alive. "God's hand," Rolfe insisted, "hath been mighty in the preservation" of Virginia.[35]

No one pointed more forcefully to God's work in Virginia than Rev. Richard Buck. From his prayers on board the *Sea Venture* and makeshift religious services in Bermuda to the new church built for him in Jamestown ("wholly at the charge of the inhabitants of that cittie"), Buck offered a daily testimony to how, thanks to this Atlantic voyage, God and England were working wonders in America. According to John Rolfe, over whose wedding Buck presided, Rev. Buck was "a verie good preacher." William Crashaw and Thomas Gates similarly praised his piety and devotion. And well they should have: few men worked harder to deepen the Christian presence in English America. In perhaps the crowning moment of Buck's career, the first General Assembly of English representatives convened in America on July 30, 1619, in Buck's new church. As one witness observed, "forasmuche as men's affaires doe little prosper where God's service is neglected, all the Burgesses stood in their places, untill a prayer was said by Mr. Bucke, that it would please God to guide and sanctifie all our proceedings to his owne glory and to the good of the Plantation."[36]

The unmistakable goal of the *Sea Venture* voyage may have been to save Virginia, but as we have seen, the shipwreck and subsequent ten months on Bermuda ignited among some men a powerful desire for the "ease and plenty" of a different destination. The unexpected crash landing awakened new hopes for life on this tropical, uninhabited island chain, and the men drawn to Bermuda left a legacy of ambition and affection for their accidental home.

Christopher Carter, one of the "three kings of Bermuda," spent his years chasing wealth and happiness on Bermuda. It is not known how well he succeeded, but in his death there is perhaps a clue to the precarious path he followed. On April 15, 1623, the *Seaflower*, bound for Virginia from England, stopped over in Bermuda. It had been "a bad trip out, and, after dropping anchor in Castle Harbour, the passengers were glad to disembark and to spend some time on shore." Several members of the crew, along with some Bermudians, including Christopher Carter and his wife, boarded the ship for an impromptu party with the "locals supplying Tobacco and the crew supplying *aquavitae.*" One of the partygoers, "by negligence of their fire blew up the ship," killing fourteen people. Among the dead were Carter and his wife. An accidental landing had first brought Carter to Bermuda, and he was the only one of the *Sea Venture* castaways who never left. Years later, another shipboard accident ended his life on the island.[37]

The second of the "three kings," Edward Chard, largely disappears from the historical record not long after the surrender of the ambergris in 1612. But we do know a bit about the third "king,"

Edward Waters, longtime assistant to George Somers. Waters had likely imagined that he would acquire land and start an independent life on Bermuda as compensation for his devotion to Somers. But with Somers's death in November 1610 and the seizure of the ambergris in 1612, Waters soon found himself without either a grateful patron or a profit source. He left Bermuda for Virginia in 1618, got married, and had two children before dying near Elizabeth City in 1629. Although eventually he built a life in Virginia, his years of loyalty to Somers at sea and on the Bermuda islands went unpaid.[38]

Another *Sea Venture* passenger, the carpenter Richard Moore, found distinction for himself on Bermuda. Moore became the colony's first governor in 1612, and he immediately focused on creating a town on St. George's Island, building forts for protection and enough houses to shelter the settlers, and cultivating a profitable tobacco crop. He also insisted that settlers strictly adhere to Church of England practices, keep the Sabbath, express loyalty to King James, and promise never to embezzle the profitable goods of the island. Here, like Carter, Waters, and Chard, he was thinking of ambergris. When Virginia Company officials got wind of the remarkable chunk of ambergris found in Bermuda, they ordered Moore to immediately send it all to them. Moore cleverly decided to ship only a third, realizing that the ambergris was "the onely loadstone to draw from England still more supplies." A few months later another ship arrived from London demanding the remaining ambergris. After meditating on this order, Governor Moore sent a second third, keeping the rest for himself and the settlers in Bermuda. Moore's defiance angered the cash-poor Virginia Company, but London promoters had to be excited at what they received: the ambergris that Moore sent to England fetched over eight thousand pounds—an enormous sum that made the Bermuda part of the Virginia Company's western enterprise profitable in less than a year! After completing his three-year term,

Governor Moore left Bermuda and returned to England, having learned the importance of good leadership in a distant colony: privileging the care of matters close to home over the financial demands of faraway promoters and investors.[39]

The story of the *Sea Venture* was only a small part—but a pivotal moment—in England's early efforts in the Atlantic world. Before 1610, England's attempts at colonization had nearly all met with disaster, from Roanoke to Jamestown. But the shipwreck, the castaways' experience in Bermuda, and their timely arrival in Jamestown helped inspire a wave of English expansion in the New World. Just when Virginia seemed doomed to failure, the passengers and crew of the *Sea Venture*, aided by the propitious arrival of Lord De La Warr, breathed critical new life into the enterprise. From that moment on, whatever problems remained—and there were many—England never again seriously considered abandoning its overseas "plantation" in America. And from there English settlement expanded with little hesitation. A few short years after the *Sea Venture* odyssey, England planted colonies throughout the West Indies. Despite the strong Spanish presence in the Caribbean, the English, after their successful settlement of Bermuda in 1612, spread their own colonies throughout the islands. Within twenty years of colonizing Bermuda, the English oversaw successful colonies in the Leeward Islands, St. Kitts, Barbados, Nevis, Montserrat, and Antigua, while sharing portions of St. Croix and the Virgin Islands with the Dutch. Meanwhile, on mainland North America, English settlers founded Plymouth Colony in Massachusetts and Connecticut. By the 1660s, the English colonies were in place in New York, New Jersey, Pennsylvania, Jamaica, and Carolina.

Fueling much of this expanding empire in the early years were the private resources of wealthy merchants like Sir Thomas Smythe and the individual ambitions of countless promoters and settlers, rather than any sort of grand imperial design from the king or Parliament. It was an empire that grew from the bottom up, so that the personal desires of a Lewis Hughes or Christopher Carter on Bermuda, or those of Rev. Richard Buck or John Rolfe in Virginia, sometimes meant as much as the goals of political leaders like Thomas Gates or Thomas Smythe.[40] And, as the remarkable experience of the *Sea Venture* reveals, we should not forget the power of unexpected and unintended events in shaping the course of English America.

Colonial Virginia's path would continue to be filled with tumult and conflict. In *The Tempest*, Shakespeare unknowingly anticipated much of what would play out in the struggles over race and power in the New World. Indeed, much of what took place on stage in Shakespeare's visionary play served as a metaphor for English perceptions of native peoples. Since the 1580s, Londoners had seen their share of Indians—when English explorers kidnapped them and brought them back to England to display them like exotic exhibits. Likewise, in *The Tempest*, Stephano contemplates capturing the native islander Caliban: "If I can recover him and keep him tame, and get to Naples with him, he's a present for any emperor." Depicted in these spectacles as barbarous savages prone to cannibalism, Indians were believed to embody all things heathen and uncivilized—all of which served to embolden English explorers already feeling entitled by an imperialistic culture to conquer and dominate them. *The Tempest* gives voice to this spirit of colonial power. Prospero, we learn, had "most strangely" landed on the island "to be the lord on 't." His dreams and ambitions, like those of so many colonists, propelled him to seize the island and dispossess Caliban.[41]

What Shakespeare, of course, could not have imagined was how violent the racial struggle would become in Virginia. A ferocious war with the Indians in 1622 nearly decimated the colony, worsening relations between settlers and Indians. John Rolfe's successful experimentation with tobacco both saved the colony's economic future and opened the door to slave labor, forever altering Virginians' perceptions of race and power.[42]

Virginia's tobacco fields, worked by poor English servants in the early seventeenth century, were, by the turn of the eighteenth century, converted to plantations cultivated by African slaves. Once the colony's white tobacco barons began extracting rich profits from their plantations, Virginia would finally pay off, even more handsomely than the Virginia Company's propagandists had originally envisioned—but at the expense of enslaved black laborers.[43]

Bermuda benefited for a time from its enticing reputation for "ease and plenty." As one early settler observed, the island's environment was "agreeable to our English constitutions." Life expectancy was high, and infant and child mortality rates extremely low; Bermuda was a place where young children "doe thrive and grow up exceeding well." But the shortage of available land proved to be a disincentive for immigration of English servants. And with many other colonies to consider, over time few chose Bermuda. Even earlier than Virginia, Bermuda began relying upon slaves, mainly from the West Indies, as well as imported Indian laborers, to work the islands' tobacco fields. Company investors, familiar with slavery in Spanish America, introduced slavery on Bermuda by 1616. The idyllic climate, fertile tobacco plantations cultivated by slave labor, and generally pious, self-sufficient English settlers all helped guarantee early, strong success for Bermuda.[44]

Company restrictions on shipping and travel would ultimately leave Bermudians isolated from the England their parents had left behind. Increasingly, Bermuda would be drawn into the much closer orbit of the West Indies and England's North American colonies. Eventually, Bermuda evolved into an economy heavily dependent on tourism. But even today, four hundred years removed from the *Sea Venture*, the connections to this much earlier world of London dreams and shipwrecked castaways lie just beneath the surface.

If you walk through the charming streets of St. George's today and enter the town's largest green space shaded by palm trees, you will find in the southwest corner of the park a modest tomb. Beneath it is buried the heart and entrails of Sir George Somers. As he lay near death in November 1610, Somers was rumored to have asked to be buried in the garden he had planted while a castaway on Bermuda. He also directed his nephew Matthew Somers and all his men to return to Virginia with the fish and hogs they had gathered. They did not heed his dying wishes. After his uncle passed, Matthew Somers removed his heart and entrails for burial. But he surreptitiously put George Somers's body in a cedar cask of whiskey that he loaded onto the *Patience*. He kept his cargo a secret because superstitious sailors believed "the portage of dead bodyes extreamley, prodigiously, ominous." Leaving Edward Waters, Christopher Carter, and Edward Chard behind, Matthew Somers, instead of heading back to Virginia as his uncle had wanted, sailed to England, his uncle's remains on board the very ship built by his own hands and at his own direction. In England, Matthew Somers, hoping to trade on his uncle's fame, attempted, but failed, to extract money from the Virginia Company. And he finally laid the admiral to rest. The body of Sir George Somers was buried in his hometown of Lyme Regis with great ceremony that included "many volies of shot, and the rights of a souldier." But Somers's heart, literally and figuratively, remained in Bermuda. Today Lyme Regis and St. George's are twin cities.[45]

The man who grew up among daring English mariners and privateers and helped lead a troubled but successful expedition to Jamestown left his heart where he ended his life: on Bermuda, an island paradise he called "the most plentifull place, that ever I came to."[46] How George Somers came to Bermuda on board the ill-fated *Sea Venture* became the means for saving English America.

NOTES

Prologue

1. Silvester Jourdain, *A Discovery of the Bermudas, Otherwise Called the Isle of Devils* (London, 1610), reprinted in Louis B. Wright, ed., *A Voyage to Virginia in 1609* (Charlottesville: University Press of Virginia, 1964), 105 (first quotation); William Strachey, *A True Reportory of the Wreck and Redemption of Sir Thomas Gates, Knight, upon and from the Islands of the Bermudas: His Coming to Virginia and the Estate of that Colony Then and After, under the Government of the Lord La Warr, July 15, 1610, written by William Strachey, Esquire* (London, 1625), reprinted in Wright, *Voyage to Virginia*, 3 (second quotation). A few sources refer to the flagship as the *Sea Adventure.*

2. Daniel Price, *Savles Prohibition Staid: or, The Apprehension, and Examination of Savle. And to the Inditement of all that persecute Christ with a reproofe of those that traduce the Honourable Plantation of Virginia* (London, 1609) in Alexander Brown, ed., *The Genesis of the United States*, 2 vols. (New York: Russell and Russell, 1964), 1:315. See also John Parker, "Religion and the Virginia Colony, 1609–1610," in K. R. Andrews, N. P. Canny, and P.E.H. Hair, eds., *The Westward Enterprise: English Activities in Ireland, the Atlantic, and America, 1480–1650* (Liverpool: Liverpool University Press, 1978), 245, 270.

3. Strachey, *True Reportory*, 4. For analysis of hurricanes in this era, see

Matthew Mulcahy, *Hurricanes and Society in the British Greater Caribbean, 1624–1783* (Baltimore: Johns Hopkins University Press, 2006).

4. Strachey, *True Reportory*, 4–8.

5. Ibid., 6–8.

6. Ibid., 8–9.

7. Strachey, *True Reportory*, 10 (first quotation), 13–14; Jourdain, *Discovery of the Bermudas*, 105–6 (second quotation).

8. Jourdain, *Discovery of the Bermudas*, 106.

9. Strachey, *True Reportory*, 10, 6, 11, 15; Jourdain, *Discovery of the Bermudas*, 106 (last quotation).

10. Edmund S. Morgan, *American Slavery, American Freedom: The Ordeal of Colonial Virginia* (New York: W. W. Norton, 1975), 19; Kenneth R. Andrews, *Trade, Plunder and Settlement: Maritime Enterprise at the Genesis of the British Empire, 1480–1630* (Cambridge: Cambridge University Press, 1984), 195–96; Peter C. Mancall, *Hakluyt's Promise: An Elizabethan's Obsession for an English America* (New Haven, Conn.: Yale University Press, 2007), 126. For the history of English efforts before Jamestown, see also Karen Ordahl Kupperman, *The Jamestown Project* (Cambridge, Mass.: Harvard University Press, 2007).

11. For Roanoke, see David B. Quinn, *Set Fair for Roanoke: Voyages and Colonies, 1584–1606* (Chapel Hill: University of North Carolina Press, 1985); and Karen Ordahl Kupperman, *Roanoke: The Abandoned Colony* (Lanham, Md.: Rowman and Littlefield, 2007).

12. April Lee Hatfield, *Atlantic Virginia: Intercolonial Relations in the Seventeenth Century* (Chapel Hill: University of North Carolina Press, 2004), 141.

13. For a differing perspective on the efforts and successes in early Virginia, see Kupperman, *Jamestown Project*.

14. See, for example, James Horn, *A Land as God Made It: Jamestown and the Birth of America* (New York: Basic Books, 2005); Morgan, *American Slavery, American Freedom*; David Price, *Love and Hate in Jamestown: John Smith, Pocahontas, and the Start of a New Nation* (New York: Knopf, 2003); and Camilla Townsend, *Pocahontas and the Powhatan Dilemma* (New York: Hill and Wang, 2004).

Chapter i: London Dreams

1. Stanley Spurling, *Sir Thomas Smythe, Knight: Governor of the East India Company and Patron of Bermuda* (New York: Newcomen Society, 1955), 15–16;

Basil Morgan, "Sir Thomas Smythe," *Oxford Dictionary of National Biography* (Oxford University Press, 2004).

2. Spurling, *Sir Thomas Smythe*, 16; Morgan, "Sir Thomas Smythe"; Wesley Frank Craven, *The Southern Colonies in the Seventeenth Century, 1607–1689* (Baton Rouge: Louisiana State University Press, 1949), 60; Charles M. Andrews, *The Colonial Period of American History*, 4 vols. (New Haven, Conn.: Yale University Press, 1964), 1:104–5.

3. Spurling, *Sir Thomas Smythe*, 8–10; Morgan, "Sir Thomas Smythe."

4. Samuel Purchas, *Hakluytus Posthumus, or Purchas His Pilgrimes Contayning A History of the World in Sea Voyages and Land Travells by Englishmen and others*, 20 vols. (New York: AMS Press, 1965), 14:133–39 (quotations); Spurling, *Sir Thomas Smythe*, 10; Andrews, *Trade, Plunder and Settlement*, 311; David B. Quinn, *North America from Earliest Discovery to First Settlements: The Norse Voyages to 1612* (New York: Harper and Row, 1977), 440.

5. *Thomas Platter's Travels in England, 1599*, quoted in W. D. Robson-Scott, *German Travellers in England, 1400–1800* (Oxford: Basil Blackwell, 1953), 64. The translation is slightly altered in Lena Cowen Orlin, ed., *Material London, ca. 1600* (Philadelphia: University of Pennsylvania Press, 2000), 3, as "London is not said to be in England, but rather England to be in London." For London's centrality to commercial pursuits, see also Theodore K. Rabb, *Empire and Enterprise: Merchant and Gentry Investment in the Expansion of England, 1575–1630* (Cambridge, Mass.: Harvard University Press, 1967). Rabb found that nearly 6,300 people participated in the various overseas commercial ventures launched out of London between the 1570s and the 1620s, and, except for the investors in the East India Company, most lost what they wagered. Rabb, *Empire and Enterprise*, 26, 34.

6. The Banqueting House is all that survives today of Whitehall, and St. Paul's had to be rebuilt after the fire of 1666. The Middle Temple and the Gray's Inn Gardens remain today much as they were at the turn of the seventeenth century.

7. Derek Keene, "Material London in Time and Space," in Orlin, *Material London*, 57; Stephen Greenblatt, *Will in the World: How Shakespeare Became Shakespeare* (New York: W. W. Norton, 2004), 163.

8. John Stow, *Survey of London* (1598), republished in Ernest Rhys, ed., *Everyman's Library* (London: J. M. Dent and Sons, 1912); Patrick Collinson, "John Stow and Nostalgic Antiquarianism," in J. F. Merritt, ed., *Imagining Early*

Modern London: Perceptions and Portrayals of the City from Stow to Strype, 1598–1720
(Cambridge: Cambridge University Press, 2001), 32; Peter Ackroyd, *London:*
The Biography (New York: Anchor Books, 2003), 92, 66–68; Thomas Dekker,
The Seven Deadly Sinnes of London (1606), excerpted in R. E. Pritchard, ed.,
Shakespeare's England: Life in Elizabethan and Jacobean Times (Gloucestershire, UK:
Sutton Publishing, 1999), 156 (quotation).

9. T. H. Breen articulated this individualistic ethic in his study of early Virginia: "Looking Out for Number One: The Cultural Limits on Public Policy in Early Virginia," in Breen, *Puritans and Adventurers: Change and Persistence in Early America* (New York: Oxford University Press, 1982). For sartorial laws, see David Kuchta, *The Three-Piece Suit and Modern Masculinity: England, 1550–1850* (Berkeley: University of California Press, 2002).

10. Quoted in Greenblatt, *Will in the World*, 166.

11. Stow, *Survey of London*, 93–95; Robson-Scott, *German Travellers in London*, 41, 44, 72; Greenblatt, *Will in the World*, 177 (quotation).

12. Stationers' Hall remains in the same location today. Peter W. M. Blayney, *The Bookshops in Paul's Cross Churchyard* (London: The Bibliographical Society, 1990); Blayney, "John Day and the Bookshop That Never Was," in Orlin, *Material London*, 325–27.

13. Greenblatt, *Will in the World*, 12; Peter Ackroyd, *Shakespeare: The Biography* (New York: Doubleday, 2005), 417–18.

14. See, for example, William Crashaw, *A Sermon Preached at the Crosse* (1607); and William Symonds, *A Heavenly Voyce* (1606). See also William Symonds, *Virginia. A Sermon Preached at White-Chappel* (1609), for an example of seeing God's will in Virginia. And see William Crashaw's dedication to Alexander Whitaker, *Good News from Virginia* (1613), for the "calumnies and slanders raised upon our colony . . . by Papists, players, and suchlike." The "vagrant and lewd persons" comment was quoted in Ackroyd, *London*, 161.

15. Alice Hogge, *God's Secret Agents: Queen Elizabeth's Forbidden Priests and the Hatching of the Gunpowder Plot* (New York: Harper Collins, 2005), 10, 46–47; Kupperman, *Jamestown Project*, 18–20; Hugh Ross Williamson, *The Gunpowder Plot* (London: Faber and Faber, 1951), 29–30. See also Susan Bridgen, *New Worlds, Lost Worlds: The Rule of the Tudors, 1485–1603* (New York: Penguin Press, 2001); and C. Haigh, *English Reformations* (London: Oxford University Press, 1993).

16. Hogge, *God's Secret Agents*, 310, 328–33, 379–80; Williamson, *Gunpow-*

der Plot, 62, 245–46. See also Antonia Fraser, *Faith and Treason: The Story of the Gunpowder Plot* (New York: Doubleday, 1996); and Mark Nicholls, *Investigating Gunpowder Plot* (Manchester: Manchester University Press, 1991). Some contemporaries and a few scholars have argued that the plot was exaggerated to destroy English Catholicism.

17. Hogge, *God's Secret Agents*, 373–75.

18. Robert Gray, *A Good Speed to Virginia* (London, 1609), 296. Richard Hakluyt the elder had listed those same goals in his 1584 report for Queen Elizabeth I. Richard Hakluyt, "Inducements to the Liking of the Voyage intended towards Virginia," reprinted in David B. Quinn, ed., *New American World: A Documentary History of North America to 1612*, 5 vols. (New York: Arno Press, 1979), 3:62–69. Scholars have long disagreed over what issue most shaped the Virginia Company. Perry Miller argued that religion was paramount in "The Religious Impulse in the Founding of Virginia: Religion and Society in the Early Literature," *William and Mary Quarterly* 5 (October 1948): 492–522; Edmund Morgan emphasized national interests in *American Slavery, American Freedom*, as did Wesley Frank Craven in *Southern Colonies*. Others, including Kenneth Andrews, pointed to the economic interests of company leaders. For the latest interpretations, focusing on an English "Atlantic world," see David Armitage and Michael J. Braddick, eds., *The British Atlantic World, 1500–1800* (New York: Palgrave Macmillan, 2002); Elizabeth Mancke and Carole Shammas, eds., *The Creation of the British Atlantic World* (Baltimore: Johns Hopkins University Press, 2005); and Robert Appelbaum and John Wood Sweet, eds., *Envisioning an English Empire: Jamestown and the Making of the North Atlantic World* (Philadelphia: University of Pennsylvania Press, 2005).

19. For typical promises about commodities, see Thomas Harriott, *A Brief and true report of the new found land of Virginia* (1588, 1600), reprinted in Quinn, *New American World*, 3:139–55. For discussions of the passage east, see *Virginia, Richly Valued, By the description of the main land of Florida, her next neighbor*, reprinted in Peter Force, ed., *Tracts and Other Papers Relating Principally to the Origin, Settlement, and Progress of the Colonies in North America, from the Discovery of the Country to the Year 1776*, 4 vols. (New York, 1947), 4:5; "Orders for First Expedition," in Edward D. Neill, *History of the Virginia Company of London, with Letters to and from the First Colony Never Before Printed* (New York: Burt Franklin, 1968), 9; William Strachey, *The History of Travel into Virginia Britannia*, in Edward Wright Haile, ed., *Jamestown Narratives: Eyewitness Accounts of the Virginia*

Colony, The First Decade: 1607–1617 (Champlaine, Va.: RoundHouse, 1998), 683. See also Quinn, *North America*, 369–84; Craven, *Southern Colonies*, 31–32; Wesley Frank Craven, *The Virginia Company of London, 1606–1624* (Williamsburg: Virginia 350th Anniversary Celebration Corporation, 1957), 9–10.

20. "Reasons for raising a fund for the support of a Colony at Virginia," ca. 1605, in Brown, *Genesis of the United States*, 1:39 (first quotation), 37; Andrews, *Trade, Plunder and Settlement*, 9 (second quotation).

21. In reality, spreading Protestantism among native Virginians never came close to matching the promises made in London sermons and publications. David Quinn, for example, pointed out that despite many lengthy discussions of converting Indians to Christianity in the first five to six years, "the company made no attempt to implement its pious promises." Quinn, *New American World*, 5:233.

22. Harriott, *Brief and true report of the new found land*, 145 (first quotation); Ferdinando Gorges, "A Briefe Narration of the Originall undertakings of the Advancement of Plantations into the parts of America," quoted in Brown, *Genesis of the United States*, 1:50 (second quotation). For examples of typically strident anti-Catholicism, see Symonds, *Heavenly Voyce*; and Crashaw, *Sermon Preached at the Crosse*.

23. Letters Patent, 10 April 1606, in Brown, *Genesis of the United States*, 1:52–63.

24. Letters Patent, 10 April 1606, 52–53; R. N. Worth, ed., *Calendar of the Plymouth Municipal Records* (Plymouth, 1893), 223.

25. David B. Quinn and Alison M. Quinn, eds., *The English New England Voyages, 1602–1608* (London: Hakluyt Society, 1983), introduction, 75; Quinn, *New American World*, 3:403, 425; Quinn, *North America*, 441, 445, 403–9; Andrews, *Trade, Plunder and Settlement*, 326–28.

26. Mancall, *Hakluyt's Promise*; Morgan, *American Slavery, American Freedom*, 14–18.

27. John Hooker on Sir Humphrey Gilbert, 1586, in Quinn, *New American World*, 3:259; George Peckham, *A true reporte of the late discoveries and possession, taken in the right of the Crown of Englande, of the Newfound Landes: by that valiant and worthye gentlemen, Sir Humphrey Gilbert Knight* (London, 1583), in Quinn, *New American World*, 3:34–60; Quinn, *North America*, 366, 368.

28. Brown, *Genesis of the United States*, 1:15–21; Morgan, *American Slavery, American Freedom*, 25–43; Alan Taylor, *American Colonies* (New York: Viking, 2001), 123–24. A brief release from the tower and a final Atlantic voyage to

Guiana concluded with another arrest, which led to Raleigh's execution in 1618. Brown, *Genesis of the United States*, 2:977.

29. Andrews, *Trade, Plunder and Settlement*, 2. For the connections between the conquest of Ireland and America, see Nicholas P. Canny, "The Ideology of English Colonization: From Ireland to America," *William and Mary Quarterly* 30 (October 1973): 575–98.

30. K. N. Chaudhuri, *The English East India Company: The Study of an Early Joint-Stock Company, 1600–1640* (London: Routledge, 1999), 3–4; Quinn, *North America*, 439–40; Rabb, *Empire and Enterprise*, 83. For earlier commercial pursuits, see Douglas R. Bisson, *The Merchant Adventurers of England: The Company and the Crown, 1474–1564* (Newark: University of Delaware Press, 1993); and Andrews, *Trade, Plunder and Settlement*.

31. John Brereton, *A Brief and True Relation of the Discoverie of the North Part of Virginia* (London, 1602), reprinted in Quinn and Quinn, *English New England Voyages*, 139–203, 168, 172 (quotations); Neill, *History of the Virginia Company*, 1–2.

32. Thomas Canner, "A Relation of the Voyage made to Virginia, in the Elizabeth of London, a Barke of fiftie tunnes by Captaine Bartholomew Gilbert, in the yeere 1603," in Quinn, *New American World*, 5:166.

33. Quinn and Quinn, *English New England Voyages*, introduction, 73–74; High Court of Admiralty trial transcript, September 1607, in Quinn, *New American World*, 3:396–402, 399 (quotations).

34. Brown, *Genesis of the United States*, 1:29–32, 31 (quotations); Louis B. Wright, ed., *The Elizabethans' America: A Collection of Early Reports by Englishmen on the New World* (Cambridge, Mass.: Harvard University Press, 1965), 155.

35. William Crashaw, quoted in Neill, *History of the Virginia Company*, 64 (first and second quotations); Ackroyd, *Shakespeare*, 116 (third quotation).

36. Quinn, *New American World*, 5:159; Andrews, *Colonial Period of American History*, 1: 83.

37. James I, *Counterblaste to Tobacco* (1604); Mancall, *Hakluyt's Promise*, 257.

38. Andrews, *Trade, Plunder and Settlement*, 11; Elizabeth Mancke, "Empire and State," in Armitage and Braddick, *British Atlantic World*, 238, 188; Brown, *Genesis of the United States*, 1:27.

39. Letters Patent, 10 April 1606, in Brown, *Genesis of the United States* 1: 55–56; Instructions for the Government of the Colonies, 20 November 1606, in Brown, *Genesis of the United States*, 1:66. See also Miller, "Religious Impulse in

the Founding of Virginia," 493; and Parker, "Religion and the Virginia Colony," 245–70.

40. Letters Patent, 10 April 1606, 56–57; Instructions for the Government of the Colonies, 69, 74.

41. Orders in Council, 10 December 1606, in Brown, *Genesis of the United States*, 1:75–85.

42. Letters Patent, 10 April 1606, 53–54.

43. "Reasons for raising a fund," 38, 40.

44. Letters Patent, 10 April 1606, 58; Andrews, *Trade, Plunder and Settlement*, 313; Andrews, *Colonial Period of American History*, 1:88; Craven, *Virginia Company of London*, 3, 17; Brown, *Genesis of the United States*, 1:49 (quotations).

45. President of the Council of the Indies to Charles Cornwallis, May 1607, in Brown, *Genesis of the United States*, 1:101 (quotation); Zúñiga to Philip III, 16 March 1606, in Brown, *Genesis of the United States*, 1:45–46.

46. Zúñiga to Philip III, ca. January 1607; Philip III to Zúñiga, 8 March 1607 (first quotation), both in Brown, *Genesis of the United States*, 1:88–91; Juan de Ciriza to Andres de Pedrastra, 7 May 1607, in Brown, *Genesis of the United States*, 1:100 (second quotation).

47. Philip III to Zúñiga, ca. June 1607, in Brown, *Genesis of the United States*, 1:102–3.

48. Zúñiga to Philip III, 8 October 1607, in Brown, *Genesis of the United States*, 1:120.

49. Orders in Council, 10 December 1606, 76. See also Kenneth R. Andrews, "Christopher Newport of Limehouse, Mariner," *William and Mary Quarterly* 11 (January 1954): 28–41.

50. Craven, *Southern Colonies*, 65; Brown, *Genesis of the United States*, 1:85; Quinn, *North America*, 447; Price, *Love and Hate in Jamestown*, 15.

51. For depositions relating to the lawsuit, see Quinn, *New American World*, 5:171–81.

52. Mancall, *Hakluyt's Promise*, 265; Mark Nicholls, ed., "George Percy's 'Trewe Relacyon,'" *Virginia Magazine of History and Biography* 113 (2005), 1–2. For modernized spelling, see George Percy, "A True Relation of the proceedings and occurents of moment which have hap'ned in Virginia from the time Sir Thomas Gates was shipwrack'd upon the Bermudes, anno 1609, until my departure out of the country, which was in anno Domini 1612," in Haile, *Jamestown Narratives*, 497–519.

53. Instructions for the Government of the Colonies, 67.

54. Oath of Allegiance and Supremacy, Records of the Virginia Company, 1607, reprinted in Susan Myra Kingsbury, ed., *The Records of the Virginia Company of London*, 4 vols. (Washington, D.C., 1906), 3:4.

55. Michael Drayton, "Ode to the Virginian Voyage," in Brown, *Genesis of the United States*, 1:86; Orders in Council, 10 December 1606, 79–85, 85 (quotation).

Chapter 2: "A Grand Enterprise"

1. Christopher Newport to Earl of Salisbury, 29 July 1607, in Brown, *Genesis of the United States*, 1:105–6.

2. Gabriel Archer, "A relation of the discovery of our river from James Fort into the main, made by Captain Christofer Newport, and sincerely written and observed by a gentleman of the colony," in Haile, *Jamestown Narratives*, 101–18; and Gabriel Archer, "The description of the now-discovered river and country of Virginia, with the likelihood of ensuing riches by England's aid and industry," in Haile, *Jamestown Narratives*, 118–21. Archer's biographical information is from Haile, *Jamestown Narratives*, 42; and Brown, *Genesis of the United States*, 2:814.

3. The Council in Virginia to the Council in England, 22 June 1607, in Brown, *Genesis of the United States*, 1:107 (first and third quotations); William Brewster letter, June 1607, in Haile, *Jamestown Narratives*, 127; Archer, "description of the now-discovered river," 119–21.

4. Horn, *Land as God Made It*, 49–50; William M. Kelso, *Jamestown: The Buried Truth* (Charlottesville: University of Virginia Press, 2006), 13–14.

5. Council in Virginia to Council in England, 22 June 1607, 107.

6. Archer, "discovery of our river," 117; Council in Virginia to Council in England, 22 June 1607, 108; William Brewster letter, June 1607, 127. For Newport's career, see also Andrews, "Christopher Newport," 28–41; and David B. Quinn, "Christopher Newport in 1590," *North Carolina Historical Review* 29 (July 1952): 305–16.

7. William Brewster letter, June 1607, 127; Dudley Carleton to John Chamberlain, 18 August 1607, in Brown, *Genesis of the United States*, 1:113; George Percy, "Observations gathered out of a Discourse of the Plantation of the Southerne Colonie in Virginia by the English, 1606," in Brown, *Genesis of the United States*, 1:167–68.

8. Council in Virginia to Council in England, 22 June 1607, 107; Archer,

"discovery of our river," 115–16 (quotations). The unfortunate colonist some-how managed to survive.

9. Horn, *Land as God Made It*, 44, 47.

10. Orders in Council, 10 December 1606, 85 (quotation); Walter Cope to Lord Salisbury, 13 August 1607, in Philip L. Barbour, ed., *The Jamestown Voyages Under the First Charter, 1606–1609*, 2 vols. (London: Cambridge University Press for the Hakluyt Society, 1969), 1:111; Carleton to Chamberlain, 18 August 1607, 113.

11. Orders in Council, 10 December 1606, 85; Kelso, *Jamestown*, 11–12. Extensive investigation of Powhatan culture is beyond the scope of this work. See Horn, *Land as God Made It*; Helen C. Rountree, *Pocahontas, Powhatan, and Opechancanough: Three Indian Lives Changed by Jamestown* (Charlottesville: University of Virginia Press, 2005); and Townsend, *Pocahontas and the Powhatan Dilemma*.

12. Percy, "Observations gathered out of a Discourse," 166–67; John Smith, *A True Relation of such occurences and accidents of note, as hath hapned in Virginia, since the first planting of that Collony, which is now resident in the South part thereof, till the last returne.* (London, 1608), in Philip L. Barbour, ed., *The Complete Works of Captain John Smith*, 3 vols. (Chapel Hill: University of North Carolina Press, 1986), 1:33; Horn, *Land as God Made It*, 56–57.

13. Percy, "Observations gathered out of a Discourse," 167; Smith, *True Relation*, 33, 35 (quotation).

14. Smith, *True Relation*, 33–35; Horn, *Land as God Made It*, 46, 58; Kelso, *Jamestown*, 132; Price, *Love and Hate in Jamestown*, 30.

15. Smith, *True Relation*, 61; Edward Maria Wingfield, "A Discourse of Virginia," in Haile, *Jamestown Narratives*, 191, 197. For a thoughtful exploration of Smith's rescue tale and Pocahontas's real life, see Townsend, *Pocahontas and the Powhatan Dilemma*.

16. Wingfield, "Discourse of Virginia," 191, 196–97.

17. Francis Perkins, 28 March 1608, in Brown, *Genesis of the United States*, 1:175; Smith, *True Relation*, 61.

18. John Smith, "The Proceedings of the English Colony in Virginia," in Quinn, *New American World*, 5:315–17. It is also possible that Smith wanted to beat his rival Newport to the gold and glory. Horn, *Land as God Made It*, 104.

19. Brown, *Genesis of the United States* 1:191–94.

20. Thomas Smythe to Lord Salisbury, 17 August 1607, in Barbour, *Jamestown Voyages*, 1:112; Horn, *Land as God Made It*, 79, 81; Price, *Love and Hate in*

Jamestown, 84; Zúñiga to Philip III, 16/26 June 1608, in Brown, *Genesis of the United States*, 1:172. In one bit of hopeful but inaccurate news, Newport passed along the rumor that the Virginians had a lead in finding the lost Roanoke colonists. This would have been of terrific public relations value to the company, but, like so many other positive reports from Virginia, it turned out to be untrue. Horn, *Land as God Made It*, 101–3.

21. Wingfield, "Discourse of Virginia," 183–201.

22. Smith, *True Relation*, 33–35; Brown, *Genesis of the United States*, 1:181.

23. John Smith, Letter sent to the Treasurer and Councell of Virginia, ca. November 1608, in Karen Ordahl Kupperman, ed., *Captain John Smith: A Select Edition of His Writings* (Chapel Hill: University of North Carolina Press, 1988), 112–14.

24. Resolution of the States General, 24 April 1608, in Brown, *Genesis of the United States*, 1:148; Natalie Zacek, "Sir Thomas Gates," *Oxford Dictionary of National Biography* (Oxford University Press, 2004); Horn, *Land as God Made It*, 133.

25. Second Charter of the Virginia Company, in Brown, *Genesis of the United States*, 1:206–37. See also Craven, *Virginia Company of London,* 15; and Andrews, *Trade, Plunder and Settlement*, 315.

26. Second Charter of the Virginia Company, 232, 235, 233.

27. *A True and Sincere Declaration of the purpose and ends of the Plantation begun in Virginia . . .* (London, 1610), in Haile, *Jamestown Narratives*, 360, 363–64.

28. Second Charter of the Virginia Company, 234; Company Instructions to Thomas Gates, May 1609, in Quinn, *New American World*, 5:213.

29. Zúñiga to Philip III, 12 April 1609, in Brown, *Genesis of the United States*, 1:259. Zúñiga was quoting one of his anonymous sources.

30. Second Charter of the Virginia Company, 207, 229.

31. Company Instructions to Thomas Gates, 213.

32. Ibid., 213, 214.

33. Second Charter of the Virginia Company, 236 (first quotation); Company Instructions to Thomas Gates, 213 (second and third quotations).

34. For the unprecedented scope of the effort, see also Craven, *Southern Colonies*, 85, 93; and Andrews, *Colonial Period of American History*, 1:108–9.

35. *New Britain*, in Brown, *Genesis of the United States* 1:264. This is a summary of *Nova Britannia*, translated for the king of Spain.

36. Craven, *Virginia Company of London*, 17–19.

37. For the centrality of religion in 1609 contrasted to disinterest in religion in 1607, see also Parker, "Religion and the Virginia Colony," 245–70.

38. G.P.V. Akrigg, *Shakespeare and the Earl of Southampton* (Cambridge, Mass.: Harvard University Press, 1968), 143, 149, 160; Brown, *Genesis of the United States*, 2:1063; Worth, *Calendar of the Plymouth Municipal Records*, 203; Council of Virginia to Plymouth, 17 February 1609, in Brown, *Genesis of the United States* 1:239–40.

39. Robert Johnson, *Nova Britannia: offering most excellent fruites by planting in Virginia* (London, 1609), in Quinn, *New American World*, 5:236, 239, 243, 245.

40. *Concerning the Plantation of Virginia New Britain*, in Brown, *Genesis of the United States*, 1:248–49.

41. Virginia Council to Lord Mayor of London, ca. March 1609, in Brown, *Genesis of the United States*, 1:252–53.

42. Lord Mayor of London to the London Companies, ca. March 1609, in Brown, *Genesis of the United States*, 1:254; Second Charter of the Virginia Company, 210, 226 (for Weld's investment); Brown, *Genesis of the United States*, 2:1044 (biographical information).

43. Fishmongers' Records, 20 March 1609, in Brown, *Genesis of the United States*, 1:254 (first quotation); miscellaneous company records, in Brown, *Genesis of the United States*, 1:257, 277–78 (second quotation), 292, 302–9; Second Charter of the Virginia Company, 209–28.

44. Lord Salisbury to Customs Officers, 3 May 1609, in Brown, *Genesis of the United States*, 1:307.

45. Zúñiga to Philip III, 5 March 1609, in Brown, *Genesis of the United States*, 1:245–46 (first and second quotations); Zúñiga to Philip III, 12 April 1609, 259 (last quotation). See also Zúñiga to Philip III, 1 April 1609, 254–55.

46. Zúñiga to Philip III, 5 March 1609, 246; Gray, *Good Speed to Virginia*, 296.

47. Zúñiga to Philip III, 5 March 1609, 245–46; Gray, *Good Speed to Virginia*, 296; David B. Quinn, "Notes by a Pious Colonial Investor, 1608–1610," *William and Mary Quarterly* 16 (October 1959): 553. James Horn provides a slightly different calculation of investors (55 companies and 619 individuals) in *Land as God Made It*, 137. David Price gives the same figures as we counted in Brown, *Genesis of the United States*, 1:209–28 (659 individuals and 56 companies), in Price, *Love and Hate in Jamestown*, 110.

48. Gray, *Good Speed to Virginia*, 296.

49. Johnson, *Nova Britannia*, 239. For further analysis of this, see also Edward L. Bond, *Damned Souls in a Tobacco Colony: Religion in Seventeenth-Century Virginia* (Macon, Ga.: Mercer University Press, 2000); Kupperman, *Jamestown Project*, 244–46; Miller, "Religious Impulse in the Founding of Virginia," 492–522; and Parker, "Religion and the Virginia Colony," 245–70.

50. Zúñiga to Philip III, 12 April 1609, 258–59; Price, *Savles Prohibition Staide*, 314. See also Crashaw, *A Sermon Preached in London before the right honorable the Lord Lavvarre, Lord Governour and Captaine Generall of Virginea, and others of his Maiesties Counsell for that Kingdome, and the rest of the Adventurers in that Plantation* (London, 1610), in Brown, *Genesis of the United States*, 1:361–73.

51. Gray, *Good Speed to Virginia*, 298; Price, *Savles Prohibition Staide*, 313.

52. Symonds, *Virginia. A Sermon Preached at White-Chappel*, 1, quoting Genesis 12:1–2.

53. Price, *Savles Prohibition Staide*, 315; Gray, *Good Speed to Virginia*, 295–96.

54. Price, *Savles Prohibition Staide*, 313; Gray, *Good Speed to Virginia*, 301, 296.

55. Symonds, *Virginia. A Sermon Preached at White-Chappel*, 15; Johnson, *Nova Britannia*, 239; Price, *Savles Prohibition Staide*, 315. See also Gray, *Good Speed to Virginia*, 298; Richard Crankanthorpe sermon, 24 March 1609, in Brown, *Genesis of the United States*, 1:256; and Symonds, *Virginia. A Sermon Preached at White-Chappel*, 26.

56. Second Charter of the Virginia Company, 236; Johnson, *Nova Britannia*, 243.

57. Symonds, *Virginia. A Sermon Preached at White-Chappel*, dedication, 4, 19.

58. Second Charter of Virginia Company, 209–28; Crashaw's name is on page 214. See also Peter John Wallis, *William Crashawe, the Sheffield Puritan* (Newcastle-upon-Tyne: Transactions of the Hunter Archaeological Society, 1963).

59. Symonds, *Virginia. A Sermon Preached at White-Chappel*, 18.

60. Ibid., 9, 32.

61. Symonds, *Virginia. A Sermon Preached at White-Chappel*, 19–20, 26. See also Gray, *Good Speed to Virginia*, 297–98.

62. Johnson, *Nova Britannia*, 243–44; Gray, *Good Speed to Virginia*, 298. See also Virginia Council to Lord Mayor, ca. March 1609, 252.

63. Johnson, *Nova Britannia*, 243 (first quotation); Gray, *Good Speed to Virginia*, 302 (second quotation).

64. Robert Johnson, *The New Life of Virginea: Declaring the former success and present estate of that plantation, being the second part of Nova Britannia* (London, 1612), reprinted in Force, *Tracts and Other Papers*, 1:10.

65. Wingfield, "A Discourse of Virginia," 191 (quotation); Smith to Councell of Virginia, ca. November 1608, 114.

66. Craven, *Virginia Company of London*, 20; Breen, "Looking Out for Number One."

67. Strachey, *True Reportory*, 42–43 (quotations); Margaret Hodges, *Hopkins of the Mayflower: Portrait of a Dissenter* (New York: Farrar, Straus and Giroux, 1972), 106. On the theological differences between Puritans and Anglicans in the Church of England, see Patrick Collinson, *The Religion of Protestants* (Oxford: Oxford University Press, 1982); and Peter Lake, *Anglicans and Puritans?: Presbyterianism and English Conformist Thought from Whitgift to Hooker* (London: Unwin Hyman, 1988). For a biographical sketch of Rev. Buck, see Brown, *Genesis of the United States*, 2:835.

68. Brown, *Genesis of the United States*, 2:1018–19; Owen H. Darrell, "Admiral George Somers," *Bermuda Historical Quarterly* 16 (Autumn 1959): 117; Jean Kennedy, *Isle of Devils: Bermuda under the Somers Island Company, 1609–1685* (London: William Collins Sons & Co., 1971), 27; William Sears Zuill, "Sir George Somers," *Oxford Dictionary of National Biography* (Oxford University Press, 2004).

69. Brown, *Genesis of the United States*, 2:1042–43; Wright, *Voyage to Virginia in 1609*, xix–xx.

70. S. G. Culliford, *William Strachey, 1572–1621* (Charlottesville: University Press of Virginia, 1965); Charles Richard Sanders, "William Strachey, the Virginia Colony, and Shakespeare," *Virginia Magazine of History and Biography* 57 (April 1949): 115–32; Betty Wood, "William Strachey," *Oxford Dictionary of National Biography* (Oxford University Press, 2004); Wright, *Voyage to Virginia in 1609*, xii–xiii.

Chapter 3: Voyage to Hell

1. Quinn, "Notes by a Pious Colonial Investor, 1608–1610," 554 (quotations); Letter of Gabriel Archer, 31 August 1609, in Brown, *Genesis of the United States*, 1:328.

2. Letter of Gabriel Archer, 31 August 1609, 328 (quotation); Ferdinando Gorges biography, Brown, *Genesis of the United States*, 2:903.

3. John Smith, *The Generall Historie of Virginia, New-England, and the Summer Isles with the names of the Adventurers, Planters, and Governours from their first beginning An:1584 to this present 1624* (London, 1624), in Barbour, *Complete Works of Smith*, 2:219.

4. Company Instructions to Thomas Gates, 212 (first quotation); *True and Sincere Declaration*, 343.

5. Company Instructions to Thomas Gates, 212. The fleet turned west at 26° latitude, "a course that would keep them well to the north of the Spanish West Indies." Horn, *Land as God Made It*, 158.

6. *New Britain*, 264 (first and second quotations); Bond, *Damned Souls in a Tobacco Colony*, 17 (third quotation).

7. Kennedy, *Isle of Devils*, 27–28.

8. Letter of Gabriel Archer, 31 August 1609, 328. There is some confusion about the number of ships in the fleet, because some contemporaries include the second, apparently unnamed pinnace (sometimes called a ketch) in their count, numbering the ships in the fleet at nine, and others do not, counting only eight. Further complicating things are contradictory stories regarding the *Virginia*. Archer reported that it left the fleet a week out of Falmouth and returned to England. But it was in the Virginia colony by June 1610. It was not there in August 1609 when Archer wrote home, or in October of that same year when Ratcliffe sent his letter. And the *Virginia* was not brought later in the De La Warr fleet, because the colonists were already using it when he arrived. All of this suggests that the 1609 return to England was only a delay and that the *Virginia* somehow made its way on to Jamestown. Council in Virginia to Virginia Company Council, 7 July 1610, in Brown, *Genesis of the United States*, 1:406; John Ratcliffe to Earl of Salisbury, 4 October 1609, in Brown, *Genesis of the United States*, 1:334. For examples of how this confusion shows up in recent Virginia works, see Horn, *Land as God Made It*, 157, 305n1; and Price, *Love and Hate in Jamestown*, 114, 130.

9. Letter of Gabriel Archer, 31 August 1609, 328.

10. Alison Games, *Migration and the Origins of the English Atlantic World* (Cambridge, Mass.: Harvard University Press, 1999), 60.

11. Hodges, *Hopkins of the Mayflower*, 96–97, 105–6; Craven, *Southern Colonies*, 20.

12. Games, *Migration and Origins*, 60. For more on the character of the first colonists, see Breen, "Looking Out for Number One."

13. Kennedy, *Isle of Devils*, 28 (first quotation); Nicholls, "George Percy's 'Trewe Relacyon,'" 2 (second quotation).

14. *Concerning the Plantation*, 249.

15. Craven, *Southern Colonies*, 94–96; Games, *Migration and Origins*, 61, 64–65; Strachey, *True Reportory*. Games notes that New England–bound ships in the early seventeenth century normally carried fewer passengers—on average about sixty-nine—and tended to bring more livestock and other provisions.

16. Andrews, *Trade, Plunder and Settlement*, 27; Company Instructions to Thomas Gates, 212–18.

17. Bryan Bevan, *The Great Seamen of Elizabeth I* (London: Robert Hale Publishers, 1971), 45–46; N.A.M. Rodger, *The Safeguard of the Sea: A Naval History of Britain, 660–1649* (New York: W. W. Norton, 1997), 319–20. Note that in Shakespeare's *The Tempest* the boatswain cries, "Heigh, my hearts! Cheerly, cheerly my hearts! Yare, yare! Take in the topsail. Tend to the master's whistle. Blow, till thou burst thy wind, if room enough!" (*The Tempest*, Act One, Scene One).

18. Rodger, *Safeguard of the Sea*, 319; Florence E. Dyer, "The Elizabethan Sailorman," *Mariner's Mirror* 10 (1924): 134 (quotation).

19. Price, *Love and Hate in Jamestown*, 19; Smith, *Generall Historie of Virginia*, 137.

20. J. J. Keevil, C. C. Lloyd, and J.L.S. Coulter, *Medicine and the Navy, 1200–1900*, 4 vols. (Edinburgh: E. & S. Livingstone, 1957–1963), 1:183; Mike Dash, *Batavia's Graveyard* (New York: Three Rivers Press, 2002), 94–95; Percy, "Observations gathered out of a Discourse," 87; Rodger, *Safeguard of the Sea*, 408.

21. Games, *Migration and Origins*, 66–67.

22. Rodger, *Safeguard of the Sea*, 318.

23. Bevan, *Great Seamen of Elizabeth I*, 39, 257.

24. Percy, "True Relation," 519 (quotation); Dash, *Batavia's Graveyard*, 98, 104.

25. Miscellaneous depositions, 1608, in Quinn, *New American World*, 3:450–54, 450 (first quotation); Percy, "True Relation," 519 (second quotation); Percy, "Observations gathered out of a Discourse," 88 (third quotation). Andrews, *Trade, Plunder and Settlement*, 27, notes that Henry Hudson was set adrift

by his mutinous men and that sailors working on the East India Company's pinnace *Good Hope* "murdered their master for victuals."

26. *A True Declaration of the estate of the colonie in Virginia, with a confutation of such scandalous reports as have tended to the disgrace of so worthy an enterprise* (London, 1610), in Quinn, *New American World*, 5:252.

27. Games, *Migration and Origins*, 67.

28. Henry Spelman, "Relation of Virginia," in Haile, *Jamestown Narratives*, 482 (first quotation); Strachey, *True Reportory*, 3 (second quotation).

29. Letter of Gabriel Archer, 31 August 1609, 329. The terms "calenture" and "yellow fever" were sometimes used synonymously; other times "calenture" referred generally to fevers contracted from traveling in hot climates.

30. Dash, *Batavia's Graveyard*, 137–38.

31. Wallace T. MacCaffrey, *Elizabeth I, War and Politics, 1588–1603* (Princeton: Princeton University Press, 1992), 64–68; Bevan, *Great Seamen of Elizabeth I*, 48 (first quotation); Rodger, *Safeguard of the Sea*, 321 (second quotation).

32. W. R. Thrower, *Life at Sea in the Age of Sail* (London: Phillimore, 1972), 86–87.

33. See Dash, *Batavia's Graveyard*, 100, regarding Drake's pastime.

34. Symonds, *Virginia. A Sermon Preached at White-Chappel.* On how English ships of this era were commonly peopled with vigorously anti-Catholic Protestant passengers and crew, see Rodger, *Safeguard of the Sea*, 407.

35. Andrews, "Christopher Newport," 28–41; Andrews, *Trade, Plunder and Settlement*, 27; Kenneth R. Andrews, *Ships, Money, and Politics: Seafaring and Naval Enterprise in the Reign of Charles* (Cambridge: Cambridge University Press, 1991), 63, 66–67; Rodger, *Safeguard of the Sea*, 322, 403.

36. Andrews, *Ships, Money, and Politics*, 71.

37. Andrews, *Trade, Plunder and Settlement*, 27; Dash, *Batavia's Graveyard*, 118.

38. Russell Shorto, *The Island at the Center of the World* (New York: Random House, 2004), 35. For another fascinating case, see Dash, *Batavia's Graveyard*.

39. Strachey, *True Reportory*, 4–6.

40. Letter of Gabriel Archer, 31 August 1609, 330.

41. Strachey, *True Reportory*, 6. See also Mulcahy, *Hurricanes and Society*, 15, 38.

42. Strachey, *True Reportory*, 8–9.

43. Ibid., 7.

44. Ibid., 8.

45. Strachey, *True Reportory*, 9; George Somers to Earl of Salisbury, 15 June 1610, in Brown, *Genesis of the United States*, 1:400.

46. Strachey, *True Reportory*, 10–11 (quotations); Somers to Earl of Salisbury, 15 June 1610, 400.

47. Jourdain, *Discovery of the Bermudas*, 105; Strachey, *True Reportory*, 10; Robert Rich, *News from Virginia* (London, 1610), reprinted Amsterdam/New York: De Capo Press, 1970. The author of this poem is sometimes listed as Richard Rich. This Robert/Richard Rich is not the Robert Rich, Earl of Warwick, who was a central figure in the Virginia and Somers Island Companies.

48. Strachey, *True Reportory*, 10–11.

49. Ibid., 10–12.

50. Ibid., 12.

51. Ibid., 12–13.

52. Ibid.

53. Strachey, *True Reportory*, 13–14; Jourdain, *Discovery of the Bermudas*, 106 (last quotation).

54. Jourdain, *Discovery of the Bermudas*, 106 (first and third quotations); Strachey, *True Reportory*, 15 (second quotation).

Chapter 4: Distressing News

1. Lewis Hughes, *A Plaine and Trve Relation of the Goodnes of God Towards the Sommer Ilands* (London, 1612), reprinted in Wesley Frank Craven, ed., *William and Mary Quarterly* 17 (January 1937): 75 (first quotation); *True Declaration of the estate of the Colonie*, 252; William Box quoted in Smith, *Generall Historie of Virginia*, 220 (second quotation); Nathaniel Butler, *The Historye of the Bermudaes or Summer Islands*, ed. J. Henry Lefroy (London: Hakluyt Society, 1882), 11 (third quotation). See also Horn, *Land as God Made It*, 164.

2. *True and Sincere Declaration*, in Haile, *Jamestown Narratives*, 364 (first quotation); Letter of Gabriel Archer, 31 August 1609, 330 (second quotation).

3. *True Declaration of the estate of the Colonie*, 252 (the defense of the captains); *True and Sincere Declaration*, 365.

4. Ratcliffe to Earl of Salisbury, 4 October 1609, 334 (first and second quotations); Letter of Gabriel Archer, 31 August 1609, 330 (third quotation); *True and Sincere Declaration*, 365 (fourth quotation).

5. William Box, quoted in Smith, *Generall Historie of Virginia*, 220.

6. Letter of Gabriel Archer, 31 August 1609, 330. See also Neill, *History of the Virginia Company*, 31; and Horn, *Land as God Made It*, 164.

7. Spelman, "Relation of Virginia," 482.

8. The Ancient Planters of Virginia, "A Brief Declaration," in Haile, *Jamestown Narratives*, 893, 894; Barbour, *Complete Works of Smith*, 1:127.

9. "The Answer of the General Assembly in Virginia to a 'Declaration of the state of the colony in the 12 years of Sir Thomas Smith's government'— exhibited by Alderman Johnsone and others," Virginia General Assembly, 20 February 1624, in Haile, *Jamestown Narratives*, 913 (first quotation); Ancient Planters of Virginia, "Brief Declaration," 895 (second quotation); Horn, *Land as God Made It*, 151.

10. Ancient Planters of Virginia, "Brief Declaration," 895 (quotations); Spelman, "Relation of Virginia," 482.

11. Craven, *Southern Colonies*, 99–100.

12. Smith quoted in Craven, *Southern Colonies*, 100. For drought, see Kupperman, *Jamestown Project*, 251.

13. Ancient Planters of Virginia, "Brief Declaration," 895.

14. Smith, "Proceedings of the English Colony," 342.

15. Letter of Gabriel Archer, 31 August 1609, 330. Archer claimed that the situation had been improved upon by Captain Argall's arrival in Jamestown shortly before his own.

16. *True Declaration of the estate of the Colonie*, 255 (first quotation); Smith, "Proceedings of the English Colony," 341.

17. Percy, "True Relation," 500.

18. Smith, "Proceedings of the English Colony," 340, 341.

19. Quoted in Horn, *Land as God Made It*, 152. Most likely the supplies were for Argall's crew, but it is also possible that he intended to personally profit from trading his cargo to the hungry colonists.

20. Smith, "Proceedings of the English Colony," 341.

21. Company Instructions to Thomas Gates, 213.

22. Ibid., 218.

23. Horn, *Land as God Made It*, 75, 82.

24. Letter of Gabriel Archer, 31 August 1609, 331, 332; Smith, "Proceedings of the English Colony," 341.

25. Percy, "True Relation," 500; Letter of Gabriel Archer, 31 August 1609, 331.

26. Smith, *Generall Historie of Virginia*, 219–20.

27. Crashaw's dedication to Whitaker, *Good News*, 703.

28. Johnson, *New Life of Virginea*, 10 (first and second quotations); Taylor, *American Colonies*, 131 (third quotation). See also Craven, *Southern Colonies*, 98.

29. Johnson, *New Life of Virginea*, 10.

30. *True and Sincere Declaration*, 365 (first quotation); *True Declaration of the estate of the Colonie*, 255 (second quotation). See also Letter of Gabriel Archer, 31 August 1609, 331.

31. Smith, *Generall Historie of Virginia*, 225 (quotations); Neill, *History of the Virginia Company*, 33.

32. Ancient Planters of Virginia, "Brief Declaration," 895. Difficulty in feeding everyone was a significant factor in this dispersal. Horn, *Land as God Made It*, 129.

33. This is an idea proposed in Horn, *Land as God Made It*, 168.

34. Percy, "True Relation," 501.

35. Percy, "True Relation," 502 (quotations); Spelman, "Relation of Virginia," 482–83.

36. Smith, "Proceedings of the English Colony," 342–43. James Horn flatly maintains that the explosion "was no accident but a deliberate attempt to kill him." Horn, *Land as God Made It*, 169.

37. Smith, "Proceedings of the English Colony," 342.

38. Percy, "True Relation," 502 (first quotation); Letter of Gabriel Archer, 31 August 1609, 328–32; Ratcliffe to Earl of Salisbury, 4 October 1609, 334 (second quotation); Horn, *Land as God Made It*, 170.

39. Nicolls, "George Percy's 'Trewe Relacyon,'" introduction.

40. Horn, *Land as God Made It*, 170.

41. Zúñiga to Philip III, 23 November 1609, in Brown, *Genesis of the United States*, 1:333.

42. *True Declaration of the estate of the Colonie*, 256; "A Publication by the Counsell of Virginea, touching the Plantation there," December 1609, in Brown, *Genesis of the United States*, 1:355 (last quotation only).

43. Brown, *Genesis of the United States*, 1:327–32.

44. Johnson, *New Life of Virginea*, 10; "Publication by the Counsell of Virginea," December 1609, 355 (last quotation only).

45. Smith, "Proceedings of the English Colony," 344–45 (quotation); Kupperman, *Captain John Smith*, 11; Barbour, *Complete Works of Smith*, 1:lx.

46. *True Declaration of the estate of the Colonie*, 252 (first quotation); John Beaulieu to William Trumbull, 30 November 1609, in Barbour, *Jamestown Voyages*, 2:287 (second quotation).

47. Ancient Planters of Virginia, "Brief Declaration," 906.

48. Craven, *Virginia Company of London*, 22; *True and Sincere Declaration*, 356–71.

49. John Beaulieu to William Trumbull, 7 December 1609, in Barbour, *Jamestown Voyages*, 2:288; Brown, *Genesis of the United States*, 1:333; Johnson, *New Life of Virginea*, 10 (quotation).

50. Johnson, *New Life of Virginea*, 10 (first quotation); Zúñiga to Philip III, 23 November 1609 and 10 December 1609 (second quotation), both in Brown, *Genesis of the United States*, 1:332–33, 336–37; John More to William Trumbull, 9 November 1609, in Barbour, *Jamestown Voyages*, 2:285 (third quotation); Emanuel van Meteren, *Commentarien Ofte Memorien Van-den Nederlandtschen Staet* (London, 1610), extracted in Barbour, *Jamestown Voyages*, 2:270–79.

51. John Ratcliffe to Earl of Salisbury, 4 October 1609, 334.

52. See also Craven, *Southern Colonies*, 100.

53. *True and Sincere Declaration*, 356–71, 358, 363, 369 (quotations). While the publication date was 1610, it was commonplace for printers to begin the publication year at Michaelmas (in September). The document was entered at Stationers' Hall on 14 December 1609, but dated 1610. Brown, *Genesis of the United States*, 1:337–38.

54. *True and Sincere Declaration*, 366, 358.

55. Ibid., 356, 360, 361.

56. Ibid., 365.

57. *True and Sincere Declaration*, 366. For analysis of how England's rivalry with Spain affected support for Virginia, see Appelbaum and Sweet, *Envisioning an English Empire*. See also Hatfield, *Atlantic Virginia*.

58. *True and Sincere Declaration*, 367, 365, 368.

59. Ibid., 370.

60. *True and Sincere Declaration*, 369. See also Craven, *Virginia Company of London*, 22.

61. "Publication by the Counsell of Virginea," December 1609, 354–56.

62. Earl of Southampton to Earl of Salisbury, 15 December 1609, in Barbour, *Jamestown Voyages*, 2:288.

63. Craven, *Southern Colonies*, 101; Johnson, *New Life of Virginea*, 11 (first quotation); Quinn, "Notes by a Pious Colonial Investor," 554 (second quotation).

64. Percy, "True Relation," 505.

Chapter 5: The "Isle of Devils"

1. Strachey, *True Reportory*, 4, 15 (quotation); Jourdain, *Discovery of the Bermudas*, 106. See also Hughes, *Plaine and Trve Relation of the Goodnes of God*, 74; Somers to Earl of Salisbury, 15 June 1610, 400; and Edmund Howes, "The Annales or Generall Chronicle of England, begun first by Maister John Stow, and after him continued and augumented with forreyne and domestique, auncient and moderne, unto the ende of this present yeere 1614, by Edmond Howes, gentleman" (London, 1615), in Brown, *Genesis of the United States*, 2:753.

2. Wesley Frank Craven and Walter B. Hayward, eds., *The Journal of Richard Norwood: Surveyor of Bermuda* (New York: Bermuda Historical Monuments Trust, 1945), lxix (first quotation), lxx; Butler, *Historye of the Bermudaes*, 12 (second quotation); Silvester Jourdain, *A Plaine Description of the Barmvdas, now called Sommer Ilands. With the manner of their discouerie Anno 1609* (London, 1613), revised and expanded from Jourdain, *Discovery of the Bermudas*, 10 (third quotation); Wesley Frank Craven, "An Introduction to the History of Bermuda," *William and Mary Quarterly* 17 (April 1937): 183.

3. Archer, "discovery of our river," 107–9, 116–17; Andrews, "Christopher Newport," 28–41; Smith, *Generall Historie of Virginia*, 345 (quotation).

4. Howes, "Annales or Generall Chronicle of England," 753.

5. Smith, *Generall Historie of Virginia*, 348 (first quotation); Crashaw's dedication to Whitaker, *Good News*, 701 (second quotation); J. H. Lefroy, ed., *Memorials of the discovery and early settlement of the Bermudas or Somers Islands, 1515–1685*, 2 vols. (London, 1877–79), 2:572 (third quotation).

6. Michael J. Jarvis, " 'In the Eye of All Trade': Maritime Revolution and the Transformation of Bermudian Society, 1612–1800" (PhD diss., William and Mary, 1998), 8.

7. Strachey, *True Reportory*, 15. The story of the *Virginia Merchant* comes from the Bermuda Maritime Museum artifacts display.

8. Howes, "Annales or Generall Chronicle of England," 753; Jourdain, *Plaine Description*, 10 (first quotation). Jourdain calculated the distance at one-half mile, while Strachey said it was three-fourths mile. Somers held them to be

only one-fourth mile from land. Strachey, *True Reportory*, 15; Somers to Earl of Salisbury, 15 June 1610, 400. In 1958, the remains were found one-half mile east of St. George's Island.

9. Strachey, *True Reportory*, 16.

10. Craven, *Southern Colonies*, 94–96; George Somers's chest, Bermuda Historical Society Museum; archaeological report, Bermuda Maritime Museum; Strachey, *True Reportory*, 46.

11. Somers to Earl of Salisbury, 15 June 1610, 401 (quotation); Jourdain, *Discovery of the Bermudas*, 107.

12. *True Declaration of the estate of the Colonie*, 252.

13. Howes, "Annales or Generall Chronicle of England," 753.

14. For sartorial laws and practices, see Kuchta, *Three-Piece Suit*. For shipwreck motifs, see John G. Demaray, *Shakespeare and the Spectacle of Strangeness: The Tempest and the Transformation of Renaissance Theatrical Forms* (Pittsburgh: Duquesne University Press, 1998).

15. Zacek, "Sir Thomas Gates"; David F. Raine, *Sir George Somers: A Man and His Times* (Bermuda: Pompano Publications, 1984), 121–22.

16. Butler, *Historye of the Bermudaes*, 12 (quotation); Kennedy, *Isle of Devils*, 35.

17. Taylor, *American Colonies*, 125, 53 (Cortés quotation). For analysis of European colonization and Indian-white encounters in the Americas, see, for example, James Axtell, *The Invasion Within: The Contest of Cultures in Colonial North America* (New York: Oxford University Press, 1986); Anthony Pagden, *Lords of All the World: Ideologies of Empire in Spain, Britain, and France, c. 1500–c. 1800* (New Haven, Conn.: Yale University Press, 1995); and Patricia Seed, *Ceremonies of Possession in Europe's Conquest of the New World, 1492–1640* (Cambridge: Cambridge University Press, 1995). For colonial Virginia, see the classic Morgan, *American Slavery, American Freedom*; and most recently Horn, *Land as God Made It*.

18. Kennedy, *Isle of Devils*, 18; Lefroy, *Memorials of the discovery*, 1:2, 7–8 (quotations).

19. Strachey, *True Reportory*, 25 (quotation); Kennedy, *Isle of Devils*, 35–37.

20. Jourdain, *Discovery of the Bermudas*, 109.

21. Company Instructions to Thomas Gates, May 1609, 212–18, 213 (quotation).

22. Company Instructions to Thomas Gates, May 1609, 216; Strachey, *True Reportory*, 46.

23. Company Instructions to Thomas Gates, May 1609, 213.

24. Butler, *Historye of the Bermudaes*, 13 (quotation). Butler said the hogs came the first night. Jean Kennedy calculated it as the second night. Kennedy, *Isle of Devils*, 36.

25. Strachey, *True Reportory*, 32 (quotations); Lefroy, *Memorials of the discovery*, 1:9; Rich, *News from Virginia*, 420–26. For Strachey's life, see Wood, "William Strachey"; and Sanders, "William Strachey," 115–32.

26. Strachey, *True Reportory*, 30–31 (quotations); Lefroy, *Memorials of the discovery*, 2:578; Smith, *Generall Historie of Virginia*, 342; Jourdain, *Discovery of the Bermudas*, 110–11.

27. Jourdain, *Discovery of the Bermudas*, 111.

28. Smith, *Generall Historie of Virginia*, 343, 341 (quotations about bugs and poison ivy); Strachey, *True Reportory*, 41 (last quotation). See also Butler, *Historye of the Bermudaes*, 2; Craven and Hayward, *Journal of Richard Norwood*, lxxxi.

29. William Crashaw's dedication to Jourdain, *Plaine Description*, 5 (first quotation); Butler, *Historye of the Bermudaes*, 2 (second quotation). See also Craven and Hayward, *Journal of Richard Norwood*, lxxxii; Strachey, *True Reportory*, 24–26; Howes, "Annales or Generall Chronicle of England," 755.

30. Jourdain, *Discovery of the Bermudas*, 109, 112; Strachey, *True Reportory*, 24–25, 27–28 (quotations).

31. Strachey, *True Reportory*, 33.

32. Jourdain, *Discovery of the Bermudas*, 111; Jourdain, *Plaine Description*, 18–19; Craven and Hayward, *Journal of Richard Norwood*, lxxxiii; Strachey, *True Reportory*, 33–34.

33. Lefroy, *Memorials of the discovery*, 2:579 (first quotation); Strachey, *True Reportory*, 41 (second quotation). For climate figures, see Bermuda Government, Department of Statistics, *Facts and Figures 2005*. For comparisons to England and Virginia, see Lefroy, *Memorials of the discovery*, 2:578–79; Craven and Hayward, *Journal of Richard Norwood*, lxxx; and Jourdain, *Plaine Description*, 21.

34. Jourdain, *Plaine Description*, 20. For the dietary habits of Londoners in the early seventeenth century, see Stow, *Survey of London*, 81–83.

35. Smith, *Generall Historie of Virginia*, 348–49; Strachey, *True Reportory*, 27–28; Jourdain, *Discovery of the Bermudas*, 109 (quotation).

36. Henry C. Wilkinson, *The Adventurers of Bermuda: A History of the Island from Its Discovery until the Dissolution of the Somers Island Company in 1684* (Lon-

don: Oxford University Press, 1958), 45; Strachey, *True Reportory*, 23; Jourdain, *Discovery of the Bermudas*, 110.

37. Howes, "Annales or Generall Chronicle of England," 749; William Brewster letter, June 1607, 127; Wingfield, "Discourse of Virginia," 196.

38. Andrews, "Christopher Newport," 30.

39. Strachey, *True Reportory*, 35. Nathaniel Butler put the number of men at fourteen. Butler, *Historye of the Bermudaes*, 13.

40. Strachey, *True Reportory*, 38; map on vellum (xiii.45), British Library.

41. Craven and Hayward, *Journal of Richard Norwood*, lxxvi; Jourdain, *Discovery of the Bermudas*, 112–13; Hughes, *Plaine and Trve Relation of the Goodnes of God*, 72 (quotation). The hope for large numbers of pearls did not materialize, but early settlers did find ambergris.

42. Howes, "Annales or Generall Chronicle of England," 754 (first quotation); Lewis Hughes, *A Letter from the Summer Islands* (London, 1615), Library of Congress (second quotation). For further examples of this pervasive theme, see Hughes, *Plaine and Trve Relation of the Goodnes of God; True Declaration of the estate of the Colonie*; Whitaker, *Good News*, including William Crashaw dedication; and Lefroy, *Memorials of the discovery*, 1:13.

43. Strachey, *True Reportory*, 35. See also Smith, *Generall Historie of Virginia*, 349; and Butler, *Historye of the Bermudaes*, 13–14.

44. Strachey, *True Reportory*, 36–37.

45. Company Instructions to Thomas Gates, May 1609, 212–18; Strachey, *True Reportory*, 37.

46. Strachey, *True Reportory*, 37–38.

47. Strachey, *True Reportory*, 36 (quotation); Butler, *Historye of the Bermudaes*, 13; Kennedy, *Isle of Devils*, 40. They miscalculated by some 45 leagues or 155 miles.

48. Strachey, *True Reportory*, 36.

49. Ibid., 37.

50. Strachey, *True Reportory*, 54; Jourdain, *Discovery of the Bermudas*, 113; Rich, *News from Virginia*. James Swift also witnessed the christening of Bermudas Eason.

51. Educated elite women typically spurned public writing because their class defined it as an exclusively masculine pursuit, and servants like Persons were almost always illiterate. For women writers in this era and in early America, see Catherine Kerrison, *Claiming the Pen: Women and Intellectual Life in the Early American South* (Ithaca, N.Y.: Cornell University Press, 2005).

52. Strachey, *True Reportory*, 54–55, 49.

53. Strachey, *True Reportory*, 53–54 (quotations); Kennedy, *Isle of Devils*, 36–37; Craven, "History of Bermuda," 183.

54. Strachey, *True Reportory*, 40 (first quotation); Butler, *Historye of the Bermudaes*, 13 (second quotation). See also Jourdain, *Discovery of the Bermudas*, 108; Crashaw's dedication to Whitaker, *Good News*, 702; and, for interpretation, Neil MacRae Kennedy, "Anglo-Bermudian Society in the English Atlantic World, 1612 to 1701" (PhD diss., University of Western Ontario, 2002).

Chapter 6: Trouble in Paradise

1. Quoted in Peter Linebaugh and Marcus Rediker, *The Many-Headed Hydra: Sailors, Slaves, Commoners, and the Hidden History of the Revolutionary Atlantic* (Boston: Beacon Press, 2000), 10.

2. Strachey, *True Reportory*, 42.

3. Ibid., 41.

4. Ibid., 40.

5. Ibid., 40–42.

6. Ibid., 41.

7. Ibid., 42.

8. Ibid., 42–43.

9. Gray, *Good Speed to Virginia*, 302 (first and third quotations); Brown, *Genesis of the United States*, 1:364 (second quotation).

10. Zúñiga to Philip III, 5 March 1609, 244.

11. Strachey, *True Reportory*, 39.

12. Strachey, *True Reportory*, 37–39 (quotations), 53; Company Instructions to Thomas Gates, May 1609, 212–18.

13. Strachey, *True Reportory*, 40.

14. Company Instructions to Thomas Gates, May 1609, 214–15.

15. Ibid., 216.

16. On Edward Waters as Somers's long-term friend and aide, see Brown, *Genesis of the United States*, 2:1042–43; Raine, *Sir George Somers*, 49, 123–24, 134, 142; and Wilkinson, *Adventurers of Bermuda*, 36. The quotation is given in Bevan, *Great Seamen of Elizabeth I*, 256.

17. See Terry Tucker, *Bermuda: Unintended Destination* (Bermuda: Bermuda Book Store, 1968).

18. Strachey, *True Reportory*, 38–39.

19. Ibid., 50.

20. Ibid., 39.

21. Ibid., 41–42.

22. Bermuda Maritime Museum. Cedar would last fifty years, while oak lasted around twelve.

23. Smith, *Generall Historie of Virginia*, 349.

24. Quoted in Kennedy, *Isle of Devils*, 61.

25. Strachey, *True Reportory*, 50–51.

26. Ibid., 43.

27. Raines, *Sir George Somers*, 121–22.

28. Strachey, *True Reportory*, 44.

29. Ibid., 44, 42.

30. Linebaugh and Rediker, *Many-Headed Hydra*, 13.

31. For further analysis, see Charles H. George and Katherine E. George, *The Protestant Mind of the English Reformation* (Princeton: Princeton University Press, 1961); Christopher Hill, *Puritanism and Society in Pre-Revolutionary England* (London: Secker and Warburg, 1964); and J. F. Merritt, "The Pastoral Tightrope: A Puritan Pedagogue in Jacobean London," in Thomas Cogswell, Richard West, and Peter Lake, eds., *Politics, Religion, and Popularity in Early Stuart Britain* (Cambridge: Cambridge University Press, 2002), 143–61.

32. Strachey, *True Reportory*, 45 (quotation). For an excessively radical but still useful interpretation of the harsh punishment of Gates and the Virginia Company, see Linebaugh and Rediker, *Many-Headed Hydra*, 10–35. On discipline and punishment for mutinies, see Rodger, *Safeguard of the Sea*, 322, 406–7; and Andrews, *Ships, Money, and Politics*, 67–71. For Virginia Company orders allowing martial law, see Quinn, *New American World*, 5:213.

33. The remaining pages draw on Strachey, *True Reportory*, 45–60.

Chapter 7: *Jamestown Starving*

1. Smith, *Generall Historie of Virginia*, 225.

2. Ratcliffe to Earl of Salisbury, 4 October 1609, 334–35.

3. Ibid.

4. Smith, "Proceedings of the English Colony," 342–44; Percy, "True Relation," 502 (first quotation); George Percy to Earl of Northumberland, 17 August 1611, in Haile, *Jamestown Narratives*, 559 (second quotation); Price, *Love and Hate in Jamestown*, 123 (third quotation).

5. Horn, *Land as God Made It*, 176, 174. See also Carville V. Earle, "Environment, Disease and Mortality in Early Virginia," in Thad W. Tate and David L. Ammerman, eds., *The Chesapeake in the Seventeenth Century: Essays on Anglo-American Society* (Chapel Hill: University of North Carolina Press, 1979).

6. Percy, "True Relation," 503.

7. Ibid.

8. Percy, "True Relation," 504. See also Price, *Love and Hate in Jamestown*, 124; and Kelso, *Jamestown*, 22–27.

9. Ralph Hamor, *A True Discourse of the Present Estate of Virginia, and the Success of the Affairs there till the 18 of June, 1614; together with a Relation of the Several English Towns and Forts, the assured Hopes of that Country, and the Peace concluded with the Indians; the Christening of Powhatan's Daughter and her Marriage with an Englishman* (London, 1615), in Haile, *Jamestown Narratives*, 827 (first quotation); Don Diego de Molina to Don Alonso de Velasco, 28 May 1613, in Haile, *Jamestown Narratives*, 749. See also Kelso, *Jamestown*, 22–27; and Strachey, *True Reportory*, 79–81.

10. Percy, "True Relation," 504; Horn, *Land as God Made It*, 175.

11. Spelman, "Relation of Virginia," 483 (first quotation); Percy, "True Relation," 504 (second quotation); Horn, *Land as God Made It*, 175; Price, *Love and Hate in Jamestown*, 125.

12. Percy, "True Relation," 504 (quotations); Spelman, "Relation of Virginia," 484.

13. Percy, "True Relation," 504–5. Other sources, including Smith, "Proceedings of the English Colony," 344, put the number of men with Ratcliffe at thirty.

14. Percy, "True Relation," 504–5; Horn, *Land as God Made It*, 175.

15. Percy, "True Relation," 505.

16. Ibid.

17. Price, *Love and Hate in Jamestown*, 127; Horn, *Land as God Made It*, 175.

18. Percy, "True Relation," 505.

19. "Answer of the General Assembly," 913; Percy, "True Relation," 505.

20. "Answer of the General Assembly," 913; Ancient Planters of Virginia, "Brief Declaration," 896 (quotations about fleeing to the Indians); Percy, "True Relation," 506 (last quotation).

21. Ancient Planters of Virginia, "Brief Declaration," 895–96.

22. Price, *Love and Hate in Jamestown*, 128 (first quotation); Percy, "True Relation," 505 (second quotation).

23. Ancient Planters of Virginia, "Brief Declaration," 896 (first quotation); Percy, "True Relation," 505 (second quotation); Ancient Planters of Virginia, "Brief Declaration," 896 (remaining quotations). For perceptions of cannibalism in this era, see Philip P. Boucher, *Cannibal Encounters: Europeans and Island Caribs, 1492–1763* (Baltimore: Johns Hopkins University Press, 1992).

24. Ancient Planters of Virginia, "Brief Declaration," 896 (first and third quotations); Percy, "True Relation," 505 (second quotation).

25. *True Declaration of the estate of the Colonie*, 256.

26. "Answer of the General Assembly," 913.

27. Percy, "True Relation," 507.

28. Ibid., 506.

29. Ibid.

30. Virginia Bernhard, " 'Men, Women and Children' at Jamestown: Population and Gender in Early Virginia, 1607–1610," *Journal of Southern History* 58 (November 1992): 613–18.

31. Bernhard, "Population and Gender in Early Virginia," 609 (first quotation); Smith, "Proceedings of the English Colony," 344 (second quotation). For a slightly different calculation of mortality, see Horn, *Land as God Made It*, 176.

32. Brown, *Genesis of the United States*, 2:814.

33. Smith, "Proceedings of the English Colony," 344.

34. Crashaw's dedication to Whitaker, *Good News*, 703; Johnson, *New Life of Virginea*, 10.

35. Ancient Planters of Virginia, "Brief Declaration," 894.

36. "Answer of the General Assembly," 913. Observers back in London echoed this criticism in the Virginia Company's waning years and after its collapse. See, for example, D. R. Ransome, ed., *Sir Thomas Smith's Misgovernment of the Virginia Company, by Nicholas Ferrar* (Cambridge: Cambridge University Press, 1990); and Arthur Woodnoth, *A Short Collection of the Most Remarkable Passages from the Originall to the dissolution of the Virginia Company* (London, 1651), 3–5.

37. Bernhard, "Population and Gender in Early Virginia," 616–17.

38. Percy, "True Relation," 506.

Chapter 8: Redemption in Virginia

1. Strachey, *True Reportory*, 60.

2. Ibid.

3. Ibid., 60–61.

4. Bernhard, "Population and Gender in Early Virginia," 612.

5. Strachey, *True Reportory*, 63.

6. Ibid., 61–62.

7. Quinn, *North America*, 456; Percy, "True Relation," 506–7 (quotations).

8. Strachey, *True Reportory*, 62.

9. Ibid., 62–63.

10. Percy, "True Relation," 507.

11. Bernhard, "Population and Gender in Early Virginia," 616–17.

12. Crashaw's dedication to Whitaker, *Good News*, 704.

13. Strachey, *True Reportory*, 63–64.

14. Strachey, *True Reportory*, 63. Strachey gives the date as May 23, while others, including Silvester Jourdain, say it was May 24. Jourdain, *Discovery of the Bermudas,* 115.

15. Haile, *Jamestown Narratives*, 54, 67; Barbour, *Complete Works of Smith*, 1: xlviii, l; Company Instructions to Thomas Gates, 212; Strachey, *True Reportory*, 63 (quotation).

16. Strachey, *True Reportory*, 64, 71; Governor and Council of Virginia to the Virginia Company of London, 7 July 1610, in Brown, *Genesis of the United States*, 1:405. Here and in numerous places throughout his *True Reportory*, Strachey repeats the stories and sometimes even the exact language from the letter to the Virginia Company which, as secretary, he would have helped craft.

17. Strachey, *True Reportory*, 71, 64.

18. Strachey, *True Reportory*, 64 (first and third quotations); Hughes, *Plaine and Trve Relation of the Goodnes of God*, 75 (second quotation).

19. Strachey, *True Reportory*, 64–65. For the later legal code, see William Strachey, *For the Colony of Virginea Britannia, Lawes Divine, Morall and Martiall* (London, 1612).

20. Strachey, *True Reportory*, 75.

21. Strachey, *True Reportory*, 71 (first quotation); Somers to Earl of Salisbury, 15 June 1610, 401 (second quotation); Governor and Council to Virginia Company, 7 July 1610, 405 (third quotation).

22. Ancient Planters of Virginia, "Brief Declaration," 896.

23. Strachey, *True Reportory*, 64–65 (first quotation); Percy, "True Relation," 508 (second quotation); Crashaw's dedication to Whitaker, *Good News*, 704 (third quotation). Crashaw wrote that he got all his information directly from Gates: "if

any man ask how I know it, for their satisfaction I answer I have it from the faithful relation of that religious, valorous and prudent gentleman, SIR THOMAS
GATES . . . [who] hath since related this and much more unto me, face to face."

24. Strachey, *True Reportory*, 65.

25. Ancient Planters of Virginia, "Brief Declaration," 896 (quotation); Strachey, *True Reportory*, 76.

26. Percy, "True Relation," 508 (first quotation); Ancient Planters of Virginia, "Brief Declaration," 896 (second quotation).

27. Strachey, *True Reportory*, 76.

28. Strachey, *True Reportory*, 76; Ancient Planters of Virginia, "Brief Declaration," 896 (quotation).

29. Strachey, *True Reportory*, 76 (first and third quotations); Percy, "True Relation," 508 (second quotation).

30. Crashaw's dedication to Whitaker, *Good News*, 702.

31. Strachey, *True Reportory*, 77.

32. Jourdain, *Discovery of the Bermudas*, 115.

33. Quinn, *North America*, 456–58. The principal tract in this campaign was
True and Sincere Declaration, 356–71.

34. *True and Sincere Declaration*, 368 (quotation); Brown, *Genesis of the United
States*, 2:1048.

35. Strachey, *True Reportory*, 77 (first quotation); Lord De La Warr to Lord Salisbury, ca. July 1610, in Brown, *Genesis of the United States*, 1:414.

36. Brown, *Genesis of the United States*, 2:833.

37. Strachey, *True Reportory*, 77 (first quotation); Somers to Earl of Salisbury,
15 June 1610, 401; Rich, *News from Virginia*; Crashaw's dedication to Whitaker,
Good News, 702.

38. Ancient Planters of Virginia, "Brief Declaration," 897 (first and second
quotations); Crashaw's dedication to Whitaker, *Good News*, 702 (third quotation).

39. Smith, *Generall Historie of Virginia*, 234; Crashaw's dedication to Whitaker,
Good News, 702–3. See also Bond, *Damned Souls in a Tobacco Colony;* Miller, "Religious Impulse in the Founding of Virginia," 492–522; and Parker, "Religion
and the Virginia Colony," 245–70.

40. Lord De La Warr to Lord Salisbury, ca. July 1610, 415; *The Relation of the
Right Honourable the Lord De-La-Warre, Lord Governour and Captaine Generall of
Colonie, planted in Virginea* (London, 1611), in Quinn, *New American World*, 5:263.

41. Strachey, *True Reportory*, 84.

42. Ibid., 84–85.

43. Governor and Council to Virginia Company, 7 July 1610, 404.

44. Strachey, *True Reportory*, 85 (first quotation); Governor and Council to Virginia Company, 7 July 1610, 407.

45. Lord De La Warr to Lord Salisbury, ca. July 1610, 415.

46. Jourdain, *Discovery of the Bermudas*, 115; Smith, *Generall Historie of Virginia*, 236 (second quotation); Quinn, *North America*, 459.

47. Virginia Company Instructions to De La Warr, 1610, in Quinn, *New American World*, 5:219–20, 220 (quotations); Governor and Council to Virginia Company, 7 July 1610, 407–8.

48. Smith, *Generall Historie of Virginia*, 235.

49. Strachey, *True Reportory*, 80.

50. Ibid, 80–81.

51. Governor and Council to Virginia Company, 7 July 1610, 408–9 (quotations); Price, *Love and Hate in Jamestown*, 140; Strachey, *True Reportory*, 86.

52. Governor and Council to Virginia Company, 7 July 1610, 408 (first quotation); *True Declaration of the estate of the Colonie,* 258 (second quotation); Strachey, *True Reportory*, 87; Jourdain, *Discovery of the Bermudas*, 116.

53. Jourdain, *Discovery of the Bermudas*, 115 (first quotation); Smith, *Generall Historie of Virginia*, 236 (second quotation).

54. Jourdain, *Discovery of the Bermudas*, 116; Lord De La Warr to Lord Salisbury, ca. July 1610, 415, printed also in *Calendar of State Papers, Colonial Series* (London, 1860), 1:10.

55. Townsend, *Pocahontas and the Powhatan Dilemma*, 99; Brown, *Genesis of the United States*, 2:815.

56. Somers to Earl of Salisbury, 15 June 1610, 401–2.

57. *True Declaration of the estate of the Colonie*, 258 (first quotation); Jourdain, *Discovery of the Bermudas*, 116 (second quotation).

58. "The Voyage of Captaine Samuel Argal, from James Towne in Virginia, to seeke the Ile of Bermuda, and missing the same, his putting over toward Sagadahoc and Cape Cod, and so back againe to James Towne, begun the nineteenth of June, 1610," in Brown, *Genesis of the United States*, 1:429–33.

59. Ibid., 433–34.

60. Smith, *Generall Historie of Virginia*, 236.

61. Lord De La Warr to Lord Salisbury, ca. July 1610, 415.

62. Strachey, *True Reportory*, 88–89.

63. Horn, *Land as God Made It*, 184 (including quotation).

64. Strachey, *True Reportory*, 88–89.

65. Percy, "True Relation," 508.

66. Percy, "True Relation," 510. This story is also recounted in Smith, *Generall Historie of Virginia*, 236.

67. Percy, "True Relation," 510.

68. Ibid., 511, 508.

69. Quinn, *North America,* 459; Ancient Planters of Virginia, "Brief Declaration," 897–98 (quotations).

70. Lord De La Warr to Lord Salisbury, ca. July 1610, 413–15.

Chapter 9: God Is English

1. Don Alonso de Velasco to Philip III, 14 June 1610, in Brown, *Genesis of the United States,* 1:392; Irene A. Wright, "Spanish Policy toward Virginia, 1606–1612: Jamestown, Ecija, and John Clark of the Mayflower," *Journal of American History* 25 (April 1920): 458. Information about Virginia was also often contradictory, which further complicated Spain's developing a firmer position. Kupperman, *Jamestown Project*, 261–63.

2. "Voyage of Captaine Samuel Argal," 429, 433–34; Brown, *Genesis of the United States*, 2:1019.

3. Butler, *Historye of the Bermudaes*, 15.

4. Smith, *Generall Historie of Virginia,* 236 (first quotation); Butler, *Historye of the Bermudaes*, 15 (second and third quotations); "Voyage of Captaine Samuel Argal," 434.

5. Butler, *Historye of the Bermudaes*, 15.

6. Howes, *Annales or Generall Chronicle of England*, 750.

7. Butler, *Historye of the Bermudaes*, 16.

8. Butler, *Historye of the Bermudaes*, 16 (quotations); Craven, "History of Bermuda," 185; Brown, *Genesis of the United States*, 2:1042–43. Washington Irving wrote about the "three kings" in a short story. Irving, "Wolfert's Roost," in Roberta Rosenberg, ed., vol. 27 *The Complete Works of Washington Irving* (Boston: Twayne Publishers, 1979), 67.

9. Don Alonso de Velasco to Philip III, 14 June 1610, 392.

10. Brown, *Genesis of the United States*, 1:400.

11. Rich, *News from Virginia*; Jourdain, *Discovery of the Bermudas,* 106, 114;

Johnson, *Nova Britannia*, 239 (last quotation). Jourdain's account was first published in London in 1610; a second edition with a preface by William Crashaw and added commentary on Bermuda's environment appeared in 1613 under the title *A Plaine Description of the Barmvdas, now called Sommer Ilands*. For further discussions of the growing importance of religious language and providential appeals, see Bond, *Damned Souls in a Tobacco Colony*; Miller, "Religious Impulse in the Founding of Virginia," 492–522; Parker, "Religion and the Virginia Colony," 245–70.

12. Strachey, *True Reportory*. See also Miller, "Religious Impulse in the Founding of Virginia," 505.

13. Crashaw's dedication to Whitaker, *Good News*, 700, 703 (first and second quotations); Whitaker, *Good News*, 730; Smith, "Proceedings of the English Colony," 345.

14. Howes, *Annales or Generall Chronicle of England*, 753 (first quotation); Crashaw's dedication to Jourdain, *Plaine Description*, 5.

15. Howes, *Annales or Generall Chronicle of England*, 754.

16. Whitaker, *Good News*, 730 (first quotation); Smith, *Generall Historie of Virginia*, 234–35; Crashaw's dedication to Whitaker, *Good News*, 702 (second quotation); Smith, *Generall Historie of Virginia*, 234–35 (third quotation).

17. Smith, *Generall Historie of Virginia*, 237.

18. Ibid.

19. Thomas Smythe to Ralph Winwood, April 1611, in Kingsbury, *Records of the Virginia Company*, 3:33; Somers to Earl of Salisbury, 15 June 1610, 401 (second quotation); Governor and Council to Virginia Company, 7 July 1610, 402–13, 402 (quotation).

20. Crashaw's dedication to Whitaker, *Good News*, 700, 705; Whitaker, *Good News*, 736-37.

21. *True Declaration of the estate of the Colonie*, 250, 262, 260. See also Whitaker, *Good News*, 737.

22. Hamor, *True Discourse*, 839 (first quotation); "Virginias Verger: Or a Discourse shewing the benefits which may grow to this Kingdome from American English Plantations, and specially those of Virginia and Sommer Ilands," in Purchas, *Hakluytus Posthumus*, 19:266 (second quotation).

23. Smith, *Generall Historie of Virginia*, 235 (first quotation); Crashaw's dedication to Jourdain, *Plaine Description*, 3 (subsequent quotations). See also Julie Sievers, "Drowned Pens and Shaking Hands: Sea Providence Narratives in Seventeenth-Century New England," *William and Mary Quarterly* 63 (October 2006): 753–54.

NOTES

24. Whitaker, *Good News*, 744–45; Crashaw's dedication to Whitaker, *Good News*, 708.

25. Circular Letter of Walter Cope, 10 March 1610, quoted in Andrews, *Colonial Period of American History*, 1:106. See also Miller, "Religious Impulse in the Founding of Virginia."

26. Ralph Winwood to Lord Salisbury, 6 February 1611, in Brown, *Genesis of the United States*, 1:448–49.

27. Horn, *Land as God Made It*, 193–95; Price, *Love and Hate in Jamestown*, 146.

28. Broadside of the Virginia Council, January 1611, in Brown, *Genesis of the United States*, 1:445; Edwin Sandys to Mayor of Sandwich, 21 March 1611, in Brown, *Genesis of the United States*, 1:462.

29. Craven, *Virginia Company of London,* 23–24; Brown, *Genesis of the United States*, 1:461.

30. *Relation of Lord De-La-Warre,* 263 (first quotation); Lord De La Warr to Lord Salisbury, 22 June 1611, in Haile, *Jamestown Narratives*, 525–26.

31. *Relation of Lord De-La-Warre,* 263; Johnson, *New Life of Virginea,* 11 (second quotation); Craven, *Virginia Company of London,* 26. The exact date of Matthew Somers's return is not known. Alexander Brown calculated the date as sometime between 28 February and 26 July 1611, most likely in early July.

32. Third Charter of the Virginia Company, 12 March 1612, in Quinn, *New American World,* 5:226–32, 226, 227 (quotations).

33. Price, *Love and Hate in Jamestown*, 145–46; Robert C. Johnson, "The 'Running Lotteries' of the Virginia Company," *Virginia Magazine of History and Biography* 68 (April 1960): 156–65.

34. David R. Ransome, "Christopher Newport," *Oxford Dictionary of National Biography* (Oxford University Press, 2004).

35. Smith, *Generall Historie of Virginia*, 237, 239 (first quotation); Thomas Dale to Council of Virginia, 25 May 1611, in Haile, *Jamestown Narratives*, 521 (second quotation); Morgan, *American Slavery, American Freedom*, 73 (third quotation).

36. Percy, "True Relation," 514.

37. Strachey, *Lawes Divine, Morall and Martiall.*

38. Strachey, *Lawes Divine, Morall and Martiall*, 21, 10.

39. Percy, "True Relation," 515, 518.

40. Ancient Planters of Virginia, "Brief Declaration," 899–900.

41. Smith, *Generall Historie of Virginia*, 241 (first quotation); Ancient Planters

of Virginia, "Brief Declaration," 900 (second quotation). For Gates and Dale's regime, see also Kupperman, *Jamestown Project*, 257–59.

42. For the death of Gates's wife, see John Chamberlain to Dudley Carleton, 18 December 1611, in Brown, *Genesis of the United States*, 2:532, printed also in *Calendar of State Papers,* 12. For lessons learned about the need for strict oversight, see also Kupperman, *Jamestown Project*, 255.

43. Thomas Dale to Lord Salisbury, 17 August 1611, in Haile, *Jamestown Narratives*, 557; Molina to Velasco, 28 May 1613, 749, 747; Purchas, *Hakluytus Posthumus,* 18:457. For the character of early Virginians, see especially Breen, "Looking Out for Number One." For the waning interest in religion, see Parker, "Religion and the Virginia Colony," especially 268–70.

44. Strachey, *True Reportory*, 82; Anne Lash Jester, *Adventurers of Purse and Person: Virginia, 1607–1625* (Princeton: Princeton University Press, 1956), xiv.

45. John Chamberlain to Dudley Carleton, 22 June 1616, in Brown, *Genesis of the United States*, 2:789–90; Rabb, *Empire and Enterprise*, 34, 69. As historian Edmund Morgan assessed things, "The adventurers who ventured their capital lost it. Most of the settlers who ventured their lives lost them. And so did most of the Indians who came near them. Measured by any of the objectives announced for it, the colony failed." Morgan, *American Slavery, American Freedom*, 48. For the end of the company, see Wesley Frank Craven, *Dissolution of the Virginia Company: The Failure of a Colonial Experiment* (New York: Oxford University Press, 1932).

46. *Relation of Lord De-La-Warre*, 264.

47. *A Briefe Declaration of the present state of Things in Virginia* (London, 1616), in Brown, *Genesis of the United States*, 2:776.

48. Strachey, *True Reportory*, 83.

49. John Rolfe, "A True Relation of the State of Virginia," (1616), in Haile, *Jamestown Narratives*, 865–77. For the effect of tobacco on Virginia, see Morgan, *American Slavery, American Freedom*.

50. Morgan, *American Slavery, American Freedom*, 96.

51. Crashaw's dedication to Whitaker, *Good News*, 708; Rolfe, "True Relation," 866, 877. For a similar outlook, see Alexander Whitaker to William Crashaw, 9 August 1611, in Haile, *Jamestown Narratives*, 550.

52. Hughes, *Letter from the Summer Islands*; Crashaw's dedication to Jourdain, *Plaine Description*, 6; Hamor, *True Discourse*, 799, 813. See also Hughes, *Plaine and Trve Relation of the Goodnes of God*, 74. The history of Bermuda has received far

less scholarly attention than most British colonies; it fits easily neither into the framework of analysis of the mainland colonies nor the Caribbean settlements. Early exceptions to this pattern include Craven, "History of Bermuda"; Kennedy, *Isle of Devils*; and Wilkinson, *Adventurers of Bermuda*. More recent important works include Jarvis, " 'In the Eye of All Trade' "; and Kennedy, "Anglo-Bermudian Society."

53. Howes, *Annales or Generall Chronicle of England*, 755 (first and second quotations); 29 June 1611 newsletter, in David B. Quinn, ed., "Advice for Investors in Virginia, Bermuda, and Newfoundland, 1611," *William and Mary Quarterly* 23 (January 1966): 144; Crashaw's dedication to Whitaker, *Good News*, 702; David B. Quinn, "Bermuda in the Age of Exploration and Early Settlement," *Bermuda Journal of Archaeology and Maritime History* 1 (1989): 16; Diego de Molina to Alonso de Velasco, 28 May 1613, 748 (third quotation).

54. 29 June 1611 newsletter, 144. See also Velasco to Philip III, 22 August 1611, 495.

55. Don Francisco de Varte Ceron to Council of War, 24 May 1611, in Henry C. Wilkinson, ed., "Spanish Intentions for Bermuda, 1603–1615," *Bermuda Historical Quarterly* 7 (May 1950): 52 (first quotation); Letter from Duque de Medina Sidonia, 20 June 1613, in Wilkinson, "Spanish Intentions for Bermuda," 61 (second quotation); Philip III to Council of the Indies, ca. August 1613, Council of the Indies to Philip III, 1 September 1613, both in Wilkinson, "Spanish Intentions for Bermuda," 68–69.

56. John Smith quoted in Craven and Hayward, *Journal of Richard Norwood*, xxxvii; Duque de Medina Sidonia to Philip III, 22 June 1613, in Wilkinson, "Spanish Intentions for Bermuda," 62; Council of the Indies to Philip III, 6 July 1613, in Wilkinson, "Spanish Intentions for Bermuda," 66. See also Michael J. Jarvis, "Maritime Masters and Seafaring Slaves in Bermuda, 1680–1783," *William and Mary Quarterly* 59 (July 2002): 587.

57. Purchas, *Hakluytus Posthumus*, 19:257, 260; Hughes, *Plaine and Trve Relation of the Goodnes of God*, 72. See also Howes, *Annales or Generall Chronicle of England*, 755; and Craven, "History of Bermuda," 190.

58. John Chamberlain to Dudley Carleton, 12 February 1612, in Norman Egbert McClure, ed., *The Letters of John Chamberlain*, 2 vols. (Philadelphia: American Philosophical Society, 1939), 1:334. The name of the company and colony were spelled in various ways: Somers Island, Summer Islands, Sommers Island, etc. For consistency, unless quoting, we use the term "Somers Island Company/colony."

59. Don Alonso de Velasco to Philip III, 25 January 1613, in Brown, *Genesis of the United States*, 2:602; Crashaw's dedication to Whitaker, *Good News*, 702; Jourdain, *Plaine Description*, 22.

60. Jarvis, " 'In the Eye of All Trade,' " 32; Wilkinson, *Adventurers of Bermuda*, 57–58.

61. "An addition sent home by the last ships from our Colonie in the Barmudas," in Jourdain, *Plaine Description*, 17.

62. "An addition sent home," 17–18. See also Jarvis, " 'In the Eye of All Trade,' " 33.

63. Virginia Company Instructions to Governor Richard Moore, 27 April 1612, in A. C. Hollis Hallett, ed., *Bermuda Under the Sommer Islands Company, 1612–1684*, 3 vols. (Bermuda: Juniperhill Press, 2005), 1:1; Governor Richard Moore, 2 August 1612, in Jourdain, *Plaine Description*, 23.

64. Governor Richard Moore, 2 August 1612, 23–24 (quotations); Company Instructions to Richard Moore, 2.

65. Company Instructions to Richard Moore, 1; Jarvis, " 'In the Eye of All Trade,' " 34n5.

66. Wilkinson, *Adventurers of Bermuda*, 59; Jarvis, " 'In the Eye of All Trade,' " 34–37; John Chamberlain to Dudley Carleton, 27 October 1613, in McClure, *Letters of John Chamberlain*, 1:483.

67. Jarvis, " 'In the Eye of All Trade,' " 39–40; Wilkinson, *Adventurers of Bermuda*, 64–65.

68. Crashaw's dedication to Jourdain, *Plaine Description*, 6; Lewis Hughes to Nathaniel Rich, 19 May 1617, in Vernon A. Ives, ed., *The Rich Papers: Letters from Bermuda, 1615–1646* (Toronto: University of Toronto Press, 1984), 10. For the Puritan leanings of Bermudians, see also Games, *Migration and Origins*, 132–34; and Gregory Shipley, "Turbulent Times and Troubled Isles: The Rise and Development of Puritanism in Bermuda and the Bahamas, 1609–1684," (PhD diss., Westminster Theological Seminary, 1989).

69. Hughes, *Letter from the Summer Islands*.

70. Craven, "History of Bermuda," 450–51; Hughes, *Plaine and Trve Relation of the Goodnes of God*, 87–88; Craven and Hayward, *Journal of Richard Norwood*, lxxii–lxxv.

71. Craven, "History of Bermuda," 212 (quotation); Jarvis, " 'In the Eye of All Trade,' " chap. 1.

72. Robert Brenner, *Merchants and Revolution: Commercial Change, Political*

Conflict, and London's Overseas Traders, 1550–1653 (Princeton: Princeton University Press, 1993), 100; John Chamberlain to Dudley Carleton, 26 July 1623, in McClure, *Letters of John Chamberlain*, 2:509.

73. Virginia Bernhard, "Bermuda and Virginia in the Seventeenth Century: A Comparative View," *Journal of Social History* 19 (1985): 57–70; Jarvis, "'In the Eye of All Trade,'" 28–31; Jarvis, "Maritime Masters and Seafaring Slaves," 588; Morgan, *American Slavery, American Freedom*, 101.

74. Hughes, *Plaine and Trve Relation of the Goodnes of God*, 77 (first quotation); "An addition sent home," 22 (second quotation).

Chapter 10: *"O Brave New World"*

1. See Culliford, *William Strachey*, 154. A recent book by journalist Benjamin Woolley suggests that William Shakespeare may have got his hands on the unpublished manuscript through Mary, Countess of Pembroke, and her son, the Earl of Pembroke. See Woolley, *Savage Kingdom: The True Story of Jamestown, 1607, and the Settlement of America* (New York: HarperCollins, 2007), 296.

2. Culliford, *William Strachey*, 47–60. See also Jeffrey L. Hantman, "Caliban's Own Voice: American Indian Views of the Other in Colonial Virginia," *New Literary History* 23 (Winter 1992): 72–73. As Louis B. Wright notes, "In a small group of this sort Strachey's erstwhile friends would have heard something of his adventures. If the letter addressed to the noble lady did not circulate in manuscript in this group, they would at least have known about the substance of it." Wright, *Voyage to Virginia*, xi.

3. Ackroyd, *Shakespeare*, 487.

4. John Gillies, "The Figure of the New World in *The Tempest*," in Peter Hulme and William H. Sherman, eds., *"The Tempest" and Its Travels* (Philadelphia: University of Pennsylvania Press, 2000), 181; A. L. Rowse, *William Shakespeare* (New York: Harper and Row, 1964), 446; Gerald Graff and James Phelan, eds., *The Tempest: A Case Study in Critical Controversy* (Boston and New York: Bedford/St. Martin's, 2000), 21. See also Wright, *Voyage to Virginia*, xix.

5. Meredith Anne Skura, "Discourse and the Individual: The Case of Colonialism in 'The Tempest,'" *Shakespeare Quarterly* 40 (Spring 1989): 42–69.

6. Charles Frey, "The Tempest and the New World," *Shakespeare Quarterly* 30 (Winter 1979): 37.

7. See, for example, Canny, "Ideology of English Colonization," 575–98;

and Ronald T. Takaki, "The 'Tempest' in the Wilderness," in Graff and Phelan, *Tempest*, 140–72.

8. Graff and Phelan, *Tempest*, 35, 26; Hantman, "Caliban's Own Voice," 72. See also Alden T. Vaughan, "Shakespeare's Indian: The Americanization of Caliban," *Shakespeare Quarterly* 39 (Summer 1988): 137–53; Patricia Seed, " 'This island's mine': Caliban and Native Sovereignty," in Hulme and Sherman, *"Tempest" and Its Travels*, 202–11.

9. Graff and Phelan, *Tempest*, 81.

10. Frey, "Tempest and the New World," 34, 39.

11. Hantman, "Caliban's Own Voice," 72–73.

12. See Linebaugh and Rediker, *Many-Headed Hydra*.

13. For recent important analysis of Virginia and the Atlantic world, see Hatfield, *Atlantic Virginia*; Appelbaum and Sweet, *Envisioning an English Empire*; Kupperman, *Jamestown Project*; and Mancke and Shammas, *Creation of the British Atlantic World*.

14. Purchas quoted in Morgan, "Sir Thomas Smythe." See also Rabb, *Enterprise and Empire*; and Spurling, *Sir Thomas Smythe*.

15. D. R. Ransome, ed., *Sir Thomas Smith's Misgovernment of the Virginia Company, by Nicholas Ferrar* (Cambridge: Cambridge University Press, 1990), 3–4 (quotations); Kupperman, *Jamestown Project*, 284; Theodore K. Rabb, *Jacobean Gentleman: Sir Edwin Sandys, 1561–1629* (Princeton: Princeton University Press, 1998), part 3; Haile, *Jamestown Narratives*, 891–92; Morgan, "Sir Thomas Smythe."

16. Brown, *Genesis of the United States*, 2:1013 (quotation); Spurling, *Sir Thomas Smythe*, 17–18.

17. Morgan, "Sir Thomas Smythe"; Brown, *Genesis of the United States*, 2:1017.

18. Quoted in Akrigg, *Shakespeare and the Earl of Southampton*, 165.

19. Akrigg, *Shakespeare and the Earl of Southampton*, 165. Quotation is from Park Honan, "Henry Wriothesley," *Oxford Dictionary of National Biography* (Oxford University Press, 2004).

20. For other examples of this popular voyage literature, see James Rosier, *A true relation of the most prosperous voyage made this present yeere 1605, by Captaine George Waymouth, in the discovery of the land of Virginia* (London, 1605); Richard Hakluyt, *Divers voyages, touching the discoverie of America* (London, 1582); and Richard Willies, *The History of travayle in the West and East Indies, and other countreys lying eyther way, towardes the fruitfull and rych Moluccaes* (London, 1577).

21. Culliford, *William Strachey*, 148–63, 149 (quotation); Strachey, *History of*

Travel into Virginia, 563–689; John Smith, *A Map of Virginia with a Description of the Countrey, the Commodities, People, Government and Religion* (London, 1612), in Barbour, *Complete Works of Smith*, 1:119–90.

22. Culliford, *William Strachey*, 140, 162–63.

23. Two petitions from Gates's destitute daughters to the Privy Council in 1632 suggest he had died in Virginia or the Low Countries. Brown, *Genesis of the United States*, 2:895; Zacek, "Sir Thomas Gates."

24. Brown, *Genesis of the United States*, 2:895.

25. On Newport, see Andrews, "Christopher Newport," 28–41; Thomas Roe quoted in Ransome, "Christopher Newport."

26. Brown, *Genesis of the United States*, 2:957–58 (quotation); Ransome, "Christopher Newport."

27. Percy, "True Relation," 497–519, 499 (quotation). See also J. W. Shirley, "George Percy at Jamestown," *Virginia Magazine of History and Biography*, 57 (1949): 227–43; Mark Nicholls, "George Percy," *Oxford Dictionary of National Biography* (Oxford University Press, 2004).

28. J. Frederick Fausz, "Thomas West," *Oxford Dictionary of National Biography* (Oxford University Press, 2004); *Relation of Lord De-La-Warre*, 263–65.

29. Brown, *Genesis of the United States*, 2:1043.

30. Nathaniel Philbrick, *Mayflower: A Story of Courage, Community, and War* (New York: Viking Press, 2006), 25–26, 39 (quotations), 105–10, 119.

31. Percy, "True Relation," 504–5; Brown, *Genesis of the United States*, 2:814.

32. Brown, *Genesis of the United States*, 2:1021 (first quotation); Woolley, *Savage Kingdom*, 362–63 (subsequent quotations); Kingsbury, *Records of the Virginia Company*, 3:175; Smith, *Generall Historie of Virginia*, 320–21.

33. Smith, *Generall Historie of Virginia*, 196; Horn, *Land as God Made It*, 216–23, 249–50. See also J. Frederick Fausz, "Powhatan," *Oxford Dictionary of National Biography* (Oxford University Press, 2004).

34. John Rolfe to Thomas Dale, ca. 1614, in Haile, *Jamestown Narratives*, 851.

35. Rolfe, "True Relation," 877. On Rolfe's life, see also Phillip Barbour, *Pocahontas and Her World* (New York: Houghton Mifflin, 1970); Robert S. Tilton, *Pocahontas: The Evolution of an American Narrative* (Cambridge: Cambridge University Press, 1994); and Townsend, *Pocahontas and the Powhatan Dilemma*.

36. Rolfe, "True Relation," 874; Whitaker, *Good News,* including Crashaw's dedication, 707; Brown, *Genesis of the United States*, 2:835 (first and last quotations).

37. Hallett, *Bermuda Under the Sommer Islands Company*, 1:23.

38. Brown, *Genesis of the United States*, 2:1042–43.

39. Jarvis, "'In the Eye of All Trade,'" 35, 37 (quotation), 43. See also Craven, "History of Bermuda," 176–215. St. George's Island became home to the town of St. George, both of which are in St. George's Parish.

40. See Steven Sarson, *British America, 1500–1800: Creating Colonies, Imagining an Empire* (London: Hodder Arnold, 2005), 186; Alison Games, "Beyond the Atlantic: English Globetrotters and Transoceanic Connections," *William and Mary Quarterly* 63 (October 2006): 675–92.

41. Takaki, "'Tempest' in the Wilderness," 148–49, 153.

42. Analyses of Virginia's challenges in the seventeenth century can be found in Morgan, *American Slavery, American Freedom*; and Horn, *Land as God Made It*.

43. For the transition from servitude to slavery, see Ira Berlin, *Many Thousands Gone: The First Two Centuries of Slavery in North America* (Cambridge, Mass.: Harvard University Press, 1998); Morgan, *American Slavery, American Freedom*; and Philip Morgan, *Slave Counterpoint: Black Culture in the Eighteenth-Century Chesapeake and Lowcountry* (Chapel Hill: University of North Carolina Press, 1998).

44. Jarvis, "'In the Eye of All Trade,'" 136–37 (quotations), 164; Hughes, *Letter from the Summer Islands*. See also Kennedy, "Anglo-Bermudian Society."

45. Butler, *Historye of the Bermudaes*, 16 (first quotation); Smith, "Proceedings of the English Colony," 277–78 (second quotation). See also Raine, *Sir George Somers*.

46. Somers to Earl of Salisbury, 15 June 1610, 401–2.

ACKNOWLEDGMENTS

Like our *Sea Venture* castaways, we've been on an adventure far different from the one we first imagined. We began this project simply curious to learn the circumstances surrounding a shipwreck occasionally mentioned in historical studies of Jamestown's founding. We hoped we might find a lively tale to share with our students. But the more we learned, the stronger our curiosity grew. And a story became a book. Our friend Jeff Norrell encouraged us to conceive of our project as a narrative history for a broad audience; he introduced us to our agent, Geri Thoma, and helped us sharpen the proposal we shared with her. Our first and greatest gratitude is owed to Jeff.

As we pursued our exploration of the *Sea Venture* ordeal we received aid and encouragement from many quarters. Natalie Zacek and Heather Hirschfeld pointed us in the right initial direction. Jeri McIntosh and Paul Cobb opened their London home to us, making a research trip far more delightful than it ought to have been. Jeri also happily answered myriad questions about Tudor-Stuart England. Tom Granger, a total stranger to us, took pity on two lost souls seeking Plymouth Sound. The staffs at the British Library, Public Records Office, Plymouth Public Library, and Library of Congress fielded all our inquiries and offered invaluable assistance. David Wingate shared his boundless knowledge of Bermuda's natural environment and those amazing cahows. Gerry Swan helped us make the most of our first trip to his native Bermuda. The eighteenth-century reading group at the University of Tennessee kindly tolerated a seventeenth-century diversion, and Misty Anderson, Denise Phillips, and Mary McAlpin offered much-needed encouragement at a critical juncture. Steve Ash, Richard Bailey, Tracy Campbell, Mary McAlpin, Jeff Norrell, Cynthia Tinker, and Steve Wrinn all read early chapters; each helped us refine our ideas and make the book stronger. We enjoyed sharing our research with Steve Sarson and the British Group in Early American History at their 2007 conference in Wales. Fashion Bowers reviewed the whole manuscript, saving us from several errors and keeping us faithful to that often vexing seventeenth-century style of language.

Tim Breen, April Hatfield, James Horn, Karen Kupperman, and Natalie Zacek read the entire manuscript and graciously shared with us their capacious knowledge of early American history. The book is far stronger for their suggestions. Of course, whatever mistakes that remain are ours alone.

The University of Kentucky and the University of Tennessee generously subsidized our many travels in pursuit of the *Sea Venture* story and then gave us time off from teaching to write the book. This book would be years from publication without that support. And it might never have happened without the encouragement and hard work of Geri Thoma, who believed enough in the project to help us find our way.

Finally, it has been an honor to work with so wise and thoughtful an editor as Jack Macrae. He and the wonderful staff at Henry Holt, particularly Lisa Fyfe, Michelle Daniel, and Supurna Banerjee, made our long journey worthwhile and ensured our safe arrival home.

INDEX

Entries in italics indicate illustrations.

Archer, Captain Gabriel, 38–40, 44–45, 49,
    101, 183, 259
  expedition of 1609, 70, 79, 86, 97, 98
  political infighting, 103–107, 110, 111,
    112, 173
Argall, Captain Samuel, 78, 104, 107, 112,
    119, 205–207, 209, 213, 214

Bacon, Sir Francis, 12, 52
Bennett, Nicholas, 71, 72, 88, 151, 162
Bermuda, 78, *126,* 150, 266–67
  boats taking castaways to Virginia from,
    see *Deliverance; Patience*
  castaways of shipwrecked *Sea Venture* in,
    125–70
  colonizing of, 214–15, 225–26, 234–44,
    235, 262–63, 264
  compact signed by settlers, 239–40
  coral reefs, *127,* 127–28, 142, 236–37
  differences among the leadership in,
    140–42, 159–60
  discovery and naming of, 133

dissension among castaways, 149–53,
    159–64, 165–68, 250
fish and wildlife, abundance of, 133–38,
    139, 140, 142, 150, 204–205
Frobisher's Bay, 140
memorial erected by Gates in, 169–70
planning of escape from, 139, 140, 141–42,
    143–46, 147, 148, 149, 153–60
religious observance in, 134, 146, 147,
    238, 239, 241–42, 263
reputation of, 125–28, 136, 148
riches of, 142, 148, 150, *157,* 234, 240,
    263
St. Catherine's Beach, 129
St. George's Island, 128, 238, 241, 263,
    267
Sea Venture arrives at, 125–29
shelter in, 133–34, 150
Smith's Island, 238, 241, 252
surveyed by Somers, 140–41, 142,
    155–56, *157*
"three kings of," 215, 238, 240, 250, 262

Bermúdez, Juan de, 133
Blackfriars Theatre, 74, 246
Blessing, 76, 79, 86, 98, 99, 185
Blunt, Humphrey, 208
Book of Martyrs (Foxe), 88
Box, William, 99
Brewster, Captain Edward, 196
Brewster, William, 38, 40
Briars, Jeffrey, 147
Browne, Robert, 162–63
Buck, Rev. Richard, 2, 71, 80, 88, 124, 261–62
   in Bermuda, 134, 146, 147, 161
   in Jamestown, 190, 200, 203

cannibalism, 180–81, 189, 204, 212
Cape Cod, 27, 206
Cape Henry, 187, 206
Carter, Christopher, 150–51, 167, 168, 170, 262
   colonizing of Bermuda and, 214, 215, 238, 240, 250, 262
Catholicism, 5, 17–19, 21, 43, 66–67
Cecil, Robert, Earl of Salisbury, 19, 37, 43, 111, 116, 122, 172–73, 200, 205, 224
Challons, Henry, 23
Chamberlain, John, 231
Champlain, Samuel de, 127
Chard, Edward, 215, 238, 240, 250, 262
Church of England, *see* religion
Collines (Collins), 180–81
Concerning the Plantation of Virginia New Britain, 59
Cortés, Hernán, 133
Crashaw, Rev. William, 17–18, 20, 56, 63, 67, 153, 184, 198, 199–200, 218, 220–21, 222–23, 233, 237, 261
Cromwell, Oliver, 52

Dale, Sir Thomas, 202, 223–24, 226–29, 243, 255, 260, 261
Davis, Captain James, 177, 178, 182, 183, 185, 195, 209, 238, 240
   castaways' arrival and, 185, 188
De La Warr, Lord (Thomas West), 52, 53, 224–25, 231, 249, 257
   expedition of 1610, 120–23, 145, 196–200, 212–13, 264
   as governor of Jamestown, 200–10, 213, 220
   health of, 200, 207, 209–10, 224–25, 257
Deliverance, 168–70, *169,* 170, 192
   building of, 153–54, 156, 157, 158, 165
   journey of May 1610, 170, 186–89
   plan to abandon Virginia and, 194–96, 198, 199
Diamond, 79, 85, 86, 97, 99, 144
"Discourse of Virginia," 47
Discovery, 34, 194–96, 206
Discovery of the Bermudas, Otherwise Called the Isle of Devils, A (Jourdain), 217, 253
Donne, John, 74
Drake, Sir Francis, 14, 76, 83, 87, 88
Drayton, Michael, 36

Eason, Mrs. Edward, 146
East India Company, 9, 10, 26–27, 227, 253, 255, 258
Eastward Hoe!, 28, 29
Elizabeth I, Queen, 5, 10–11, 18, 25
England, 31, 131
   history of New World exploration and settlement, 4–7, 23, 24–29, 264–65
   rivalry with Spain, *see* Spain, empire in America, and rivalry with England
expedition of 1609, 1–4
   arrival of fleet in Virginia, 98–102
   departure of, 76–79
   the hurricane, 2–4, 8, 90–96, 97, 112, 113, 124–25
   leadership of, 70
   lead ship, *see Sea Venture*
   navigational methods, 86–87
   planning for, 50–56
   public relations campaign to finance and recruit settlers for, 55–70, 71, 80
   the route, 77–78, 90, 113
   separation of the ships, 91, 97–98, 116
   the voyagers, 70–75, 79–81
   see also individual ships and passengers

expedition of 1610, 120–23, 145, 196–200, 210–11, 264

expedition of 1611, 223–24, 226, 229

Falcon, 79, 98, 99, 185

Fawkes, Guy, 19

Fishmongers' Company, 28

Fort Algernon, *see* Point Comfort, settlement at

Foxe, John, 88

Frobisher, Richard, 72, 140, 141, 153–54, 156, 168, 169

Garnet, Henry, 19–20

Gates, Sir Thomas, 1, 23, 24, 50, *51,* 71, 98, 254–55, 261
  arrival in Bermuda, 125–26, 129
  asserts authority while in Bermuda, 131–32, 134–35, 139–40, 147, 148, 152, 153–55, 163–64, 165–67, 250
  Bermuda-Jamestown journey in May 1610, 170, 187, 188–89
  De La Warr's expedition and, 196–98, 200
  as designated governor of Virginia colony, 52–53, 54, 70, 75, 104, 119, 120, 131–32, 134
  expedition of 1611 and, 223–24, 229
  as governor of Jamestown, 190–93, 200, 229, 254
  hurricane faced by the *Sea Venture* and, 3–4, 92–93, 94
  Indian policy and, 207–208
  as lieutenant governor, 202, 203, 213
  London trip of 1610, to ensure continued support for Virginia, 210–11, 216, 217, 220, 223
  memorial erected by, 169–70
  planning of escape from Bermuda, 139, 140, 141–42, 147, 148, 149, 153–60
  plan to abandon Virginia, in spring of 1610, 193–96, 197–98
  plot to kill, 165–66
  reports reaching London in fall of 1609 and, 112–16
  voyage across the Atlantic, 76–77, 82, 88, 92–93, 94

Gilbert, Sir Humphrey, 5, 25, 27–28, 249

Gilbert, Raleigh, 23

Globe theater, London, 17, 56

Glover, Thomas, 74

Godspeed, 34

Golden Hinde, 14

Good News from Virginia (Whitaker), 220–21

Gosnold, Captain Bartholomew, 27, 34, 38, 41, 43

Gray, Rev. Robert, 63, 65, 67, 69, 153

Hakluyt, Richard, 17, 23, 24–25, 35, 249, 253

Hanham, Thomas, 23

Hawkins, Richard, 87

Henry, Prince (son of James I), 187, 254

History of Travel into Virginia Britannia, The (Strachey), 253, 254

Hitchman, William, 147

Hog Island, 171, 178, 196

Hope, 256

Hopkins, Stephen, 71, 80, 88, 160–64, 168, 250, 258
  family of, 258

Horton, Mistress, 72, 146

Hudson, Henry, 89–90, 253

Hughes, Rev. Lewis, 233, *234,* 237, 241–42

Hunt, Rev. Robert, 41, 83

Indians, *see* Native Americans

James I, King, 6, 11, 17, 18–19, 21, *22,* 26, 29, 32, 33, 56, 102, 226
  chartering of Virginia Company, *see* Virginia, colony of
  expedition of 1609 and, 60–61
  expedition of 1610 and, 122

James River, 38, 44, 204, 206, 256

Jamestown
  after 1611, 229–33
  Dale as governor of, 226–29, 255
  deaths in winter of 1609–10, 183, 189, 190–91, 259
  expedition of 1609 to save, *see* expedition of 1609

Jamestown (*continued*)
  expedition of 1610 to save, 120–23, 145,
    196–200, 212–13, 264
  food crisis in summer of 1610, Somers'
    Bermuda mission and, 204–206,
    213–15
  fort at, 39, 41, 44, 45, 100, 175–76, 179,
    191, 201
  founding of, 6
  map locating Bermuda and, *126*
  the original colony and its problems, 1,
    6–7, 30–50, 69, 132
  plan to abandon, in spring of 1610,
    193–96, 197–98
  political infighting among leaders of,
    102–108, 112, 144, 172–73
  reports in fall of 1609 of troubles in,
    111–16
  Smith's provisioning of, before departing
    in October 1609, 171–72
  "starving time," 179–85, 189, 191, 212
  winter of 1609–10, 123, 175–85,
    188–89, 190, 212, 259
  see also Virginia, colony of
John and Francis, 44, 45
Johnson, Robert, 57–58, 63, 68–69, 112,
  123, 184
Jonson, Ben, 12, 74, 246
Jourdain, Ignatius, 74
Jourdain, Silvester, 74, 93, 128–29, 196,
  199, 201, 205, 217, 237–38, 245, 246,
  253

Keith, Rev. George, 241
Kendall, George, 38, 43–44

Lawes Divine, Morall and Martiall, 192,
  227–28, 232
Levant Company, 9, 10
Lewis, Richard, 147
Lion, 79, 98, 99
London, 12–20, *15,* 85
Lost Flocke Triumphant, The (Rich), 217

Magellan, Ferdinand, 249
Map of Virginia (Smith), 113, 159, 253, 254

Martin, Captain John, 38, 43, 44, 108–109,
  174, 183
  political infighting, 103–107, 110, 111,
  173
Mary, Queen of Scots, 18, 19
May, Henry, 133
Mayflower, 258
Mease, Rev. William, 114
Mexico, 132–33
Middle Temple, *13,* 13–14
Molina, Don Diego de, 175
Monocan Indians, 101, 102
Montaigne, Michel de, 248
Moore, Richard, 238, 239–41, 242,
  263–64
Muscovy Company, 9, 10, 12, 252

Namontack, 46–47
Nansemond, 108, 109, 174–75
Native Americans, 258, 265
  conversion to Christianity, 21, 63, 65,
  118
  first Jamestown settlement and, 31,
  40–41, 42, 45
  see also names of individuals and tribes
Netherlands, 5, 253, 254, 257
Newfoundland, 5, 25
Newport, Captain Christopher, 90, 141,
  192–93, 202, 210, 216, 217, 226–27,
  254, 255–56
  arrival at Bermuda, 124–25, 128
  as commander of the *Sea Venture,* 1, 2, 3,
  70, 72, 75, 88–89, 90–91, 125–26,
  128
  first colony at Jamestown and, 24, 30,
  34–42, 44–49, 100, 106
  the hurricane and, 3, 90–91
  life in Bermuda, 146, 164, 250
  voyage across the Atlantic in 1609,
  76–77, 82, 88–89, 90–91
Northwest Passage, 5, 10, 26, 251, 253
Nova Britannia, 57–59, *58,* 61, 63, 66,
  68–69, 117, 231

"Of the Cannibals," 248
Opechancanough, 259, 260, 261

Paine, Henry, 72, 165, 168

Pamunkey Indians, 44

Parker, William, 23

Patawomeck Indians, 178

Patience, 169, 170, 192, 206, 215, 267
arrival at Point Comfort, 185, 187–88
building of, 156–59, 160, 165
journey of May 1610, 170, 186–89
plan to abandon Virginia and, 194–96

Pembroke, Earl of, 52, 249

Percy, George, 35, 42–43, 81, 103, 106, 108–109, 190, 192–93, 195, 198, 226, 228, 256–57
castaways' arrival and, 185, 188
described, 111, 173, 256
as president of Jamestown, 111, 173–82, 185, 191, 216
raids against the Indians, 208–209
"starving time" and, 179–82

Perkins, Francis, 45

Persons, Elizabeth, 72, 88, 146, 147

Phetiplace, Captain William, 177

Philip and Francis, 35

Philip III, King, 32–33, 61, 102, 213, 236

Phoenix, 106

Pierce, Jane (third wife of John Rolfe), 189, 261

Pierce, Joan, 185, 189

Pierce, William, 185, 261

Pilgrims, 258

piracy, 6, 26, 72

Pius V, Pope, 18

plague, 85, 86, 97, 113, 174

Plough, 238, 240

Plymouth Colony, 254–55, 258, 264

Pocahontas (Rebecca Rolfe), 7, 44, 146, 233, 260–61

Point Comfort, settlement at, 172, 175, 177, 178, 182, 183, 190, 208
Bermuda castaways arrive at, 185, 187–89
De La Warr's expedition reaches, 196, 197

Popham, George, 23, 46

Powell, Thomas, 82, 88, 146

Powhatan, 42, 44, 45, 48, 54, 75, 102, 188, 191, 259–60

De La Warr and, 207–208
fall and winter of 1609–10, 174, 176–77, 178–79, 216, 260

Powhatan Indians, 42, 48, 66, 100, 109, 132, 191, 207–209, 228, 259–60
arrival of 1609 expedition and, 100–101
fall and winter of 1609–10, 174, 175, 176–77, 178–79, 204, 260
offensive of 1622, 232, 244, 261, 266
Ravens's rescue party and, 188

Powle, Stephen, 76

Price, Rev. Daniel, 2, 63, 65, 66, 67

Pryse, Hughe, 181

Purchas, Samuel, 230, 236–37, 251

Puritans, 71, 160, 162–63, 241, 242

Raleigh, Sir Walter, 5–6, 12, 20–21, 25, 26, 253

Ratcliffe, Captain John, 34, 38, 43, 44, 49, 54, 116, 144
expedition of 1609, 70, 79, 97, 99
letter to Cecil on conditions in Jamestown, 172–73
mission to Powhatan and death of, 176–77, 183, 190, 259
political infighting, 103–107, 110–11, 144, 173

Ravens, Henry, 35, 143, 145–50, 152, 153, 156, 188

Reed, Humphrey, 161, 163

religion, 88
Bermuda castaways and colonists and, 134, 142–43, 146, 147, 151, 160, 162–63, 238, 239, 241–42, 263
Catholicism, 5, 17–19, 21, 54, 66–67
conversion of the Indians, 18, 21, 63, 65, 118
founding and promotion of Virginia colony and, 2, 4, 8, 17–18, 20, 36, 54, 56, 57, 58, 61, 62–68, 64, 71–72, 80, 118–19, 124, 171, 220–24, 230, 261–62
interpretation of experiences of English colonists as providence, 196, 199–200, 211, 216–19, 220–24, 233–34, *234,* 237–38, 244, 245

religion (continued)
in Jamestown, 200, 203, 228
Puritans, 71, 160, 162–63, 241, 242
Rich, Robert, 93–94, 198, 217, 245, 251
Richard, 23
Roanoke, "lost colony" of, 5–6, 25–26
Roe, Sir Thomas, 255
Rolfe, Bermuda, 146, 147, 260
Rolfe, John, 75, 146, 189, 233, 260–61
first wife, 146, 147, 260
tobacco economy and, 232, 261, 266
Rolfe, Thomas, 261

Sagadahoc, colony of, 23, 46, 57
St. Elmo's fire, 95, 247
St. Paul's Cathedral, 13
St. Paul's Cross, 2, 4, 17, 19, 20, 56, 63,
124
Salisbury, Earl of (Robert Cecil), 19, 37, 43,
111, 116, 122, 172–73, 200, 205, 224
Samuel, Edward, 164–65
Sandys, Edwin, 43, 52, 251, 255
Scrivener, Matthew, 144, 145, 191
Seaflower, 262
Sea Venture, 1–4, 7, 185, 241, 244, 246–51
arrival at Bermuda, 125–29
conditions on, 81–86
the crew, 2, 72, 74, 80, 82–83, 88–89
described, 78–79, 81–82
the hurricane, 2–4, 8, 90–96, 112,
124–25
illness and death, 83, 84, 85
passengers aboard, 1–2, 70–75, 79–81,
119
provisioning of, 76, 81
rumors of loss of, 112, 115–16, 171
salvaging of materials for boat to escape
Bermuda, 141, 153–54, 158–59
salvaging of supplies from, 129–30
sealed box with list of names of new
leaders, 82, 88, 103, 105, 107, 144–45
separation of other ships from, 91, 97–98,
116
story of survival of, Virginia Company's
turnaround and, 210–11, 216–24,
233–34, 245–46, 264

The Tempest and, 246–50
voyage across the Atlantic, 76–96
Shakespeare, William, 10, 17, 52, 56, 74,
217, 246–50, 265
Sharp, Samuel, 161, 163
Shelley, Henry, 140
Sicklemore, Lieutenant, 174, 175
Skinners' Company, 252
slavery, 266
Smith, Captain John, 7, 38, 41–46, 53, 70,
90, 100, 236
accounts of, 7, 44, 45, 47–50, 50, 113,
159, 183–84, 199, 218, 253, 254,
256–57, 260
arrival of 1609 expedition and, 99,
100–101
Map of Virginia, 113, 159, 253, 254
political infighting, 102–11, 112, 144,
173
return to England in 1609, 110–11,
171–72, 173
survey of New England, 113
on Virginia Colonial Council, 54, 105,
144
Smythe, Dame Sara, 246, 265
Smythe, Sir Thomas, 9–12, *11*, 20, 24, 34,
40, 49, 102, 210–11, 243, 251–52,
253
colonizing of Bermuda and, 226, 237
criticism of, 184–85, 227, 251–52
expedition of 1609 and, 52, 55, 57, 59,
60, 77, 114
expedition of 1610 and, 117, 120, 122,
123, 215–16
reorganization of Virginia Company in
1609, 50–52
support for Virginia from 1611 on, 220,
226
Somers, Admiral George, 1, 23, 24, 144,
192–93, 195, 198, 202, 220, 237
arrival in Bermuda, 124–26, 129
background of, 72–73
building of boat to escape Bermuda,
156–59, 160, 169
colonizing of Bermuda and, 214–15, 238,
263

death of, 215, 225, 258, 263, 267–68
dissension in Bermuda and, 164–65, 167, 257
exploration and mapping of Bermuda, 140–41, 142, 155–56, *157*, 214
as fleet commander in 1609, 70, 72–74, *73*, 75, 76–77, 90, 91, 94–96
food crisis in summer of 1610, Bermuda mission and, 204–206, 213–15
Gates' authority in Bermuda and, 140–41, 159–60
hurricane faced by the *Sea Venture* and, 4, 91, 94–96, 124–25
Patience piloted from Bermuda to Virginia by, 170, 187, 188
voyage across the Atlantic, 76–77, 82, 88, 91, 124–25
Somers, Joan, 72
Somers, Matthew, 79, 215, 225, 258, 267
Somers Island Company, 242–43, 252, 253
Southampton, Earl of (Henry Wriothesley), 10, 52, 56–57, 62, 122, 223, 249, 252–53
Spain, 25, 26, 29
    Catholicism and, 5, 21
    empire in America, and rivalry with England, 5, 6, 21, 32–33, 120–21, 132–33, 175, 212, 235–36, 240–41, 264
    see also Zúñiga, Don Pedro de
Spelman, Henry, 99, 100, 207, 259
Squirrel, 5
Strachey, William, 7–8, 74–75, 80, 186, 189–90, 200, 203, 230, 253–54
    in Bermuda, 136, 146, 148, 151, 163–64, 165, 168
    family of, 75
    on hurricane faced by *Sea Venture,* 3, 4, 91–92, 93, 94, 95
    as secretary of Jamestown, 191, 202, 227–28
    A True Reportory . . . , 217, 245, 246, 254
Susan Constant, 34–35, 37, 41, 90
Swallow, 79, 99, 108, 112, 178, 212
Symonds, Rev. William, 17–18, 20, 63, *64,* 64–68

Tempest, The, 246–50, 265
tobacco, 232, 233, 238, 241, 261, 266
True and Sincere Declaration of the purposes and ends of the plantation begun in Virginia, 117–21, 122
True Declaration of the Estate of the Colonie in Virginia, A, 221, 245
True Relation, A (letter of John Smith), 47–50
True Reportory of the Wreck and Redemption of Sir Thomas Gates, A (Strachey), 217, 245, 246, 254
Tucker, Daniel, 176, 241, 242

Unity, 79, 85, 97, 98–99

van Meteren, Emanuel, 116
Velasco, Don Alonso de, 212–13
Verney, Tom, 79–80
Virginia, 23, 79, 194–96
Virginia, colony of
    after 1611, 229–33, 243–44, 254–55
    boundaries, 21–23
    charter of 1606, 9, 10, 21–23, *22,* 29–30, 31
    charter of 1609, 52, 54, 55, 56, 66, 70, 103, 107
    Jamestown settlement, *see* Jamestown
    outlying settlements, after 1610, 231
    outlying settlements, before 1610, 108–109, 171, 172, 174–75, 177, 178
    plan to abandon, in spring of 1610, 193–96, 197–98
    religion and, *see* religion, founding and promotion of Virginia colony and
    royal authority over, 229
Virginia Colonial Council, 173, 204
    original, 35–36, 38, 41, 42, 43, 44
    reorganized, in 1609, 53–54
    sealed list on the *Sea Venture,* 82, 88, 103, 105, 107, 144–45
Virginia Company, 26–28, 254–55
    Bermuda colony and, 225–26, 235–44, 263
    boundaries and purposes of two colonies, chartered in 1606, 21

Virginia Company (*continued*)
  charter for Bermuda colony, 225–26, 238
  charters for Virginia colony, *see* Virginia, colony of
  dissolution of, in 1624, 229, 231, 232, 244, 252
  expedition of 1609, *see* expedition of 1609
  expedition of 1610, 120–23, 145, 196–200, 212–13, 264
  expedition of 1611, 223–24, 226, 229
  London group, 21–23, 24, 46, 50
  lotteries to fund, 226
  Plymouth group, 21–23, 46, 57
  reorganization of 1609, 50–52
  Sea Venture's survival and revival of the, 210–11, 216–24, 245–46, 264
  troubling reports in fall of 1609, 111–16
  see also Jamestown
Virginia Company Council (London), 202, 252
  in 1606, 30, 38, 39–40, 50
  in 1609, 52, 56, 57, 59–60, 105, 111, 113, 116–23
  Gates' assurances and continued support of Virginia by, 210–11, 219–20, 223
Virginia House of Burgesses, 75, 232, 259, 261–62
Virginia Merchant, 128

Walsingham, Robert, 140
Want, John, 71, 88, 150–53, 250
Waters, Edward, 74, 214, 215, 238, 240, 250, 262–63
Waters, Robert, 164–65, 167, 168, 170, 214, 215, 257–58
Webster, William, 79–80
Weld, Humphrey, 59–60, 62
West, Francis, 106, 108, 109, 173, 175, 178, 198, 212
West, Thomas, *see* De La Warr, Lord (Thomas West)
Whitaker, Rev. Alexander, 218, 221, 222
Wingfield, Edward Maria, 23, 24, 35, 38, 40, 43, 44–45, 47, 70
Winne, Peter, 144, 145, 190–91
Winwood, Sir Ralph, 221
Wittingham, Thomas, 143, 144, 145
Wriothesley, Henry, Earl of Southampton, 10, 52, 56–57, 62, 122, 223, 249, 252–53

Yeardley, Captain George, 75, 185, 189, 232, 259
Yeardley, Temperance, 185, 189

Zúñiga, Don Pedro de, 32–33, 47, 61, 63, 115–16, 212

LORRI GLOVER is the author of two books on the early South, in-cluding *Southern Sons: Becoming Men in the New Nation.* She is a pro-fessor of early American history at the University of Tennessee at Knoxville.

DANIEL BLAKE SMITH is the author of *Inside the Great House: Planter Family Life in Eighteenth-Century Chesapeake Society.* He is the author of a dozen articles in early American social history and a produced screenwriter. His documentaries and docudramas have appeared on PBS. Smith is a professor of colonial American history at the University of Kentucky.